Sergeant Guillemard

Sergeant Guillemard
The Man Who Shot Nelson?
A Soldier of the Infantry of the
French Army of Napoleon on
Campaign Throughout Europe

Robert Guillemard

Sergeant Guillemard: the Man Who Shot Nelson? A Soldier of the Infantry of the French Army of Napoleon on Campaign Throughout Europe
by Robert Guillemard

Published by Leonaur Ltd

Originallt published in 1826 under the title:
Adventures of a French Serjeant During His Campaigns in Italy, Germany, Spain, Russia &c. from 1805 to 1823

Content original to this edition and the presentation of the text in this form copyright © 2007 Leonaur Ltd

ISBN: 978-1-84677-262-7 (hardcover)
ISBN: 978-1-84677-261-0 (softcover)

http://www.leonaur.com

Publisher's Note

The opinions expressed in this book are those of the author and are not necessarily those of the publisher.

Contents

English Editors Preface	9
Departure for the Army	13
I Shoot Admiral Nelson	26
My Interview with Napoleon	35
Siege of Stralsund	45
Oudet	59
Spain	73
A Prisoner at Cabrera	86
Escape	104
My Native Village	114
Russia & Borodino	121
Siberia	137
Wassili and Daria	146
Return to France	158
Campaign in the South	172
Lyons	181
After the One Hundred Days	192
Helping a Fugitive	200
Murat at Toulon	211
The King Of Naples	222
Court-Martialed in Corsica	232
The Trial of Valle	241
The Spanish War & My Discharge	250
Conclusion	261

To the Non-Commissioned Officers of the French Army

Fellow Soldiers,
Several generals have written an account of our campaigns; but they have only given their own history, and that of their equals.

I have worn your shoulder-knot during twenty years; it is for you that I write the narrative of my military career; it is to you that I dedicate it.

Placed in circumstances entirely similar, how many other persons are there who are well fitted to shed a new lustre upon our arms?

I shall not have fruitlessly employed my time, if I inspire even one of your number to bring to light a gallant action that has been neglected, to correct a mistake, or to point out the author of an error or a calumny.

Your fellow soldier,
Robert Guillemard

The Original English Editors Preface

The important events that have occurred in Europe for the last thirty years have been already described by a host of able writers, and we are still constantly acquiring a more intimate knowledge of the causes of those commotions and revolutions that change the fate of kingdoms. The military occurrences of the late war have also been described by officers of rank and talent; and if our knowledge of the general features of a campaign be in any respect deficient, it must arise less from the want of materials to judge by, than from the conflicting statements of observers placed in opposite situations, or from the feelings of the writers belonging to rival nations. When national vanity is excited, candour is apt to disappear.

The work now submitted to the public is very different from the formal narratives of military historians, for though it describes a variety of interesting adventures, and the campaigns of many years, it is nothing but a plain, simple, and unadorned statement of the incidents that fell immediately under the writer's eye. He pretends not to unfold the secrets of cabinets, or even the plans of a campaign; but he describes minutely the scenes that presented themselves during his diversified career, and gives a most novel and original account of the discipline, conduct, and opinions of the soldiers and non-commissioned officers of the French army, from 1805 to 1823. Among the great variety of interesting topics, the reader's attention will in all probability, be chiefly excited by his lively description of the prison depot at Cabrera, and the singular mode of life led by the prisoners: his account of the massacre of the Protestants in the South of France, in 1815, of which he was on the point of becoming one of the victims; his narrative of the escape of Murat from Toulon to Corsica; of Murats stay in that island, his expedition to re-conquer his kingdom, and his melancholy end in Calabria.

The following is a brief summary of the Sergeant's career.

Robert Guillemard was born at Sixfour, near Toulon; he was drawn as a conscript in 1805, and soon after sent on board Admiral Villeneuve's fleet. He was present at the battle of Trafalgar; and was supposed to be the man who shot Lord Nelson. After the action, he became secretary *to* Villeneuve, accompanied him on his return to France, and saw him assassinated at Rennes. Guillemard was now ordered to Paris, brought into the presence of Buonaparte, and examined respecting his knowledge of the circumstances attending the admiral's death. He then joined the army in Germany, was present at the siege of Stralsund, returned to France, fought a duel at Lyons, in which he was wounded; and then, on his recovery, marched again to Germany, fought at Wagram, under the command of the celebrated Oudet, who was mortally wounded in a nocturnal rencounter with the enemy. The Sergeant then marched to Spain, was made prisoner by a band of peasants, and sent to the Island of Cabrera, where six thousand of his countrymen were detained; after a detention of several months he escaped to the coast, joined the French army then besieging Tortosa, distinguished himself during the siege, was promoted to the rank of Sergeant, and received the then much valued cross of the legion of honour.

He again joined the army in Germany in 1812, fought in the Russian Campaign, was engaged in the battle of Borodino, after which he was made an officer by Napoleon in person; in the evening after this battle he was wounded in a skirmish with the enemy, taken prisoner and sent to Siberia. He remained in Siberia till 1814, when he was allowed to return. At the time of Napoleon's return from Elba, he was serving in the Duke of Angouleme's army in the South—and saw the massacre of the Protestants at Nismes. Soon afterwards he assisted Joachim Murat (King of Naples) in escaping from Toulon to Corsica, and accompanied him on his expedition to the coast of Calabria, where Murat lost his life. He was sent to Spain in 1823, and shortly afterwards discharged from the service.

This brief outline sufficiently indicates the variety of the incidents that are described; and it is believed that the tone of the narrative, though simple and unassuming, will not diminish the interest of the subject.

Chapter 1
Departure for the Army

It was with grief that I first left my native spot; the remembrance of it has accompanied me in all my distant marches, in following the flight of our eagles, and in my captivity; I have always returned to it with renewed pleasure; and now that I am settled in it for the remainder of my days, my imagination, by a strange contrariety, for which I cannot account, transports me incessantly to far distant scenes. After reaching the termination of so many travels, I renew them again in fancy; I traverse France, Italy, Germany, Sweden, and Spain; I feel transported to the barren rocks of Cabrera, to the interior of Siberia; I see again the friends of my youth, the companions of my toils, and see them such as then we all were, brilliant with hopes and vigour, I think I am still present at those immortal battles, which seemed to us to secure the eternal duration of the great empire, to maintain the splendour of which we were so proud in cooperating; methinks I hear the words of that king of kings, who was only the first soldier of his army, and who shared in our toils as we shared in his renown. I was then proud of my lot, and would say to myself: *I also was one of the grand army!* But suddenly, again, my reflections take another turn, and I see that the dazzling illusions, with which more than once in my life I had a right to flatter myself, have altogether disappeared amidst the solitude of a wretched village.

It is there, that, contrasting my former hopes with my actual situation, I involuntarily recur to my recollections of the past, and compare them with the recollections of those who have described the events of our times. How is it that they have often not seen things as I did? Is it because we consider things with a different eye, according to the rank we hold in society? How happens it that in reading the memoirs of so many men who have held high situations, I have never found in their narratives of facts the particulars that have appeared to me most important, and that I have often recognized neither the facts themselves, nor the actors? Surely the history of the period cannot be exact, when such differences exist between the opinions of the writers, and the view taken of it at the time by the majority of contemporaries, more fitted to appreciate the nature of the facts than to describe them. To render these materials complete, it is necessary that the recollections of all classes should be examined; and whilst so many generals, from their luxurious mansions, are addressing to their companions in arms an account of the events which they directed, cannot I, a simple soldier, from the bosom of my humble retreat, add the last touch to these pictures of the past, and render them more fit for the popular eye, by illuminating them with the shades of colour through which my rank and situation enabled me to regard these important events? Shall I receive less attention, because I am the first soldier who has raised his voice? I leave to others the pretension of writing history; I give nothing but memoirs, formed from the notes I never omitted to take during the whole course of my service, and for their faithful correctness I vouch. Since I am to speak in the first person, I may be allowed to tell who I am, and to go back a little prior to my own time, that I may notice the circumstances of my native village.

    Sixfour is built on a little mountain of a sugar-loaf form, which rises about a league from Toulon, in the midst of a plain studded with hamlets. Fifty houses falling to pieces, and an old church, which seem to form but one mass with the rocks by which they are supported, compose the humble village in which I was born. It was a sort of town in old times, it is said; but it daily loses its inhabitants and the stones of its houses, The former remove into the plain, attracted by the hope of leading a less laborious life; the latter roll into it, borne away by their own weight, and precipitated by time, which will soon have totally annihilated Sixfour, where people deign neither to build new houses nor to repair the old.

In this part of the country there formerly existed a chapter of canons, who were driven from their asylum by the gust of 1793, and did not return till the calm of 1814. An excellent ball ground, formerly frequented by the amateurs of all the villages for more than six miles round, is now abandoned as a play ground to children, or to a few old men, who go hither in winter to warm themselves in the sun; everything, in fact, seems to indicate that in less than thirty years the village will be wholly deserted. Yet its position, and the character of its inhabitants, are not without charms in the eyes of those who deem of some value a beautiful situation, a healthy air, and frank cordiality of manners. These three qualities are combined at Sixfour; its inhabitants are simple and kind-hearted. If numberless ridiculous stories circulate in the neighbourhood respecting their credulity and unsuspecting simplicity, nothing has ever been alleged against their moral character. The prospect from the village is most magnificent; in front is a vast extent of the Mediterranean, with the white rocks that form its coasts, occasionally broken by country seats, olive trees, and fine groves; on one side is Toulon, with its mountains in the form of an amphitheatre, its forts, the movement and bustle of its dockyards and arsenal, and its beautiful roads covered with ships and vessels of every species. Farther on to the left is the pretty little town of Ollioules, (at the entrance of the mountain passes of that name), as if springing up amidst arbours of orange and lemon trees, which grow in the very centre of a semicircle of volcanic mountains.

My father, Pierre Guillemard, was mayor of Sixfour before and after the revolution, and during that event; his father and grandfather had occupied the same post, which seemed, indeed, to have belonged to the family for ages, as well as the business of a public notary, which had been handed down from father to son ever since the time of Henry III., as may be seen in the registers of the place, which are still extant in the office of M. Aycard, the notary of La Seyne; some of the documents are dated so far back as 1576.

My father, like many others who have not boasted of it in after-times, and who would take especial care not to confess it at the present day, saw with pleasure the first symptoms of the revolution, without being able to foresee its results. Yet he occupied the first, or, more properly speaking, the only magisterial office in Sixfour; he was wealthy, for his business and personal property brought him in rather more than three thousand francs a year, a considerable fortune in our part of the country; but my father was not a selfish, interested man: he was delighted at the establishment of an order of things which seemed to ameliorate the lot of the great mass of his countrymen, without interfering much with the interests of the minority. All our neighbours (and everyone is a neighbour in a village containing but fifty houses) were possessed of the same sentiments; and even our worthy old *curé,* M. Berenguier, applauded in 1789 the noble firmness of the commons, and the disinterested conduct of the great majority of the clergy. He seldom failed to spend his evenings at our house, where were also assembled the politicians and best informed people of the place. The journal of Ducos was read and talked of at their meetings; and sometimes they even entered into a somewhat animated discussion till ten o'clock; but they almost invariably ended by concurring in the opinions of *Monsieur le maire,* and by separating as well pleased with each other as they were with the news they had just learned. The canons were the only persons whom this state of things could not please. As fat, and as well provided for, as their numerous brethren in other parts of France, it did not require a great effort of foresight on their part to see that they had much to lose and nothing to gain by a change; hence they did not feel quite gay, nor did they come to see us, but they endeavoured by increasing their good cheer, to compensate themselves for the privations they began to fear for the future.

These particulars were told me long afterwards, for I was too young at the time they occurred to pay the smallest attention to them. I remember, however, that my elder brother (who was eight years older than me, and intended as a successor to his father in the office) read the newspapers, and took part in the political discussions which my sister Henriette and I often enough interrupted by our noisy sports and childish quarrels.

Though our worthy curate, M. Berenguier, had taken the oath required by the constitution, he was forced to conceal himself, and afterwards to seek an asylum in foreign countries. My father provided him with the means, took a passage for him on board a Genoese schooner going to Leghorn, obtained him a passport, and lent him some money; for this excellent man was not wealthy, and divided the trifling revenues of his living among the poor of the country. When these two old friends bade each other *adieu*, they agreed that the ruling powers were adopting somewhat violent means to procure the regeneration of France, and without venturing to communicate their mutual fears, they formed sincere wishes for their speedy reunion. The canons had long before this deserted their chapter, and gone elsewhere to seek their fortunes.

Some time after the *curés* departure, the whole commune of Sixfour was denounced by Freron to the convention as guilty of the most violent *moderantisme*. The first thing done was to throw into prison the mayor, and a dozen peasants, the greater part of whom firmly believed that it was purely through mistake, as they could not make out what was meant by a charge of moderation. It was found easier to guillotine them than to make them understand the matter. My father was reserved for the same fate, but fortunately had not yet underwent it, when the ninth Thermidor restored him to liberty, and to his former functions. A long and painful imprisonment had injured his health, without in the smallest degree changing his disposition. He came back to Sixfour, to preside over affairs, to draw up his legal writings, and take care of his property, with the quietness that had hitherto distinguished every action of his life; and those who in after times had occasion for his services, never perceived that the injustice of which he had been the victim, had in any respect altered his philanthropy and kindliness of disposition. I shall not mention the services he rendered, for they do sot belong to my subject; nor need I say that he met with nothing but ingratitude—that is the natural order of things.

All these things had taken place long before, and everything was very quiet at Sixfour; I had reached my eighteenth year, when my father was called one day to draw up the marriage contract of Mademoiselle Rosalie Rymbaud, with my old companion Jauffret, a son of one of the richest individuals in Sixfour. If I notice this event, (which is altogether of a private nature, and perhaps not very interesting) let the reader pardon me, and be reassured I shall not often be guilty of this fault. But at the age I have attained, one looks back with so much pleasure on the scenes of his youth.

The Rymbaud family possessed a very pretty country seat in the neighbourhood of Ollioules. It was there that the marriage was celebrated, and there I accompanied my father. I had often seen Miette Rymbaud, the younger sister of Rosalie; but I saw her then for the first time, with the eyes of a youth of eighteen. Miette was seventeen. She had received a more careful education than what is usually given to the young ladies of our province. To this she added the natural talent which is more common among the inhabitants of the South than knowledge. I was placed at table between her and her brother, who was a year younger, and intended for the navy, I had been his companion in boyhood, and sought now to renew our intimacy; I really loved him then, as I loved every one connected with Miette. As for Miette herself I spoke little to her; but the embarrassment I felt near her was not without some hidden charms. We separated at a late hour; I withdrew enchanted with the events of the day, and thought I had begun a new existence.

Our connection with the Rymbaud family became more intimate from this moment. They did not disapprove of my inclination, since they did not seek any opportunity of preventing me from seeing Miette. But I was still very young! I had no profession, and had never even thought seriously of choosing one. An inclination very natural to young people who frequent sea-ports, had turned my ideas towards the navy. My uncle, Bernard Eyguier had served in it from his infancy; he had been master's mate for more than fifteen years, when, in consequence of the new system, he was appointed assistant lieutenant. All the accounts he gave of his cruises, and the countries he had visited, along with the valuable curiosities he was always bringing from them, inspired me with a strong desire of following him, and of becoming a sailor also. This desire became still stronger when my friend Rymbaud was appointed a midshipman, and entered on board a frigate. I went several times on board to dine with him and his companions. The authority which these young men, scarcely out of their boyhood, possessed over grown up men, their gaiety, their future prospects, the dangers to which they were exposed, and more than all, the elegance of their uniform, made me bitterly regret that I had not sooner embraced a profession for which I thought myself so well fitted. With what pleasure I should have hastened to M. Rymbaud's country house, on returning from a long voyage or an engagement! How the account of my dangers would have interested Miette!

But I was nineteen at the time, which was somewhat late to enter upon a profession which ought to be embraced in very early life, for life in it wears rapidly away. However, in spite of my father's repugnance, I was entered on the books of the sloop of war the *Rhinoceros,* and authorized to remain on shore, that I might be enabled to pass my examination as a midshipman of the second class. I studied incessantly, and joyfully anticipated the happiness I should feel when, for the first time, I should appear before Miette with a sword by my side.

This flattering perspective, and these dreams of happiness were very cruelly disappointed; the examining officer could not come to Toulon at the appointed period, the examination of the young men intended for the navy was put off for six months, and in the interval, having attained my twentieth year, I was called upon the conscription.

I still retained the hope that my number would not be among those appointed to set out. I had taken one of the last of my class, and thought myself secure, but I had reckoned without the council of revision. Almost all the numbers that were to form the contingent had fallen to young men belonging to wealthy families, or to relatives of men in place; the greater part was set aside; one man, with broad shoulders, and an Herculian form, was discharged as consumptive; another, with the sharp eye of a lynx, was discharged as short sighted, and my number was called. It was in vain that I endeavoured to excuse myself on account of my physical constitution, which was not very strong at that time; it was absolutely necessary that the contingent should be filled, and Robert Guillemard, of Sixfour, was solemnly declared by the council of revision to form part of it, and received in consequence an order to be in readiness to march on the 1st of May, 1805, to join the corps that should be assigned to him.

My father wished to purchase a substitute; but they were extremely dear at that time, and the purchase would have made a considerable breach in his fortune at a critical moment; hence I would not hear of it, and prepared for my departure. It was not without a very painful emotion that I prepared to leave my country, my family, and Miette above all. I at last opened my heart to her at the moment that I was about to lose her, perhaps forever; she found how dear she was to me. She loved me and told me so; we flattered ourselves with the hope that some fortunate event would enable us speedily to meet again; we promised each other inviolable fidelity, and formed all kinds of plans for the future; one year, or eighteen months at the utmost, I was to be absent from her, but after that period I was to return to Sixfour, obtain her from her family, and our days would glide away in peace, and with increased charms from the remembrance of our separation: I have in after times formed many other projects that were not more successful than these: but none made me ever spend such happy moments.

The conscripts of my class assembled at Toulon on the 1st of May, 1805, and I was appointed, along with a hundred and nineteen of my companions, to a regiment of the line, whose depot was at Perpignan. At the moment of our departure, the colonel made us a very fine speech upon our zeal for the service, and the ardour with which we flew to the defence of our country. This address had very little effect upon me, and I thought that if all my companions were the same, we deserved little praise for our enthusiasm; but these reflections I kept to myself, and presented, as the saying is, a stout heart to ill-fortune. Mean while, all the newspapers, and all the proclamations of the head of the government, spoke of nothing but the emulation of the young conscripts, who, on all sides, took arms of their own accord, presented themselves before they were called, and covered every road on their march to join the different corps to which they were appointed. I confess that I was at first rather ashamed at finding myself so cold amidst the general enthusiasm, the extent of which, however, I was soon enabled to appreciate, as I afterwards found the means of appreciating so many other kinds of zeal with which an army and a nation become inflamed, without even thinking of the matter.

My brother and some of my friends accompanied the detachment as far as Ollioules, where we separated after breakfast—-they to resume their peaceful occupations at Sixfour—I to begin the trade of a soldier, and that military pilgrimage which, after the lapse of twenty years, was to bring me back to my native village, covered with wounds, without fortune, and despoiled of every future prospect.

At our first halt, I was quartered along with three other conscripts of the detachment. My surprise may be easily imagined, when I heard my companions in the evening bitterly regretting their country, complaining in no very measured terms of the law that forced them to leave it, and already forming plans of desertion. One of them, who was my bedfellow till we reached the depot, was called Moutet, of Hyéres, a merry, fat soul, whom the conscription had caused the first sorrow of any kind he ever had felt in his life. I thought when I heard him talking, that he would not remain more than a fortnight in the service; yet he is in it at this moment. The nature of their conversation did not much agree with the colonel's address, the language of the newspapers, or the proclamations of the government. "Here are four of us in one detachment (I said to myself) who do not share in the general enthusiasm; I should never have suspected it, but thought I stood alone."—Assuredly there were many more. Moutet's discontent and mine were shared by all our fellow conscripts, whatever their circumstances or fortune might otherwise be. The same repugnance at their first departure was characteristic of all the young men who left their homes; and it was a foolish hoax to boast of their courageous zeal. But to tell the truth, this dislike insensibly disappeared; they gradually accustomed themselves to the service and to military habits; and the soldiers at last (to use their own language) looked to the eagle of their regiment as their village steeple, their company as their family, and sometimes their captain as their father. It is easy to find the due to this inconsistency in a national character keenly susceptible of new impressions, fond of change, enthusiastic in the love of glory, and which must have been necessarily allured and fascinated by the varied and ever moving scenes of military life.

Our detachment gave me a proof of what I have stated. The regret of the conscripts daily became less as we advanced farther from home, and gaiety came in its stead. We formed intimacies and friendships. As we all belonged to the same department, we remembered that we had occasionally met at the fêtes of the different villages; we always delighted to speak of these things, and this pleasure began already to be unalloyed with bitterness or regret. Besides, should not we be glad, on our return home, that we had seen the world, that we had been in active service, and that we could relate the battles in which we had been engaged?

We were commanded by a lieutenant about forty years of age, by two sergeants and four corporals. They had all been long in the service. The lieutenant and one of the Sergeants had been in the expedition to Egypt, and the narratives they gave us of their adventures there, made us more than once forget the length of our marches, They treated us with great mildness, and endeavoured to inspire us with predilection for military life. Care was taken in those days to give the charge of young conscripts to none but those who had seen active service; for in the army, as in every other profession, he who has done nothing, displays his superiority only by arrogance and petty vexations, so that those who are under him detest not only the individual but the orders he issues.

We reached Perpignan on the 15th of May, and after being reviewed by the major, were enrolled by the quarter-master in different companies. Shortly afterwards we put on uniforms, and began to be exercised twice a day by non-commissioned officers and corporals. Fortunately, I soon got rid of this, for a month sufficed to make me expert in the manual exercise, and I only went on parade with my company, which marched for Port-Vendres with the battalion to which it belonged, towards the end of September, that is, about four months after I entered the corps.

We had garrisoned this little sea-port only a few days, when some transports and frigates came to anchor before it; our battalion was embarked, but not without murmuring, for the French soldier always exaggerates the privations and sufferings of the sailor, and never sees his element changed but with the utmost repugnance. In spite of our murmurs, we were forced to put, as the saying is, our feet in the shoe. Our officers, who, doubtless, knew what to make of it, assured us that we should only be a short time on board, and that we were only going as far as the coast of Brittany, where we were to join a camp about to be formed there. We soon saw how much truth there was in this. On the 3rd October, at daybreak, we anchored in the bay of Cadiz, where was assembled a splendid French and Spanish squadron, commanded by Vice Admiral Villeneuve. The second in command was the Spanish Admiral Gravina, already known by his brilliant actions and distinguished bravery. On the same day, our battalion left the transports to go on board the vessels of the fleet; my company was sent on board the *Redoutable,* a seventy-four gun-ship, commanded by Captain Lucas.

The navy, which had hitherto presented so many attractions to me, seemed to me but a painful and disgusting trade, when I found myself on board as a soldier; I could feel no interest in anything around me, in objects which I was only to see for a moment, and which must forever remain foreign to the service to which I belonged. Every movement and manoeuvre made on board made me regret the more bitterly that circumstances bad kept me out of a profession, to which I was attached for a moment, only that I might more fully experience all its inconveniences.

Young Adolphe Rymbaud had been on board the *Redoutable* some time before my arrival; I was delighted with meeting him, which I had no reason to expect. I should have been highly gratified to have had a long conversation with him, to have talked of Sixfour and of our early years, and of the members of our two families; but I soon perceived that he felt a certain constraint when I addressed him, that he was extremely cold and reserved towards me, and that without seeking openly to avoid me, he seized the slightest opportunity of changing his place when I was near him. Hence, our intimacy was not great. Yet Adolphe had an excellent heart; and assuredly he could not have forgotten the friend of his infancy; but he had already adopted a portion of the pride and arrogance of a naval officer. It would appear that, at the beginning of the revolution, the cold reserve and stately pride of our ancient nobles had sought shelter in this gallant and accomplished corps. A midshipman of eighteen speaks in the most contemptuous terms of familiarity to a grey haired boatswain, respectable by his toils, his zeal, and his long services; whilst a staff-officer in the land service, even a general, never fails to show the soldiers that respect, that sort of consideration which Frenchmen never submit to lose but with the greatest difficulty. Whence arises this difference? It is doubtless, because every post in the army is within the soldier's reach, because all the different ranks form but one chain, every link of which he may run through in succession; and that an officer never forgets that nothing prevents the soldier whom he is addressing from one day becoming his equal. But sailors and their officers form two classes for ever separate and distinct; an insurmountable barrier rises between them, which never can be passed by him who has once formed part of the crew. The revolution, which has opened such a vast career to the brave spirits of our armies, has done little or nothing for the advancement or happiness of the common sailor. For one moment only were officers taken from among them; that was when the French nobility deserted. These plebeian officers are not those who have contributed the least to the glory of the French flag. Since that period, the special schools have always supplied the navy with officers; and the rank of boatswain has been the highest point of the sailor's promotion.

CHAPTER 2

I Shoot Admiral Nelson

I was beginning to get tired of my situation; as were my companions, and nothing indicated that a speedy change would occur. It was said that we were to sail for the Channel, to protect the landing of the troops in England, which everybody talked of at the time; but an English squadron, known to be commanded by Nelson, blockaded Cadiz, and prevented us leaving the bay; and there was a report that Vice Admiral Villeneuve had received express orders to come to action. On the 20th October, however, there was a vague rumour in circulation that we were to leave our position next day and attack the English. The frequent signals made by the *Bucentaure* (the admiral's ship), the meeting of all the captains of the fleet on board it, and the manoeuvres and preparations of the different vessels, indicated that these reports were not without foundation.

In fact, on the 21st of October, at ten in the morning, the combined fleet left Cadiz to offer battle to the English. It consisted of thirty vessels, of which ten Spanish ships occupied the left flank. Six frigates, French and Spanish, formed the wings of this splendid fleet, and had orders to assist the vessels that required it during the action. Our line occupied more than a league in extent, and towards twelve o'clock, had come up within cannon shot of the English squadron, which was nearly of equal strength.

The two fleets manoeuvred for more than an hour, for

the purpose of choosing their positions and terminating the preparations for a battle that was henceforth inevitable. The *Redoutable* was in the centre, and a little in front of the French line, which by the admiral's last orders had been formed in a semi-circle. Immediately in front of him was an English three-decker, carrying a vice admiral's flag, and consequently commanded by Nelson. This vessel occupied in the English fleet the same position which the *Redoutable* did in ours. All at once it made signals, which were instantly answered, and advanced with full sail upon us, whilst the other vessels followed its example. The intention of its commander was evidently to cut our line by attacking the *Redoutable,* which presented its flank, and discharged its first broadside.

This was the signal for action. The English vessel returned the fire, and at the same moment, there began along the whole of the two lines a fire of artillery, which was not to cease, except by the extermination of one of the two squadrons. Already cries of suffering and death were heard on the decks of the *Redoutable*. By the first discharge, one officer, and more than thirty sailors and soldiers, were killed or wounded. This was the first time I had been in action; and an emotion I had never felt till now made my heart beat violently. Fear might form an ingredient in the feeling; but it was mingled with other sentiments which I could not account for. I was grieved that I was kept in a post where I had nothing else to do but to fire my gun upon the enemy's deck. I should have desired a more active duty, to be allowed to go over the ship, and to work one of the cannons. My desires were soon gratified. All our top-men had been killed, when two sailors and four soldiers, (of whom I was one) were ordered to occupy their post in the tops. While we were going aloft, the balls and grape-shot showered around us, struck the masts and yards, knocked large splinters from them, and cut the rigging in pieces. One of my companions was wounded beside me, and fell from a height of thirty feet upon the deck, where he broke his neck.

When I reached the top, my first movement was to take a view of the prospect presented by the hostile fleets. For more than a league, extended a thick cloud of smoke, above which were discernible a forest of masts and rigging, and the flags, the pendants, and the fire of the three nations. Thousands of flashes more or less near continually penetrated this cloud, and a rolling noise pretty similar to the sound of continued thunder but much stronger, arose from its bosom. The sea was calm; the wind light, and not very favourable for the execution of manoeuvres.

When the English top-men, who were only a few yards distant from us, saw us appear, they directed a sharp fire upon us, which we returned. A soldier of my company and a sailor were killed quite close to me; two others who were wounded, were able to go below by the shrouds. Our opponents were, it seems, still worse handled than we, for I soon saw the English top deserted, and none sent to supply the place of those who must have been killed or wounded by our balls. I then looked to the English vessel and our own. The smoke enveloped them, was dissipated for a moment, and returned thicker at each broadside. The two decks were covered with dead bodies, which they had not time to throw overboard. I perceived Captain Lucas motionless at his post, and several wounded officers still giving orders. On the poop of the English vessel, was an officer covered with orders, and with only one arm. From what I had heard of Nelson, I had no doubt that it was he. He was surrounded by several officers, to whom he seemed to be giving orders. At the moment I first perceived him, several of his sailors were wounded beside him, by the fire of the *Redoutable,* As I had received no orders to go down, and saw myself forgotten in the tops, I thought it my duty to fire on the poop of the English vessel, which I saw quite exposed and close to me. I could even have taken aim at the men I saw, but I fired at hazard among the groups I saw of sailors and officers. All at once I saw great confusion on board the *Victory,* the men crowded round the officer whom I had taken for Nelson. He had just fallen, and was taken below covered with a cloak. The agitation shown at this moment left me no doubt that I had judged rightly, and that it really was the English admiral. An instant afterwards the *Victory* ceased from firing; the deck was abandoned by all those who occupied it; and I presumed that the consternation produced by the admiral's fall was the cause of this sudden change. I hurried below to inform the captain of what I had seen of the enemy's situation. He believed me the readily, as the slackening of the fire indicated that an event of the highest importance occupied the attention of the English ship's crew, and prevented them from continuing the action. He gave immediate orders for boarding, and everything was prepared for it in a moment. It is even said that young Fontaine, a midshipman belonging to the *Redoutable* passed by the ports into the lower deck of the English vessel, found it abandoned, and returned to notify that the ship had surrendered. As Fontaine was killed a few moments afterwards, these particulars were obtained from a sailor, who said he had witnessed the transaction.

However, as a part of our crew, commanded by two officers, were ready to spring upon the enemy's deck, the fire recommenced with a fury it never had had from the beginning of the action. Meanwhile, an English eighty gun ship placed herself alongside of the *Redoutable* to put it between two fires; and a French ship of the same force placed itself abreast of the *Victory,* to put it in the same situation. There was then seen a sight hitherto unexampled in naval warfare, and not since repeated—four vessels, all in the same direction, touching each other, dashing one against another, intermingling their yards, and fighting with a fury which no language can adequately express. The rigging was abandoned, and every sailor and soldier put to the guns; the officers themselves had nothing to provide for, nothing to order, in this horrible conflict, and came likewise to the guns. Amidst nearly four hundred pieces of large cannon all firing at one time in a confined space— amidst the noise of the balls, which made furious breaches in the sides of the *Redoutable*—amongst the splinters which flew in every direction with the speed of projectiles, and the dashing of the vessels, which were driven by the waves against each other, not a soul thought of anything but destroying the enemy, and the cries of the wounded and the dying were no longer heard. The men fell, and if they were any impediment to the action of the gun they had just been working, one of their companions pushed them aside with his foot to the middle of the deck, and without uttering a word, placed himself with concentrated fury at the same post, where he soon experienced a similar fate.

In less than half an hour our vessel, without having hauled down her colours, had in fact surrendered. Her fire had gradually slackened, and then ceased altogether. The mutilated bodies of our companions encumbered the two decks, which were covered with shot, broken cannon, matches still smoking, and shattered timbers. One of our thirty-six pounders had burst towards the close of the contest. The thirteen men placed at it had been killed by the splinters, and were heaped together round its broken carriage. The ladders that led between the different decks were shattered and destroyed; the mizzen-mast and main-mast had fallen, and encumbered the deck with blocks and pieces of rigging. Of the boats placed forward, or hung on the sides of our vessel, there remained nothing but some shattered planks. Not more than a hundred and fifty men survived out of a crew of about eight hundred, and almost all these were more or less severely wounded. Captain Lucas was one of the number.

It was five o'clock when the action ceased. I went over the ship where everything presented a prospect of desolation. Calm despair was painted on the countenances of those who had escaped from this terrible scene, where I had just made my military *debut*. Amongst the dead I saw the ill-fated Rymbaud, the friend of my infancy; at the utmost he was not more than eighteen. His sword had been broken in his fall; he was wounded by a chain-shot in the right breast, and fell against the wheel of a cannon; the disordered state of his features indicated that his sufferings had been great. His disfigured remains inspired me with painful reflections, and brought to my mind a host of bitter recollections. I left the spot, and, I must confess, felt my eyes filled with tears. I had not yet been able to acquire that indifference which the soldier displays from a constant habit of witnessing similar scenes.

In the evening, English long-boats came to take away the remainder of our crew, to be divided among the vessels of the fleet; and I was taken on board the *Victory*. There I learned the death of Nelson: he had been wounded on the right shoulder by a ball, which penetrated obliquely, and broke the spine of the back. When taken to the cock-pit, he ordered his surgeon, Mr. Betty, to inform him of his situation without concealment or ceremony. He learned, without the least emotion or regret, that he had only an hour to live, called for his captain (Capt Hardy) and after inquiring about the situation of the two fleets, expressly forbid him to let the English fleet know of his death, and directed the vessels to be brought to anchor as soon as the action was over, on the very spot where it was fought. Captain Hardy promised to obey his orders implicitly, but he did not like to assume the responsibility. He made signals that the admiral was dead, when Lord Collingwood took the command, and did not judge proper to come to anchor, which, perhaps, might have been dangerous on account of the gale that came on that night.

The death of Nelson was regarded by the English as a public calamity, the bitterness of which could not be allayed by the victory they had obtained. The sailors deplored him as a father; the officers as a commander, whose talents had caused the glory and prosperity of their country, and whose place would not for a long period be filled by an admiral of equal merit. He whose loss is regretted by an entire nation, he whose death is deplored by old sailors, usually little susceptible of sentiments of attachment, should necessarily inspire some interest, even in an enemy; hence, as a man, I could not help sharing in some degree the affliction that prevailed on board the *Victory;* while, as a Frenchman, I had reason to rejoice at an event that had delivered my country from one of her most dangerous enemies. At any rate, from the moment in which he received his wound, and the position of the wound itself, I could not doubt for a moment that I was the author; and I have ever since been fully convinced of it. But though the shot that had brought down this admiral had rendered a service to my country, I was far from considering it as an action of which I had a right to boast. Besides, in the general confusion, everyone could claim the honour; I might not be believed; so that I was afraid of furnishing my companions with a subject of ridicule, and did not think proper to mention it to them nor to the French officers I saw on board the *Victory.* It was in this manner, that more than once in the course of my life, carelessness and false shame have deprived me of advantages I might have justly claimed.

A very strong gale arose in the evening, blew through the night with extreme violence, and soon scattered the wrecks of our vessels which covered the sea. We did not learn the particulars of the action till next day. Five French vessels were unable to come into action; the greater part of the Spanish ships would not fight; and the rest of the fleet sustained with the most distinguished courage the attacks of an enemy now become superior in number, for the whole of the English fleet were engaged. The Spanish three-decker, the *Santissima Trinidada,* commanded by Admiral Gravina, was sunk after an obstinate resistance against three English vessels; the admiral was taken up wounded, and died sometime afterwards at Cadiz. When he saw all the masts of the *Trinidada* shot away, he exclaimed: "I was lately in a ship, I am now in a fortress, and shall not abandon it till it sinks under me."—This he did.

The *Aigle,* a French 74, fought also against three English ships, lost almost all its crew, was taken, and was stranded during the night upon the Spanish coast, where both French and English were drowned together. The *Indomptable* foundered at sea, with fifteen hundred wounded men on board, not one of whom was saved. The *Intrepide,* commanded by the brave Infernet, was also sunk, after a terrible resistance to several vessels who came up successively to cannonade it. Infernet was picked up, along with one of his sons, and was taken on board an English vessel, where he astonished the officers by his language, equally remarkable for its freedom, bluntness, spirit, and originality. The *Achille,* in which was a detachment of the 67th regiment, was set on fire during the action. The English who were fighting it cleared off; and of eight hundred men, who formed the crew, not more than twenty found an opportunity of escaping. When all hopes of stopping the progress of the flames were gone, and death seemed inevitable, to avoid waiting for it, several officers blew out their brains; others threw themselves into the flames, that were consuming the forepart of the ship, several sailors went to the store-room, gorged themselves with brandy, and by the most complete drunkenness endeavoured to throw a veil over the disaster that was about to terminate their existence. Towards six o'clock in the evening the fire reached the gunroom, the vessel blew up, and everything disappeared. Upon any other occasion, the unfortunate crew could easily have been saved; but without troubling themselves about their fate, the two fleets in their vicinity thought of nothing but their mutual destruction.

I need not enumerate all the vessels that perished. It is sufficient to state, that the combined fleet was totally annihilated, and that it fought with such obstinacy that of all those that were engaged in action, the English could only save, I believe, one single vessel: the rest all perished at sea, on the coast, or by fire. The day after the action, they brought on board the *Victory,* Vice Admiral Villeneuve, who had displayed so much intrepidity, talents, and patriotism. The English received him with the marks of respect due to bravery and merit in misfortune. He was wounded in the right hand, and seemed quite terror-struck at his defeat, and careless of the respectful attentions that were shown him. The same day, he caused an inquiry to be made if there were any non-commissioned officers among the French prisoners on board; not one was found. He then asked for a military man of any rank, who could write easily what he should dictate; I offered myself. After a short examination, he told me that I should act as his secretary till further orders, and ordered me to come daily to the chamber that had been allotted to him.

CHAPTER 3

My Interview with Napoleon

In the evening of the 22nd, the *Victory* set sail for England, with the rest of the English fleet. The voyage was long and painful, especially to the French prisoners, some of whom already knew the guard-ships that awaited them. The duty I had to perform near Admiral Villeneuve, spared me many inconveniences to which the rest of my companions were exposed, and procured me more respect from the enemy, I saw him regularly every day; and I often passed the whole twenty-four hours in writing various parts of a long memorial, which he intended to publish on the battle of Trafalgar. The very first day, he dictated to me a summary of the whole transaction, which was immediately transmitted to Cadiz by a flag of truce.

He communicated little with the English officers, and his chagrin was far from diminishing; sometimes, however, after having been busily employed for several hours in making me recommence several times the substance of letters he wished to write, or in writing passages of his memorial, he seemed desirous of relaxation by inciting *me* to speak on subjects foreign to the task we had been performing. When he learned the province I belonged to, he often spoke to me of Toulon, where he had commanded the fleet, of all the neighbouring places, and even of Sixfour, the position of which he remembered perfectly.

On the 27th November, the *Victory* arrived at Plymouth, and set sail next day for London; but the French sailors and soldiers who had been taken prisoners at Trafalgar, were previously transported to the guard ships that were in the roads. The officers received passports to go to live on their parole in various small inland towns; and our admiral was sent to Arlesford, in Devonshire. He was granted the permission of taking me with him, along with his servant Prieur.

   The admiral's first object was to address the transport-board, to be allowed to return to France for the purpose of demanding a trial, offering to give his parole that he would return, if he was not exchanged in the interval. His petitions and various other measures produced no effect at first, and were not even honoured with an answer. At last the members of the transport board broached a host of difficulties which would prevent them, they said, from accepting his proposal. New demands and letters came from the admiral. More than five months were passed, incessantly asking a favour to which he attached the highest importance. The length of time taken up by answers, the opposition that was continually springing up in different forms, in proportion as others were conquered, visibly embittered his mind, and rendered his temper sombre and capricious. His mental sorrows doubtless affected his wound, which was not getting better, but which should, in other circumstances, have been closed long before. However, at the moment he began to despair of obtaining the object of his ardent solicitation, Mr. Chilcott, the agent for the prisoners at Arlesford, received orders to give him a passport to go to Plymouth, and to require him to sign an engagement, by which he promised to return in three months, if the French government did not provide for his exchange. Prieur and I were included in the same engagement, and marked in the admiral's passport. Our preparations were made immediately; and in three days we were at Plymouth, where a cartel waited only for the admiral to weigh anchor, and sail to a French port We went on board without delay, and got under weigh in the course of the day.

We landed at Morlaix on the 7th May, and set out the next day for Rennes, where we arrived on the 10th, and put up at the Hotel du Brésil. The air of France seemed to give a serenity to the admiral's mind I had not yet seen it enjoy since I was attached to his service. He still suffered much from his wound, and attempted to write himself; but he was forced to dictate several letters to me. I have not forgotten the smallest expression of the one I am about to notice. Several events of later date, have called back my attention to the language, and have made me suspect that they were directly connected with them: it was as follows:

To Rear Admiral Lucas
I have been in France only two days, my dear Admiral, and have this moment learned a piece of news that has given me great pleasure—it is that of the reward your bravery has just received; and the flattering, and the well merited expressions employed by the head of the government in announcing the recompense.
If every commander of a ship had acted as you did at Trafalgar, the victory would not for one moment have been doubtful. Assuredly none knows this better than I do; and I am happy that I contributed in rendering you this justice, in the short account I drew up immediately after the action. It remains for me to fulfil a very painful duty, to point out those whose conduct destroyed the effect of my arrangements, and brought about the destruction of our squadron and the humiliation of the French flag. My own justification, the honour of France, and above all, the honour of the navy, imperiously require me to surmount my repugnance to call for severe measures, where I would be most desirous of calling for nothing but honours and rewards.
Perhaps you may have received sailing orders before this letter reaches you; but as I intend to call you as a witness in the trial I am about to demand and to corroborate

my charges against those who have produced this disaster, be so good as to do your utmost to remain a few days longer in Paris, where I shall soon have the pleasure of embracing you.

I am, &c.

Rennes, 11th May, 1806.

The admiral, in fact, intended to remain only two days in Rennes, and to set out on the third day for Paris, where I was to accompany him. These two days were passed without any incident occurring worthy of notice. The admiral went out little, reflected a great deal, and I scarcely ever left him. The few arrangements required for our journey were made, the trunks were put on a *post-chaise* the admiral had bought, and at daybreak, the next morning, we were to set out.

On the afternoon of the same day, there arrived at the hotel four individuals with moustaches, in very decent plain clothes, which they did not seem accustomed to wear; in other respects, their accent and manners, and above all, their copper complexion did not allow me to think for a moment that they were Frenchmen. One of them asked me a host of questions, of an indifferent nature at first, and then connected with the admiral. He seemed greatly surprised when I said that we were to set out next morning, and inquired very minutely about the admiral's habits, and the arrangements of his apartment This circumstance struck me afterwards; at the moment I saw nothing in his inquiries, but the natural curiosity which makes a man desirous of learning the smallest particulars connected with an individual, whose actions have been distinguished; and I answered all his questions, which, as I said before, I thought wholly without consequence.

When this individual had no more questions to ask me, he left me immediately, returned to the hotel about half an hour afterwards, and brought with him an individual, whose appearance struck me forcibly. The latter was a Frenchman; at least a strongly marked pronunciation indicated that he belonged to our Southern provinces, and I even thought I could distinguish the accent of Ronergue. He seemed to be about forty-five; short, rough, with a grey powdered head, a short and pointed queue, mean features, a sharp and piercing look, a complexion indicative of the habit of drinking to excess, and spindle legs—such was the man whom I saw afterwards, by whose repulsive and vulgar look I should, independent of other circumstances, never have forgotten. He surveyed me at first from top to toe, then asked me in a commanding tone, the same questions put to me by the first individual, and added a number of his own. He asked me if I was very sure that the admiral would set out next day; I said I was. He then left me, walked for a moment with the man who had brought him, and spoke to him in a low tone with much gesticulation. They were joined by the other three, who all showed him the utmost deference and respect. They left the hotel together, returned in an hour after, went up to their rooms, had long conferences, and finally separated.

As the admiral was to rise at daybreak, he went to bed at ten o'clock. Prieur slept at the post-house, where the carriage was, and he was to come for us in the morning so as to prevent delay. I assisted the admiral in undressing; he retained me a few minutes, and finally dismissed me, by telling me to keep a light in my room, to draw the door on me only, and call him in the rooming as soon as Prieur came. I retired to a chamber in the story above, where I was lodged; and ten minutes afterwards was in a profound sleep.

I was suddenly awakened by a loud noise, which I thought came from the admiral's apartment. It increased, the noise of voices was heard, and then came cries of pain, that left no doubt of the occurrence of some catastrophe. I sprung from my bed, and only taking time to snatch the light, and a sabre the admiral had bought me at Morlaix, I rushed in a moment along the staircase that led to his room, and heard very distinctly the precipitate steps of several persons running off. I doubled my speed, and immediately under me perceived the individual who had spoken to me the evening before skulking off towards the ground floor. I have since reflected that there was no change in his dress, and that he had not been in bed. Something urged me to pursue him, but my first impulse led me to the admiral's room, the door of which I found open. I advanced a few steps, and saw the unfortunate man whom the balls of Trafalgar had respected, stretched pale and bloody on his bed, with the coverlets scattered on the floor. He was pale and livid, breathed hard, and struggled with the agonies of death. He recognised me, attempted in vain to rise, tried to speak some broken phrases, but the only words I could make out were those of *commissary* or *secretary,* and he breathed his last before I could even think of procuring him the smallest assistance. Five deep wounds pierced his breast, yet no weapon, no arms of any kind were near him. I called, and rang the bell with all my force. In a moment the master of the hotel and the travellers who occupied it filled the apartment; the confusion was very great, and the first, the only idea entertained was that the admiral had been assassinated. Yet the same day, I saw, with as much surprise as sorrow, the admiral interred without pomp or ceremony; and what was strangely inconsistent with the language of the night before, I heard every one say that he had himself shortened his days, and terminated his life by five stabs of a *poignard*. Every time that I wished to express what I had witnessed, I discovered that no-one was either interested in or gave much credence to my account.

However, I was soon recalled to Paris to present my version of events. I was ushered into a chamber, without being allowed the time to wash the dust of the road from my person, where a man, seated with his back to me, was dictating a communication of some kind. A few paces beyond him another individual was busily writing. I was standing and much embarrassed with my looks, but nobody thought of these but myself. After several minutes, the person who was seated rose abruptly, and said to the officer, "leave us." He retired with a profound bow. This word, and the gesture that accompanied it, with the respect shown by the officer, instantly struck me with the idea that I was in the emperor's presence. He turned towards me, and notwithstanding my confusion, I recognized a countenance whose features and expression were then deeply engraved in *every* soldier's thoughts.

After casting a rapid glance at me, "What is your name?" said he. At the moment I had almost forgotten my own name, and was so confounded that I opened my mouth without being able to articulate a word. He repeated his question in a tone of kindness that gave me the force of stammering out—

"Robert Guillemard."

"Were you at Rennes with Admiral Villeneuve?"

"Yes, general." I did not then know that he was styled Sire.

"What do you know about his death?"

"A great deal," replied I, with a confidence that increased every moment.

He was struck with surprise, and ordered me to relate all the particulars of that event. The account I gave was doubtless not very eloquent, but it was authentic and very circumstantial. Whilst I spoke, the emperor walked slowly up and down the cabinet, with his arms folded. He several times stopped to listen to me with more attention; but he stopped abruptly when I spoke of the five individuals whom I thought guilty of the admiral's death, and when I attempted to describe the man who seemed to be their director, he suddenly stopped me, and inquired:

"Should you be able to know him again?"

"Yes, general,"

The emperor stamped on the floor, and walked over the room with an angry aspect. He rang the bell, and said to the officer who came, "Call Decrés."

I was then taken to the hall in front of the emperor's cabinet. In about a quarter of an hour I saw a rear-admiral enter, who was immediately introduced, I was soon after introduced myself and saw that it was the minister of the marine.

The emperor, whose physiognomy had assumed a more sombre expression, ordered me to repeat my account; the moment I had finished he turned to the minister and said: "You have heard what he says, let an inquiry be instantly made—see Fouché, and let these men be tried."

The minister began to urge that official documents proved that I was mistaken. But the emperor would not let him conclude, and said to him: "It is enough—do as I tell you." The minister withdrew, and the emperor made me a sign that I might retire. When I had readied the door, he said: "From what part of the country are you?"

I stopped and answered: "From Sixfour."

"Near Toulon?"

"Yes, Sire," said I this time, for I had heard the minister.

"Ah—ah, I went there during the siege, to observe the English positions. It is quite a signal post, a complete eagle's nest. What is your father?"

"He is the notary and mayor of the village," said I, assuming a look of importance.

"How long have you been in the service?"

"Thirteen months."

"That is not much—but it's no matter—you may go."

I retired enchanted. I had no doubt but I should be made a corporal the same day, a sergeant the next, and should be pushed from rank to rank by the last look of the emperor. The only advantage, however, that I derived from this interview is the recollection of it that I retain. The brilliant hopes with which I flattered myself for a few days were overthrown by the emperor's occupations, when he was on the eve of entering into a war with the Fourth Coalition.

It is not long since I read the work of Dr. O'Meara. He relates that in his conversations with Napoleon at St. Helena, the latter spoke very fully of the admiral's death, and explained how he had killed himself by five stabs of a *poignard*. I am far from contesting the veracity of the Irish doctor; but certainly Napoleon had greatly changed his mode of thinking, or had totally forgotten the particulars of my narrative, which, however, seemed to convince him at the time, and produced the strongest impression on his mind.

Three or four days after this examination, I met on the Boulevards the individual of Rennes. He wore a dark blue uniform, with a red collar, embroidered with silver. He passed quite close to me without seeming to remark me. I would have much wished to have met him there before I had been called before the emperor. I was undecided during the whole day whether I should mention it to one of my officers. Next day I went to the major's, but he was not at home; I went again, but he had company and could not see me. Perhaps my good genius inspired me with the idea of not pushing any farther my inquiries into the subject.

Till this period I had reflected little. The events I had witnessed, of little importance in themselves, had made on me only that slight impression that glides over the minds of young people. I knew neither men nor affairs; but the violent shock given me by the battle of Trafalgar, the disastrous end of a man eminent by his rank and talents, and my singular interview with the emperor, were all events, that were not fitted to leave me in a state of indifference. I was deeply affected, could think of nothing else, and my reflections enabled me to appreciate the system of social order. In fact, I had in the space of a few months seen the fortune of England compromised by the death of Nelson, shot by a common soldier; an admiral, whose conduct and misfortunes merited rewards, assassinated in the centre of France with impunity; a minister making useless efforts to discover murderers who made no attempt at concealment; and the emperor himself ceasing after a few days to think any more of a matter that had seemed to interest him so strongly at first Yet the death of Nelson was to remain without effect; the whole of France was to believe in Villeneuve's suicide; and the truth, which Napoleon had learned from my mouth, was to lead to no result. This was the first time I had seen such things; and I henceforward adopted the habit of judging only of what

I saw with my own eyes, and appreciated at their proper value the statements of historians, and those conventional truths that are so easily palmed on the public.

These grave thoughts completely altered my views of life and manners; notwithstanding the caprices of fortune I had just witnessed, I determined to brave its rigours, and laid out for myself a rule of conduct having in view my military promotion. I saw but too much, in after times, how chance blindly determines our lot, whatever our resolutions or intrinsic value may be.

Chapter 4
Siege of Stralsund

It was rare at this period, for the soldiers who were fit for service to remain long at their depot, and our departure was already talked of. It was still rarer for them ever to return to Paris after they left it. Hence I profited by the opportunity now in my power, an opportunity that might never again occur, of seeing this capital of the world. I explored it in every sense, and saw all that a soldier can see. Unfortunately there existed at that time neither *Hermite de la Chaussée d'Antin, Hermite de la Guyanne, Hermite du Marais,* nor the *Rôdeur;* how much fatigue and how many journeys these gentlemen would have spared me by pointing out all that is worthy of a stranger's attention, without even forgetting the conversations of porters and the refinements of the ladies of the fish-market!

During the few months I remained at the depot, visiting every part of the city in turn, spending the Sundays at the barriers, fighting sometimes, and yet studying pretty attentively my military duties so as to hope for promotion, the year's levy had received sufficient instruction and discipline to join the army. On the other hand, though the French army had entered Berlin after the battle of Jena, war was still going on with Russia and Prussia. None of us would have been sorry to he engaged in it, and it was with pleasure that we saw a detachment, of which I formed a part, ordered to join our regiment in the North of Italy. But before my departure, and during my stay at Paris, I had several times received news from home by conscripts who came from that part of the country. Miette was still handsome, the conscripts said, and inconsolable for my absence, according to her own letters. My father was as active and kind as ever, which was very evident by the small remittances he continued to send me pretty regularly; my brother and sister often talked about me to the good women of the village, but my poor mother was daily declining, and had lost all hope of ever seeing me again. In other respects, Sixfour was still the finest place in the world.

We set out to join our regiment on the 20th November, and after forty days' march reached the little town of Rovata, four leagues from Brescia, where were stationed the staff and the *compagnies d'elite*. I was placed on my arrival in the light company of the first battalion. The centre companies were scattered in about twenty villages, at various distances from each other, and had little communication with each other, or with the staff; and the regiment was never assembled, except to perform those grand manoeuvres which the viceroy of Italy came often to see performed in the plain of Montechiaro, by the two divisions under his command. The various regiments of which they consisted, received the order the evening before, and set out from their quarters during the night that they might reach by daybreak the place of meeting, where more than twenty thousand men were assembled.

The prince always inspected the troops before he began to execute manoeuvres, and examined with the greatest care the smallest particulars of the soldiers situation. He stopped pretty frequently in the ranks, inquired of the soldiers about the state of their linen, shoes, pay, and clothing, listened to them with patience, replied with kindness, and set their grievances right. I twice saw the Princess, his wife, along with him at these reviews, and passing through our ranks by his side. The grand manoeuvres and mock fights then began, and were not terminated till night, apparently as much for his own instruction as for ours. After treading in every sense the arid and stony plain of Montechiaro, we returned to our quarters, where we scarcely ever remained eight days without being ordered again to the same ground. Except some trifling exercises, we passed the intervals in the most complete idleness.

We passed in this manner the early part of 1807. The regiment formed at that time a part of Molitor's division, and of the corps of observation of the grand army.

At the beginning of April, that division received sudden orders to march to Trente, where it was to receive further instructions. After marching along the banks of the beautiful lake of Garda, and passing through the city of that name, and the towns of Lonado and Teschiera, we arrived in a few days at the capital of the Italian Tyrol, which we found full of troops. Here we made a pretty long stay. At length an order of the day informed us that the division was henceforward to belong to the fourth corps of the grand army, and was to march to Magdeburgh.

We quickly marched over the German Tyrol, Bavaria, Saxony, and a part of Prussia. We made forced marches, and more than once set out some hours before sunrise, marched all day, and did not arrive till late at night at the town where we were to halt, and where we stopped only a few hours. At Lansberg, I remember going into a coffee-house with some of my companions, and finding a French newspaper; we laughed heartily at reading in it that Molitor's division was travelling post. It was right: but as we said at the time, *our shoes were our post-chaises.*

These fatigues, which in fact were very great, seemed to me at the moment to be the *ne plus ultra* of a soldiers sufferings. The campaigns I saw afterwards, particularly that in Russia, greatly altered my ideas on the subject. But how rapid so ever our movements were, often made in bad weather and along wretched roads, very few soldiers remained behind, owing to the reception we met with in the countries we traversed.

The provinces conquered by France, and those which had the honour of being its allies, had long been accustomed to maintain the French regiments that passed through their territory, or who came to garrison it; the practice seemed almost as natural to the inhabitant as to the soldier: the latter took possession of his quarters as if he had been at home, was surprised if dinner was not ready at his arrival, and inquired if by chance he was not expected. The host made excuses, gave him up his best room, and provided him with the best accommodations he could afford; and the next day the soldier met ten leagues further on the same attention and obsequiousness, whilst the inhabitant received a new guest equally troublesome with the one he had the evening before, and whom he treated in the same manner. In the countries beyond the Rhine these things went on, not during weeks or months, but during a period of twenty years.

We justly thought that the renown of our arms obtained for us a reception always full of good will and cordiality, often even mingled with marks of the warmest affection and of real enthusiasm. The recollection of our victories, might naturally produce the latter feeling; but resignation to necessity had often the greatest share in the attentions that were paid to us. This we were enabled to appreciate when, after our defeats, we passed through the same countries, which we had so often traversed when on our march to new conquests.

We arrived at Magdeburgh at last, in the beginning of July, and learned that the fourth corps was ordered to punish Sweden for its aggressions, and take possession of the city of Stralsund and the rest of Pomerania.

The regiment had a few days repose at Magdeburgh, received its camp effects, and was wakened by the drum beating to arms at two o'clock in the morning, on the 7th of July. A suspension of arms had been entered into with Sweden, and expired on the 14th, at mid-day: the same day our corps, consisting of the divisions Loison, Grandjean, Doudet, and Molitor, of a Bavarian corps, some Italian regiments, and a part of the Spanish corps of Romana, entered Pomerania, and were concentrated on Stralsund, under the command of Marshal Brune.

When the different corps had formed their junction, they connected their operations, and marched on the city. About mid-day, our division entered Pomerania by Damgarten, a village not far from Stralsund, and in a few hours we perceived the steeples of the place. Some light infantry soon appeared, but dispersed at the first discharge of musketry. In a short time a large body of English and Swedes commanded by the King of Sweden in person, seemed desirous of offering some resistance, but they were driven back, and pursued as far as the foot of the ramparts, after a contest of several hours, in which we lost but few men. Gustavus Adolphus commanded the enemy; we were led on by General Boudet

The French army soon fixed its camp, and the labours of the siege began with great activity, in spite of a continued and very sharp firing from the enemy; numerous redoubts and entrenchments in *every* direction covered the environs of Stralsund, and began already to extend very near the ramparts in the beginning of August. At that period a chain of the enemy's posts was still placed all round the city, at about a hundred paces from the fortifications; in front of each was a French post, and between them, sentinels of each nation, so close to each other that they could have shaken hands.

On the 5th August, I was on guard during the night, and formed part of a post of twelve men, commanded by Sergeant Moutet, my first companion after joining the army. An aid-de-camp came from the marshal to order him to march as soon as he heard the signal given by a cannon shot fired from the camp, to advance upon the post in front of him, inform the men they must retire into the city, and to fire on them in case of hesitation. All the posts surrounding the city received a similar order, and advanced the moment the cannon shot was fired at four o'clock in the morning.

When the Swedes saw us approaching, they hastily ran to their arms; but Moutet told them to retire, exactly in the tone he would have used in addressing a picket of his own regiment. They seemed at first to understand what was meant, hut did not seem decided till they saw we were preparing to fire on them, which we did while they were retreating. At the same moment, the numerous posts round Stralsund executed the same movement; shots were heard on all sides, and continued without intermission, gradually approaching nearer to the place, in proportion as the advanced guards of the enemy retreated.

We soon saw the drawbridges let down to allow the garrison to come out and repel our attack, while several of our regiments had already taken up positions, and were preparing to support us. The second battalion of the 67th, commanded by the intrepid Jacquemet, marched with shouldered arms, in a close column, exposed to a shower of balls that thinned their ranks, and advanced as far as one of the gates of the city, where an aid-de-camp brought the orders to halt, and sent them in another direction. Several battalions were then disposed as light infantry: we fought in the space included, a few hours before, between the enemy's posts and the place. This spot had not yet suffered the devastation that is inseparable from a siege and a camp, and was covered with charming country houses, English gardens, elegant pavilions, flowers and verdure. In one moment everything was changed; the dead bodies of Englishmen, Frenchmen, and Swedes, and the wounded of both armies dyed with their blood this spot so agreeable a moment before; and the turf was trodden down in every direction, and was strewed with remnants of cartridges.

At one o'clock the enemy had abandoned their posts, and retired into the city, after losing a great many men. We had pursued them as far as the foot of the fortifications; several of their artillerymen had been killed at their guns on the ramparts by our light infantry; and I was myself put the next morning in the order of the day of our corps, and made a corporal for having killed one of them at the moment he was going to fire a cannon.

Seven or eight windmills were enclosed in the space we had just taken possession of. Whilst the contest was going on, an officer pointed out one to me, and ordered me to take four men with me and set fire to it. We were forced to drive in the door, and were preparing to execute our orders, when we were surprised by the appearance of a woman, about thirty years of age, making a piteous lamentation, followed by two children from five to six years of age. She stretched out her arms in a tone of supplication, and threw herself at our feet; she spoke with a great deal of action, and her animated language and sobs could leave me no doubt as to her meaning, though I did not understand one word of what she said. Assuredly she was imploring me not to destroy this mill, which was perhaps the sole support of the family.

It would have been a consolation to me to have made her understand the regret I felt in executing a cruel order, of which I was only the passive instrument; to have told her that it was not in my power to dispense with my orders, and that if I did not obey, other soldiers would soon do it in my place. I wished to persuade her to retire as speedily as possible towards the city, and to take away all she could. But I could not make her understand me; I collected in a corner of the mill some wood and straw, set fire to it, and it soon spread to the building.

The poor woman's despair was then at its height. She rolled herself on the ground in convulsions, and wished to throw herself into the flames. Her children raised a terrible outcry, and hung round their mother. But there was fighting going on close to us, balls whizzed round the mill, and several cannon shots from the ramparts went through the building with a terrible crashing; I then laid hold of her, and in spite of her resistance, hurried her rapidly past various parties of our skirmishers, led her beyond the most advanced, to the interval that separated the two armies, showed her the city, and continued to follow her with my eyes till I saw her enter with her children among the enemy's skirmishers.

For some days after this skirmish, our labours were still continued, and our retrenchments extended as far as the foot of the fortifications. Several battalions worked at them night and day, exposed to the fire of the besieged; whilst others under arms, were ready to support them, and to oppose any sortie the enemy might attempt to make.

Amidst all this confusion and noise, there still were moments occupied in pleasure and in sports, which Frenchmen seek and find in every situation. The fete of St. Napoleon was celebrated by races, games, dances, and extraordinary distributions. In our regiment, in a theatre hastily erected between the two battalions, our non-commissioned officers performed plays. Without *lustres,* without curtains, without decorations, but not without spectators, we performed with universal applause, the *Fourberies de Scapin,* followed by the *Retour Imprévu* of Regnard, and the whole terminated by a cantata on the siege of Stralsund, written by one of our sergeants major, set to music by the leader of our band, and sung by the finest voices, and accompanied by the whole musical strength of the regiment.

The same day I was the object of a ceremony, that I cannot pass over without notice. In recompense of my conduct in the action of the 6th of August, I had been proposed to the Masonic lodge of the regiment, and my reception was fixed for the day of St. Napoleon; it took place accordingly, with all the splendour circumstances admitted, in a hut about fifteen feet in length and six in breadth, where there was no room to stand up, but which served as the temple notwithstanding. After having made my journeys, which were not very long ones, undergone the trials by fire and water, and the usual tricks, received the signs, words, touches and other forms, the adjutant, who was our orator, addressed me a very fine speech, in which he explained to me the sublimity of the character I had just obtained, by creating me a child of the true light, and all the happiness that I should thereby derive. I was afterwards present at the dinner, and it may be easily imagined how delighted I was on hearing myself called *brother* by our colonel and the rest of the officers. I retired quite enchanted with masonry, became a zealous partisan of the institution, and long believed that it had some meaning.

Meanwhile, our labours in carrying on the siege were finished; and we began to place pieces of heavy artillery in the redoubts, and there was some talk of an assault, when on the

20th August, after a severe fire on our skirmishers, which had continued all night, the latter perceived in the morning that the sentinels on the ramparts had been relieved, and that the most profound silence reigned in the place.

The colonel of the 67th made some of his men swim over the ditches, ordered them to haul down the drawbridge, occupied the gate with a detachment, and sent the Marshal information of what was going on. A short time after this, some regiments entered the city and found it abandoned. The garrison and the greater part of the inhabitants had retired to the Isle of Rugen. The English had long before this left the Swedes to take care of their own defence. Marshal Brune sent the inhabitants a proclamation, inviting them to return to their houses, which they hastened to comply with.

On the 7th of September, a descent was made during the night upon the Isle of Rugen; and almost without resistance, the governor of Stralsund, the garrison, and a large body of officers, were taken prisoners. It is well known that peace with Sweden was the consequence of this event, which was followed by the disgrace of Marshal Brune, who bad signed the preliminaries in the name of the French armies.

It was not till a fortnight afterwards that the fourth corps left the camp, where we already began to be tired with our situation. It rained incessantly after the taking of Rugen. Our huts had been covered with rye straw, cut while green, and long since dried up, and no longer affording us sufficient shelter. We got nothing but very unwholesome food: thousands of worms, produced by the moisture, destroyed our bread, covered our clothes, and swarmed in the cut and half rotten straw which served us to lie upon.

At last an impatiently looked for order of the day announced to the different corps the quarters they were to occupy, and they almost all set out at the same time. Some foolish wit, or rather some evil-disposed person, thought proper to terminate this short campaign in a dramatic manner, by setting fire to the camp the very day we abandoned it.

On our march to Wismar in Mecklenburgh, the town assigned to our regiment by the order I have just spoken of, we saw nothing but misery and desolation, the inevitable consequences of a siege or the stay of an enemy's army, till we reached the frontiers of Pomerania. Reibnitz, Damgarten, and the few villages we passed through were almost deserted, and we scarcely felt courage to ask the inhabitants for what we were in need of, they had been long before so completely ruined by requisitions and the passage of troops.

Rostock, the first town we came to in Mecklenburg, and all those we afterwards saw, presented us a very different aspect. All military men who have been in this fine country always remember with pleasure the affability of the inhabitants, and their gaiety, which is somewhat French in its tone; they love the regularity of its small towns, the neatness and taste displayed in the furniture, and the arrangement of even the least wealthy houses; but it is with particular emotion that they recollect the reception we met with wherever we went, and the attachments which every man in the army, from the general officer to the meanest soldier, formed with the amiable females of Mecklenburgh.

These pleasures awaited us at Wismar, with which we were enchanted, but where I was not to remain long. Three or four days after our arrival, perhaps twenty detachments of six, ten, twenty, or thirty men, commanded according to their numbers by an officer, non-commissioned officer, or corporal, received at the same time orders to occupy the villages in the neighbourhood of Wismar, and the charge of guarding the coast, in case of an attempt at landing on the part of the English, who had a fleet cruising in the Baltic. I was sent with a detachment of eight men to Wischendorf, a village on the seashore, four leagues from Wismar, and consisting of a very pretty chateau, surrounded by a dozen little houses that belonged to it. I need not say that my soldiers were quartered in the village, and that the commander of the detachment was lodged in the chateau.

I was received with much politeness and attention, but with a coldness I should not perhaps have perceived had it continued, and had it not formed a great contrast with the frankness and cordiality shown me a few days after, and kept up towards me during the whole of my stay at Wischendorf. After several interviews with the inmates of the chateau, a sort of intimacy began to arise between them and me. Instead of taking my meals in my room, where I was attended by a servant, they intimated that they would be flattered by my joining the family, and I accepted the invitation with pleasure. I doubtless owed it to the education I had received, that the humble uniform of a corporal was admitted to the table of a German lord.

M. Hartmann, the Baron of Wischendorf, was about fifty years of age, had a fine countenance, and a manner full of grace and dignity. He had been a long time in the army, was a strong admirer of the French nation, of its literature, of its character, and military exploits, and was an enthusiastic admirer of Napoleon. He had a handsome fortune, of which he made a noble use, and spoke our language with great ease and always with pleasure, as did his wife, his son Charles, and his daughter Frederica.

The large and handsome library of the Baron was at my service, and I passed many pleasant hours in it. They were far, however, from possessing the same charms as the company of Charles and his amiable sister, our hunting parties, our journeys in sledges over the snow, and above all our evening parties; the voice and the piano of Frederica, the narratives of battles given by M. Hartmann, and the accounts I gave of France, and the dangers I had already encountered, often prolonged them to a very late hour.

It is necessary for me to remember the resolution I adopted, and the promise I made to the reader, not to write on what merely relates to myself, for me to resist the recollections that crowd on my mind, and to pass over in silence the most agreeable period of my military life. I feel the more regret at this, that I am forced to notice only in a very cursory manner the expression of my gratitude, and the affection I shall always preserve for that amiable family.

My duty called me every three or four days to Wismar, but I always came back the same day, for I was always eager to be at Wischendorf. One day I had been detained later than usual, and I was surprised on my road by the approach of night; I hurried forward, and was not more than a mile or two from the chateau when I saw before me a soldier stretched out on the snow.

As I approached, he implored my assistance, and told me that he had fallen from his horse, that he suffered great pain from his leg, which he believed was broken; he added that he had become insensible the moment he fell, but had recovered his senses through the severity of the cold, though he was unable to rise up. His horse was at a short distance; I tried to catch him but could not succeed. I came back to the wounded man, whose language indicated that he belonged to the Spanish troops commanded by Romana. I took him on my shoulders, and carried him to the chateau, where he was received with a cordiality which I expected. He was a cadet serving in a cavalry corps.

The village surgeon declared that his leg was only dislocated; and in fact, in a few days afterwards, Valdejo (that was his name) was going about. His horse had been brought back by a peasant. Our new guest passed eight or ten days along with us, during which he received from the Hartmann family the most assiduous care and the most delicate attentions. He said again and again that but for my assistance, he should inevitably have died on the highway, from the effects of the cold during the night after the accident.

I should, perhaps, have forgotten this adventure, as well as many others of no greater importance; the recollection of Valdejo himself might have been effaced from my memory, like that of many others with whom one daily meets upon active service, where one contracts a sort of intimacy which ceases at the moment of separation—but chance, which had brought me into contact with him, that I might do him a service, made me meet him at a later period, that he might do me a service in his turn.

I need not mention the regret I felt on leaving Wischendorf after a residence of three months. The corps to which I belonged performed a variety of manoeuvres, by which the regiment was marched backward and forward to Stralsund, Barth, Rostock, and in fact traversed in every direction Pomerania, Mecklenburg and a part of Prussia.

In the beginning of the year 1808, a camp of instruction was formed in the neighbourhood of Stralsund, almost on the same ground which we occupied during the siege. In autumn, we resumed our quarters, our journeys, and the mode of life we had led the winter before; but in the beginning of 1809, Molitor's division, to which our regiment still belonged, received orders to march, and we soon learned that we were to go to Spain.

In traversing a part of France, we discovered how proud it was of the victories of the grand army. Fetes were given us in every town where we halted; our officers were invited to balls and public dinners. At Besançon the gate by which we entered was changed into a military triumphal arch; the magistrates of the city came out to meet the regiment, and a crown of laurel was placed on our eagle.

At the end of April we arrived at Lyons, where we were to remain till next day. It was Sunday, the greater part of which I devoted to the examination of the second city in France, for I had only slept in it on my way to Italy. I went in the afternoon, with some of my companions, into a grog-shop at Brotteaux. It was full of men belonging to the different corps, particularly of soldiers of the departmental company.

When we entered, a very keen discussion had arisen between the latter and some men of our battalion. They were bitterly reproached with the honours they received in every town, and doubts were thrown out concerning the honour which the regiment had acquired in the different actions in which it had been engaged. I had the weakness or the vanity to wish to persuade our opponents that we had done as much as others. Upon this my friend Savournin, sergeant in the battalion, a native of Provence, like myself, and pretty hot-headed withal, cried out:

"Even if we had done a great deal less than others, we should at any rate have been of more use than the departmental companies."

This was quite enough for these quarrelsome fellows, whose only object was evidently to raise a dispute. I vainly employed a great deal of moderation to prevent a duel, which might become an army question, and lead to interminable quarrels. The more desire I showed of making peace, the more insolence was shown by the other party, and the more impetuosity by Savournin.

At last the quarrel rose to such a pitch that there were no means of settling and in a quarter of an hour after we were on the ground ready for action, six against six. I have always felt too much repugnance to these sort of things, (in which the truly brave are rarely seen,) to give any particulars of this. Suffice it to say that in half an hour after I was taken to the hospital with a pretty severe wound. Savournin, on his side, was also wounded, but slightly. I do not mention the much greater injury we did to our opponents.

I learned next day that the regiment had received orders that altered its destination.

Chapter 5

Oudet

A fortnight had already elapsed since the departure of the regiment, and my regret at not being able to accompany it had been increased by learning that it was retracing its steps and marching again towards that Germany, the French soldiers' land of promise; but I was pretty well recovered, and felt myself fit to march, and join my regiment: so I asked the chief surgeon of the hospital for my discharge, which he did not make me wait long for, as he delivered it to me next day, the 18th March.

Four soldiers, who left it the same day, were sent with me to New Brisack, where the commissary was to give us further orders.

Previous to my departure I had received news and money from my family, and I had a very agreeable journey, which was much enlivened by one of our companions, an old pioneer, who had survived the wars of the revolution. His never-ending accounts of battles never fatigued us. They were given in such an original and natural way, he mingled such strange reflections with them, that the most terrible circumstances, when told by him, often made us burst into a roar of laughter, while he never for a moment lost his own imperturbable gravity. I was generally quartered along with him, and almost every day, without perceiving the lapse of time, he captivated till midnight the attention of our peasants—the name he gave to our host, and to every man not in the army, whatever his rank or fortune might be. War was, in his opinion, the grand object of civilization; to be able to read and write out a list of a troop the *ne plus ultra* of knowledge; and the honorary sabre he had received at Marengo, a reward far above all orders, or marks of distinction.

We reached New Brisack on the 6th of April; it was there that I separated from my companions, as we were sent off to join our respective corps. Mine was quartered at Ortenburgh in Bavaria, and I accordingly set off for that place. I marched, without halting, as far as Freiseigen, where I resolved to take some rest.

I had scarcely taken possession of my quarters, when I was told of a soldier who had been there for more than a fortnight, and whom they spoke highly of. I felt but little interest in this: I requested to be left quiet, and to be awakened when dinner was ready. When I went downstairs, the soldier I had been told of was already at table; he turned round when he saw me coming in, and to the great surprise of our hosts, he rose with great precipitation and embraced me. It was my friend Savournin, in the uniform of a Sergeant major.

During dinner, he informed me that on his way to join our corps he had halted at Freiseigen, where he had been urged by some of his old companions to leave it, and to enter a supplementary regiment that was forming at the time, and was to be called the *new ninth* of the line. This corps, recently formed, and with a number of posts not filled up, presented a prospect of promotion which he thought it his duty not to refuse. He concluded by urging me to imitate his example. How strong so ever my desire was of rising higher than a corporal I felt great repugnance to leave my regiment, for, in fact, we soldiers had formed a habit of considering our regiment as our family. But what Savournin told me of the. colonel of the ninth shook my resolution. He described him as a commander desirous of having round him officers and non-commissioned officers, whose knowledge would distinguish his regiment, and be of personal use to him on a day of battle.

He told me also that as the colonel knew how to appreciate services, and was fond of rewarding them, there was every prospect of promotion under his command.

This conversation, which continued till a late hour, made me reflect upon my prospects, and my mind was next day absorbed with the subject, whilst I was looking at the soldiers of the new regiment at their exercise. From the number of new epaulets and shoulder-knots, it was easily seen that plenty of promotions had been made; and all this strengthened the advice given me by Savournin.

At that moment the colonel left the burgomaster's house, which was in the grand square, and came up to the different companies that were performing the manual exercise. He was about thirty years of age, of an open and mild, yet martial physiognomy, with a look indicative both of penetration and good nature. His appearance put the seal to Savournin's endeavours. My resolution was formed in an instant: I took advantage of the first moment the colonel was left alone, went up to him, and told him frankly that the account I had received from my friend, the appearance of his men, the impression that he had himself made on my mind, and lastly, the hope of proper promotion, induced me to ask him for the honour of serving under his command.

The singularity of this address, and perhaps the praise I had mingled with it, fixed the colonel's attention. He took me aside, asked me about my education more than my services, about general studies more than the soldier's school; and being satisfied with my answers, he said to me at length:

"Young man, you shall be 'harbinger' in my regiment; no other post is at this moment vacant; but in a short time, if your conduct be correct, I promise you that you shall not be forgotten."

I accepted the offer with gratitude; the colonel engaged to get my change of regiment approved of by the minister of war; and that very day I was installed into my new post at the head of a company.

I soon began to think that my days of trial were over, and that the future would be favourable to me. A new campaign had been opened against Austria; the grand army to which we belonged, marched with enthusiasm to new triumphs; it was commanded by Napoleon in person. Our regiment was composed of new elements, and aspired to the honour of speedily becoming old in the esteem of the army, and this noble feeling was kept up by our young colonel with a skill that was well fitted to bring about great results. I became his favourite, and as always occurs when a regiment is newly formed, the non-commissioned officers were almost all employed in writing, he made me his private secretary.

This employment attached me still more to him; and I confess that there was something seductive and irresistible in his way that completely fascinated my mind. The sentiment of admiration I felt for him became still stronger when I represented in my own fancy this young commander on the battle field—everything in him announced one of those men whom nature seems to have formed for command.

I might give you a more finished portrait of Colonel Oudet, at least gratitude claims it of me; but I am also aware of the renown he obtained, and the reports that were spread of his conduct; I do not wish the justice I render him to have any influence in spreading fables already but too widely circulated.

When we left Freiseigen, the whole regiment was impatient of reaching the theatre of hostilities. We met at Osterhoven the first French troops. During the eight days we remained in that town, we fraternized with several regiments, which were all animated with the same spirit. In those times we marched to battle with a feeling of confidence and of national dignity, inspired by fifteen years of victory.

I passed a great part of my time at the colonel's, and had an opportunity of remarking that he enjoyed the same influence over everyone that approached him as he did over me and the officers of his own regiment. He was constantly receiving visits from officers of rank, and all showed him profound esteem, and often a degree of respect and deference, for which he was indebted to his superior merit rather than to his rank.

One day I had remained later than usual in the room where the colonel usually sat, when two persons came to see him; they were all three in the next room, which was only separated from mine by a thin partition, so that I could hear all that was said. My attention was first called by hearing Oudet embrace one of them, and address him by the names of colonel and friend, and express his joy at meeting him after such a long absence.

The second stranger said very little at first, but when his companion had finished, spoke in a low voice to the following effect:

"Colonel Oudet, our friend Chautard, was passing through Olmaring, not far from this; I informed him that you were in the neighbourhood, which I learned in my capacity of officer of the staff—I requested him to introduce me to you; I felt the most urgent necessity of seeing you, and your friend seized with avidity an opportunity of embracing you.

"You have not been in the army for some time, and have, perhaps, not remarked all the progress made by the institution you founded seven years ago. The *Philodelphes* prosper and increase; their leaders are at this moment far distant from the army. The *areopagus* has decided that in your capacity of founder of the order, you ought to resume the *censorship*. We are desired by them to express to you their desire."

I was greatly struck with this, to me, extraordinary address, and listened with redoubled attention.

Colonel Oudet seemed surprised at this commencement, for he was a moment before he replied—

"Gentlemen," said he, "the areopagus honours me more than I merit; there are in its own bosom, officers of higher rank than mine, and who are well qualified to preside over the institution. I have been but lately recalled to the army, and do not know its elements sufficiently well to take charge of such a heavy burden; I should fear to commit errors, to compromise the safety of the members; I cannot accept the honour they present to me."

Upon this the staff-officer and Colonel Chautard urged him very strongly; though I could not make out all they said, it was evident that they were members of an association instituted for the destruction of what they denominated tyranny. I was much embarrassed for them, for Colonel Oudet, and for myself, who thus suddenly became entrusted with their secrets. I recollected that more than one conspiracy had failed through accidents similar to the one that put me so near them; and without wishing to have any responsibility in the whole of this business my anxiety became greater and greater.

Oudet long resisted the bold appeals of his friend, and the brilliant perspective with which the staff-officer attempted to fascinate him. At last their obstinacy restored him to his wonted firmness and decision, and he told them with a moderation, skill and nobleness of manner that left them scarcely a word to say in reply:

"At the period when I founded the society of *Philadelphes* between a few young men, it was an association of friends that I formed; that enthusiasm had secretly increased afterwards, while despotism had sprung up in the consular government, and the *Philadelphes* had dared to form the project of overthrowing that power, and of restoring France to its republican liberties. At that period, one day might have restored liberty, since one man only was to be destroyed; but five years of a most extraordinary reign and of glory wholly unparalleled, had altogether changed the ideas of the French. Political parties had been extinguished; almost all the soldiers of the republic were sincerely faithful to the imperial eagles; every man saw in the present war the expiring struggle of the coalition, and the indication of a durable peace—the assurance that our country was about to make, under the aegis of a great man, the trial of its powers of industry and commerce, which it had been accumulating during a period of twenty years. In this state what Frenchman could believe that he was called upon to destroy so many bones, by overthrowing the established government? Doubtless I am a republican, and will die a republican; but I can sacrifice my wishes to the happiness of my country; its glory is secured—its repose is about to commence. Would we stain its glory and endanger its repose by new agitations? The principles of the revolution will spring up in prosperity, and our children will one day establish, without a struggle, that liberty which we could not secure except by shedding torrents of blood. My friends, let us be capable of making a greater effort than the courage of conspiring, that of renouncing projects of which the very success would be disastrous to France."

Colonel Chautard attempted to urge the binding nature of the oaths of the *Philadelphes*. Oudet reminded him that the *Philadelphes* did not in his time take such oaths as he alluded to; that duties change with times and circumstances, and resolutions with the progress of years; that an association of students does not bind a man for the whole of his life. They spoke of Brutus and Cato. He replied that the world had now no need of such ferocious virtues as these ancients displayed. They talked of republics, and mentioned the name of Sparta. He ridiculed the Grecian republics, with the exception of Athens. The liberty he wished for, was one accompanied by all the blessings of civilization, all the charms of the arts, all the riches of commerce and of science.

Finally, they asked him what was his reply to the proposal of the areopagus—"Tell them," replied he, "that my love for my country forces me to stand firm by the standard of the head of the government, when his march is in all respects favourable to our country; but that if, in future days, he became a despot, I would be one of the first to raise the cry, 'Rise lovers of your country.'"

The conference broke up, and Colonel Oudet went out with the two officers. I took advantage of his absence, to retire; these individuals so far as I know, never came again.

For some days after this incident, I remarked that an air of thought and anxiety was mingled with the colonel's wonted pleasing smile. I was afterwards told, by a Corsican major retired from the army, that reports were spread among the troops that Oudet was at the head of a secret association. I have been told that a lady, at that time possessed of great beauty and influence, asserted that the staff-officer I spoke of, had carefully spread this belief in the army, for the purpose of forcing the discontented to show themselves.

At the very time he was taking advantage of their credulity, it is said that he obtained a secret interview with the emperor, and discovered to him all the plans of the association. Napoleon listened with great anxiety to everything that was reported of Oudet. When he was told of his refusal to join the party, and ascertained that it was sincere, he resumed his serenity of countenance, and said, with a smile, that the association *was nothing more than a club of college companions.* But he too fully appreciated the merit of such conduct to allow it to remain unrewarded. In fact, a month had not expired when the colonel was promoted to the rank of general, the very evening before the battle of Wagram; yet the regiment had been doing nothing but marching and countermarching since the opening of the campaign, and had not even been engaged in the bloody engagement of Essling.

This un-looked for promotion seems to me to be a sufficient proof that the emperor had been informed, as I learned afterwards, of Oudet's refusal, I was even then satisfied of the falsehood of the report circulated of his participation in the plans of the secret society at that period; and everything combines to show the error of those who have maintained that he was completely disgraced at that very time.

Perhaps I have already said too much upon this part of Colonel Oudet's life; but so many reports have been spread in the army about his conduct, after the battle of Wagram, that I have thought it my duty to state the above mentioned particulars, which chance brought to my knowledge.

The new rank he had just obtained was a sure sign of

the promotion that would be made of every man of merit in his regiment, because previous to the battle of Wagram, General Oudet had not been employed on services conformable to his rank, and because he still continued to command the *ninth*. These arrangements, the numerous promotions going on among the superior officers, the concentration of the army, everything announced an approaching engagement. It was the battle of Wagram.

It is not to be expected that I can give the particulars of this action, which was fought on the 6th July, 1809. Besides, all that I know of it is limited to a very few things. In these grand movements, when generals can scarcely tell whether they are on the right or on the left wing of the army, what can a non-commissioned officer know? All that I can say is, that on leaving the Isle of Lobau, and in the plain at whose extremity Vienna is situated, our regiments were crowded upon each other like men of the same column, and that on the day of the battle I was present at the most brilliant review I ever saw in my life.

In the morning, the Emperor rode along the lines, and was hailed with loud exclamations by the soldiers; but the splendid staff that surrounded him, and the enthusiastic shouts that burst forth at his approach, pointed him out to the enemy, and exposed him to great danger, till an order was sent to the troops not to hail him as he passed along.

It is well known how the Emperor allowed the enemy to make several attempts on his flanks, till about ten o'clock in the morning, when he ordered a grand movement upon the Austrian centre, which decided the fate of the battle.

Our regiment was in the left wing, which was commanded by Massena; it was against it that the enemy made their strongest attacks, when they wished to cut us off from our communications with the Isle of Lobau. We had to sustain and drive back several charges of cavalry, that caused us the loss of a great many men. Our colonel was twice wounded. He was wounded in the thigh with a lance, and forced to leave the field of battle for a few minutes; but the moment he was dressed, he came back to resume his post.

The action had terminated; it was early in the day, and we were close to the gates of Vienna, which had for several days been in the hands of the French; we expected we should enter it ourselves in the course of the day, and enjoy the repose we had so much need of, when the regiment received orders to move forward on the right beyond Ebersdorf, to secure the movements of a part of the army, and to follow the enemy in their rapid retreat.

We armed ourselves with patience and set out. Night began to set in. We were to meet on our march with two or three regiments that had been called off from their positions, to whom we were to transmit orders to march back, and combine their movements with ours; but they had set off before we arrived, and we did not come up with them. Night had come on; though we were full of confidence, as the enemy had been in full retreat since the middle of the day, yet we marched forward with the usual precautions.

It was about eleven o'clock; we had just left the plain, and were entering upon some broken ground that was slightly hilly, when, on turning round a tuft of trees, we were hailed by several Austrian advanced posts, and all at once received a very sharp fire from every direction. We soon recovered the shock; our colonel displayed equal coolness and judgment, and led us on to the charge in the direction from which the hottest fire had come. We overthrew without difficulty the battalions placed on this spot, and continued our march forward; but a skirmish was not enough for us, others of the Austrian troops assembled to support the first; we were soon surrounded on all sides, and discovered too late that we had fallen into the very midst of a division of the enemy's army.

They formed round us a wall of fire and bayonets, which we fruitlessly attempted to break through. Twenty times were we thrown back upon the hollow ground where we had been surprised. The colonel hoped that the noise of our firing would bring up the regiments that ought to have occupied the same position as ourselves; but they had joined the main body of the army and we remained isolated.

Meanwhile, every discharge of musketry brought down whole ranks, and we were called upon to surrender. It was then that, formed in a square, and covering the eagle with our bodies, we heard Oudet exclaim:

"On the day of a grand victory, in which it had the glory of concurring, the ninth regiment will not dishonour eagle by surrendering. My lads, we will all conquer or die—*Vive l'Empereur.*"

This rallying word we each of us shouted with fury, we rushed upon the enemy, who gave way; but we were again thrown back upon the little wood where the enemy's troops rested. In a few moments, the greater part of those whom the great battle had spared, were cut down in the ambuscade. Some few of us still stood by the colonel, who was covered with wounds, and seemed no longer animated with the hopes of safety; but merely with the necessity of dying worthily.

Not one of the enemy dared to approach us. Our fire had almost ceased, and we received in silence and resignation the shots that were fired at us at a distance of only twenty paces; the colonel then took the eagle of the regiment, pulled it from the staff, and after making a small hole in the ground with a pioneer's hatchet, put into it our rallying signal, to prevent it falling into the enemy's hands. On the same spot, and at the same moment I fell senseless on the ground—I was wounded by a musket shot in the breast.

The coldness of the morning air revived my senses for a moment. When I opened my eyes, I saw the dead bodies of my companions around me. Two entire battalions of the regiment lay dead beside me, and the colonel was in the midst of them. The Austrians had retreated, and the silence around me was only broken by the groans of the dying.

I again became insensible, and had not fully recovered my recollection, till I was taken to the *ambulance*. At daylight several regiments had hastened towards the spot where they had heard firing during the night; but all the assistance they could give was to save the wounded, and this, unfortunately, was not a hard task, for the greater part had lost all their blood during the night, and expired towards morning.

The assistant surgeon who dressed me, assured me that my wound was not dangerous, and that I should soon get over it. As the same thing is said to every wounded man, to those even who are on the point of expiring, I had no great reason to be satisfied on this account; but the tone in which it was said, and his manner of dressing me, and more than all, a certain presentiment which I felt on more than one important occasion, made me trust in his words; hence my wound did not make more impression on me than a similar event usually does on a soldier's mind.

The day after I was sent to the ambulance it was visited by the Emperor, accompanied by Massena and two or three general officers; he was a quarter of an hour in visiting our ward. A calm and satisfied look shone on his countenance; he had no sword, and had under his arm his hat full of gold coin. He stopped at every bed, said something to every patient, inquired about his wound, and before going further, threw on the bed two or three Napoleons, according to the patient's rank. When he left our ward, we made an effort to rise up on our beds, in spite of the sufferings we felt, and saluted him with acclamations which he received with a smile of kindness and goodwill, casting a last glance round the hall before he went out. It was thus that the Emperor inspired the soldier with enthusiasm.

On the same day, Savournin came to see me; our third battalion, to which he belonged, had remained with the main body of the army, and had not been engaged in the ill-fated action of Ebersdorf. My friend was profoundly afflicted at the disaster our regiment had sustained. As soon as I embraced him, I mentioned my regret at the colonel's death.

"He is not dead," said he, "but there are small hopes of

saving him. He is in an adjoining ward covered with wounds, and surrounded by his own men. I have obtained leave to attend upon him, and have only left him for a moment, for the purpose of seeing you."

On the third day, Savournin came and informed me that the colonel was dying, and that no hopes remained. I would absolutely see him; Savournin called a soldier, and they two assisted me in getting up, and supported me as far as his bed. He knew me, as I perceived by the painful smile on his countenance; I saw but too clearly, at the very first glance, the truth of Savournin's statement. Colonel Oudet was losing his blood by a wound in the breast, which had broken open again that morning; and it was in vain that he had till this moment tried to conceal his weakness and his sufferings; his strength declined every moment, and the marks of dissolution already began to disguise the beauty of his martial figure. He seemed to recover for a moment; I was standing beside his bed; he stretched out his hand to me, and as I pressed it, several men of the *ninth* collected round us, he made a last effort to address us, and said:

"My fellow soldiers, I shall not have time to recommend you to the Emperor; I hope that he will learn your conduct, and will fully reward it. This is my consolation on leaving you."

He added some unconnected words, and expired. By the universal regret expressed by those present on this melancholy occasion, it was easy to discern what were the colonel's merits, and the affection borne to him by his regiment.

I was led away, or rather carried back to my bed. Savournin was full of sombre despair, and left me without saying a word; I scarcely thought of retaining him, I was so painfully affected at the melancholy scene I had just witnessed.

The next day, at the hour when the sad ceremony was to be paid to my colonel, I crawled to the window to see him carried by. He was to be buried in the garden belonging to the house that served us as an hospital. The persons present were all soldiers, most of them wounded. Whilst they were lowering him into the grave, the company crowded round; my eyes were fixed on this motionless group, when all at once some unforeseen event seemed to throw it into confusion. They rushed towards one spot, and I saw someone carried away. My uncertainty was not of long duration, for I learned in a few minutes afterwards that Savournin, rendered desperate by his sorrow at the colonel's loss, and perhaps disgusted with a life, in which all his best founded hopes vanished one after another, had thrown himself on the point of his sword, beside the grave of Oudet.

Thus I lost at the same moment a friend and a protector; I was again thrown back among the crowd, without hopes of reward for my past services, without being able to flatter myself with meeting another commander who would do me justice. I had reckoned on the future so confidently, that I remained for some time completely discouraged, and foresaw not that any event could ever place me in a position equally advantageous. Besides, I knew, as everyone else did, that our commanders treated us as they were themselves treated by the Emperor; success was all in all in the army; courage in misfortune was held of no avail; and as ostentation made promotion and reward to be publicly distributed to every regiment immediately after an engagement, the absent had seldom any share.

Chapter 6

Spain

I very soon perceived that the surgeon had not deceived me, when he said that my wound was not dangerous, for it healed without difficulty; I was fully convalescent in a month, and would certainly have been so much sooner, had not the deaths of the colonel and my friend, and my anxiety about my future lot affected me with a deep melancholy, and a moral uneasiness that delayed my cure.

The ambulance to which I belonged was twice sent to different villages, and consequently I had been removed with the rest of the wounded to considerable distances, which produced a violent shock upon my health. I was at Etzertorff on the 15th of August, and began to rise and walk about. I was put on full rations, and was informed that I should receive leave to quit the hospital in a few days.

The regiment that I had left to enter into the 9th was at Getzendorf, three leagues from the village where I was; it had lost a great many men at the battles of Essling and Wagram. The colonel and major, ten or twelve officers, and the half of the non-commissioned officers and privates had been killed. The vacancies were already beginning to be filled up; and a major of the young guard had just been appointed colonel.

I knew not where was the surviving battalion of the 9th whose buttons I had not yet put on; I knew nobody in it; I had no protector there, and was ignorant even if its wrecks would still continue to form the skeleton of a regiment, or would not shortly be dispersed among different corps. I was, it is true, put on the rolls of the ambulance as belonging to the 9th; but I felt no inclination whatever to join it; and at any rate I resolved to take a walk over to Getzendorf, which I was permitted to do by the head surgeon.

I saw the colonel, told him under what circumstances I had left the regiment he commanded, and showed him my desire of entering it again. He asked what company I had belonged to, and told me to come back in an hour. On seeing him again I perceived that the inquiries he had made concerning me were far from being unfavourable. He told me that there were still two posts of harbinger vacant of the five that were killed at Wagram, and that I should enter in this capacity among the light company of the second battalion, he gave me, for the director of the ambulance, a letter pretty much in the style of an order, desiring him to send me to his regiment as soon as I left his care.

A soldier sees too many events for them to produce a very durable impression on his mind; even that produced by the memorable skirmish of Ebersdorf began gradually to be effaced from my memory; and in the end of August, I joined my corps, and assumed my functions of harbinger. These were not very troublesome, in a country where the soldier was lodged, boarded, and almost entirely maintained by the inhabitants, received no rations or allowances, and was whole months without receiving a farthing of his pay. Hence our accounts did not occupy much, of our time; our exercise occupied us but a short time, and in comfortable quarters the polite attentions of the Germans, and particularly of the German females, made us soon forget all our fatigues. The different regiments were soon placed again on their full war establishment, the men perfectly equipped; and the army, recovered from its fatigues, became proud and audacious, full of devoted obedience, and of that thoughtlessness of the future, then justified by so many victories.

The peace which had just been signed between the two

sovereigns, and the report that was circulated of an alliance that was to render it perpetual, increased the good intelligence in which we lived with our guests. Towards the end of 1809, the army made a few movements, and some corps changed their positions; we occupied successively a number of villages in the environs of Vienna, and found everywhere the same reception, the same eager attentions.

We felt the more inclined to enjoy the comforts of our situation, as we were well assured that we should not enjoy them long. Besides, even comforts would soon have seemed insipid to us; people accustomed to such long and frequent marches necessarily became soon tired of repose. This, doubtless, Napoleon knew, for he was always ready to break the monotony of a life that might have seemed to us too uniform, and to supply us with objects of novelty and amusement. He doubtless thought we should see Spain with pleasure, and determined on sending us thither.

On the 15th November, in the evening:, the regiment received orders to march; on the 16th at five o'clock in the morning, I was already on the road, with my companions the harbingers, under the command of a non-commissioned officer, for the purpose of preparing quarters on our march. It would appear that the delicate attention was paid us of shortening the pain of our *adieus* with the kind hearted Austrians and their amiable partners, whose recollection was deep in our minds for two or three days march.

The list of the places we were to march through did not go so far as Spain; but the direction we took, and the political affairs of the time left us no doubt on the subject. At any rate, we cared no more about going to Spain than anywhere else; but as we had set out for it, we wished to go thither. We had been on the way to it seven or eight months before, but we had been countermarched for a short time, to win three or four battles and take a capital.

We took double marches, and halted only a few times to be inspected; and after marching through Austria and Piedmont, and traversing the South of France, we entered Spain by the valley of Aran, in the beginning of January, 1810. We had passed through Orange, which is no more than twenty-five or thirty leagues from Toulon.

This neighbourhood, the air of Provence, the dialect of the inhabitants awakened my affection for my native spot which I had not seen for four years; I could have been there in three days, passed as much there, and after embracing my family and friends, still have joined my regiment before it entered Spain—and assuredly I should have been at my post on the day appointed. It may be easily imagined how desirous I was of such an occurrence.

During the two or three days, in which we traversed Upper Provence and the Comtat, I suffered greatly from my painful reflections; but I knew too well the state of things, even to dare to ask permission to take a journey, that would have afforded me so much happiness, and which would, as I thought, have increased my zeal for the service. The colonel would have been unwilling to take upon himself the responsibility of granting me leave at such a moment, and it was too late to ask it from the minister of war. I was obliged to give up the idea, but it was not without great sorrow. My friends perceived it: for several days together their jokes and their gaiety I could not endure; I took no share in their always spirited conversation; I did not mix with them at all, but walked a short distance behind them, a prey to my own melancholy reflections.

By the wretched state of the roads, and the filthiness of the villages and the inhabitants, more perhaps than our march through the Pyrenees, we perceived that we had crossed the frontiers. France and Spain are joined together like the two halves of those masks called *night* and *day,* the one black, and the other white, without any intermediate shades.

The bad humour of our hosts, rather than their language, soon told us that we were in an enemy's country; they pretended that we were carrying on an unjust war against their country. This we had nothing to do with, soldiers are not fitted for meddling with such sort of things.

After crossing the Pyrenees, we remained for some time at Puertolas, where we learned that the third corps, commanded by Marshal Suchet, was master of almost the whole of Arragon, and of a part of Catalonia; and we flattered ourselves with the idea of aiding to take the remainder.

On the 15th of January, the regiment received orders to march; we passed through Arragon by short marches, crossed the Ebro at Alborga, and remained a few days at Galba. The general opinion was that the marshal was preparing to besiege Valentia, and that we were to form a part of the troops employed. A few days after our arrival at Galba, an order of the day informed us that about four thousand men belonging to our corps had met, between El Povo and Terruel, the Spanish corps of General Villa Campa, and had defeated them, after an engagement, where the latter suffered a great loss. This we were not surprised at: to tell us at this period that a French corps had met the enemy, was saying enough; the rest was a matter of course.

We left Galba a few days after hearing this news, persuaded that we were going to support and follow up the successes of the troops that were a-head of us. As the country we passed through had been already occupied by the French, I went forward along with the harbingers of the two battalions, accompanied by an escort, to prepare quarters for our respective companies. The morning of the day at which we were to arrive at Terruel, my companions had already been gone half an hour before I reached the guard-house, our usual place of meeting. I was obliged to set out with only two soldiers of my company who were along with me; and we hurried forward in the expectation of speedily coming up with the other harbingers.

The little we had heard of the war in Spain, and the guerrillas, gave us no desire of marching in such small numbers: we had already met some peasants, whose answers informed us that our companions were far ahead of us; and in spite of our strong desire of continuing our journey, we were obliged to halt about eight o'clock at a wretched tavern on the road to take some refreshment. At nine o'clock we were again on our route; my two men were about a hundred paces in front of me, and I was hurrying forward to join them, when I heard some shots in front.

I rushed forward, and was soon able to distinguish, at the turn of the road, about thirty persons shouting violently, and in the greatest confusion. I stopped for an instant to examine what could be the matter, when seven or eight individuals left the crowd, and hastened towards me. I had not time to think that I was about to be attacked, when I was struck, disarmed, and led, or rather dragged towards the main band, in the midst of whom I was thrown with violence.

The first object that struck me, was one of my soldiers horribly mutilated, and with his head separated from his body: the other with his clothes torn to pieces, bloody, and covered with wounds, still struggled against the blows that were showered on him, and which seemed to be given so as to make his sufferings more lingering. I was soon exposed to similar blows myself, and some strokes of the butt-end of a musket, were the commencement of the treatment reserved for me; I expected nothing but death, when suddenly one of the individuals pronounced some Spanish words, which made the rest retire a few paces; he came up to me bluntly, took me by the hand, called me by my name, and asked me in very good French if I did not recognise him.

I had not had too much time to look at him till this moment I did so now, and after a moment's hesitation I remembered having seen, and even having been acquainted with him, but where or under what circumstances I could not recollect. It was only necessary for him to mention his name to recall them to my mind in a moment. It was Valdejo, the young Spanish volunteer of the corps of Romana, to whom I had been of service when I was stationed at Wischendorf, in Mecklenburgh.

We did not remain ten minutes after the skirmish I have just mentioned on the spot where it had taken place, I should have liked that these guerrillas had stopped a little longer, as I was certain that the advanced guard of our regiment would be up in two hours, and might deliver me.

Valdejo ordered it otherwise; he commanded his men to march; they left the high road, threw themselves to the right, through fields at first, and then entered upon a wretched path, which led I knew not where. We had left on the road the body of the soldier who had been killed. The other, who for a long time was exposed to the inhuman cruelty of our guides, was covered with deep wounds, and could scarcely keep up with us; but they now began to pay some attention to him, and to spare him from further suffering; they even halted in a wood to dress his wounds. Valdejo, notwithstanding the marks of friendship he had shown me, did not think proper to restore my arms, but marched alongside of me at the head of his little band. He repeatedly expressed to me how happy he felt in having met with me, for he said that if I had fallen into the hands of any other partisan chief, I should have assuredly been massacred.

He informed me that some time after the return of Romana's corps to Spain, he felt disgusted with the army in consequence of the ill-treatment he met with from his captain, had obtained leave to quit his regiment, and had retired to Tierga, a village in Arragon, where his family had large estates; but that in a short time the aspect the war assumed, the desires of his relations, and especially of his uncle the priest, had prevailed on him to enter anew upon the career of arms, and that he was one of the officers of the partisan leader Porlier, whom he was preparing to join.

He assured me that I might be tranquil about my safety; that so far from allowing the smallest injury to be done me, he was ready to do for me everything in his power; but that at the same time his devotion to his country imperiously forbade him to give me my liberty; that he would, consequently, leave me at the first depot for prisoners we should meet on our route, where he would take care to procure me all the comforts that he was able.

After marching till four o'clock in the afternoon, we halted at a solitary farmhouse to pass the night. The inhabitants came several times and thrust their fists in my face, and would not have been satisfied with this, had not Valdejo got at last seriously angry, and threatened to draw his sabre in my defence, My soldier died the same evening from the effects of his wounds.

We again set out the next morning at daybreak. Valdejo informed me that unless unexpected circumstances occurred, we should sleep at La Puebla, where his band would rest and reprovision for a few days. I was protected by the friendship of Valdejo; and I was even treated on his account with a sort of goodwill by the officers of his corps.

He remained two days at La Puebla, during which I lodged with him and scarcely ever left his side. On the second evening he informed me that he was ordered by Porlier to go to Palma on a secret mission, that he would set out next morning with four men only; and that I was to go with him to form part of the depot of French prisoners of war at Majorca.

We took mules and a guide, Valdejo paid liberally wherever he went, and displayed a gaiety and good humour, which he fruitlessly attempted to make me share in. We slept on the first evening at Alventosa, on the second, at Almonacir, both miserable villages, as poor and as filthy as all those I had already seen in the filthy kingdom of Spain, and where, though we paid a high price, we could not obtain anything eatable, at least for a Frenchman. At Castelon de la Plana, a small seaport, which we reached on the third day, Valdejo wished to take advantage of a settled south west wind, and immediately bargained with the captain of a pink, that was about to weigh anchor, to convey us to Palma, and we arrived at that place the next morning at daybreak.

Whilst Valdejo was busy in fulfilling the objects of his mission, he advised me to walk about and visit the town, always attended, however, by two of his men. I learned that all the French prisoners who had been lately in this place, had been sent to Cabrera, a small island in the neighbourhood, and that there remained in Majorca only a few officers on parole. I had plenty of time during two days to visit the town, which is handsome and well built. It was not till the second evening that Valdejo, who since our arrival had scarcely ever shown himself at the inn where we lodged, informed me that he was to set out again for the kingdom of Valentia the following evening, and that he would come beforehand and accompany me on board a brig that was to set out at ten o'clock in the morning, to convey provisions to the prisoners of Cabrera whom I was to join.

The expectation of my departure awoke me earlier than usual. Valdejo had settled the business he came on, and had received a supply of money. We took a parting breakfast, as plentiful as delicate, and at the close he would absolutely make me accept some doubloons; but I thanked him for his kind offer, and showed him that I had still plenty of money, as I had not been plundered by his soldiers.

We then went on board the brig, into which I put some provisions, which I thought right to take with me in case of need. My Arragonese friend seemed to part from me with regret; and for myself I had too much reason to be satisfied with his conduct towards me, not to assure him how desirous I was that some opportunity might arise of reciprocating the favours I had received; we promised each other that in case the chances of war brought us again into contact, we should do each other every service in our power, that was not inconsistent with our duty and our fidelity to our colours.

I was given in charge of the captain of the brig, who was to convey me to my destination: at half past ten the vessel weighed anchor, and at two in the afternoon we were within sight of Cabrera.

When we approached the coast, we saw the rocks on the

shore crowded with people; I could soon distinguish the persons individually, who bad their eyes fixed upon us, and seemed to follow our movements with anxious care. I examined them in my turn, without being able to account for the scene before me; at last a sudden impulse which struck me with astonishment and stupefaction, told me that the men before me were Frenchmen, whose lot I was come to share. Many of them were quite naked, and as black as mulattos, with beards fit for a pioneer, dirty and out of order; some had pieces of clothing, but they had no shoes, or their legs, thighs, and part of their body were bare.

The number of these new companions of mine, I estimated to be about five or six thousand, among whom I at last saw three with pantaloons and uniforms still almost entire; the whole body were mingled together on the rocks and the beech, were shouting with joy, beating their hands, and following us as we moved along. I supposed that the arrival of provisions was the cause of their running to the shore; but other objects soon called my attention; the ground a little way from the shore was covered with groups of huts, pretty much like those we are wont to have in our camps, but neither so regular nor so clean. In front of one of these rude constructions, on a pine tree, about fifteen feet high, crossed over at top by a bar, was attached a man completely naked, and making the most violent efforts. For what reason had he been put there? This was one of the first questions I resolved to ask on my arrival at Cabrera, I shall explain it a little further on.

The brig came at last quite close to the shore, and was fastened to a rock, and a plank was put out for us to land. About twenty prisoners only were allowed to come on board, while a file of thirty Spaniards were drawn up on the shore, and were ready to fire on any of the rest who should make any sign of coming too near. The provisions were landed on the shore by the prisoners who were allowed to approach; I also landed, and in about an hour after the brig was under weigh, and was speedily out of sight.

An immense semicircle was formed round the spot where the bread and meat had been deposited. Ten or twelve persons were in the centre; one of them had a list in his hand, and called out successively for the different divisions to come forward, and likewise cried out their respective numbers. Three or four men then came forward, received the rations allotted to their mess, and carried them away; the private divisions were then made among themselves.

I should not give a just idea of the manner in which the distribution was made, by saying, that the utmost order and regularity prevailed; it was more than order, it was a kind of solemn and religious gravity, I doubt if the important and serious duties of ambassadors and ministers of state, have ever in any country been fulfilled with such dignity as was shown on the countenances, and in every movement of the distributors.

Bread seemed to be a sacred object, the smallest morsel of which could not be secreted without committing a heinous crime; the smallest pieces which had been broken off in the conveyance, were gathered with care and respect, and placed on the heap to which they belonged.

I was busily engaged in surveying this singular ceremony, and took no share in it myself; I did not know whom I was to apply to for rations, which I had an equal claim to with the rest; hence I was soon left alone, for everyone went off with his supply. This, however, I was not much concerned at; I had four loaves in my knapsack, two pounds of salt beef, and a bottle of rum; with these I could do till the next distribution of provisions.

I wandered up and down the shore with a staff in my hand, and my knapsack on my back, and I was thinking of walking into the interior of the island, when I was addressed by some of the prisoners, and in a few minutes surrounded by a considerable crowd. The distribution of provisions had been a matter of too great importance for them to pay attention to me at first; but it would seem after the staff of life, what they loved most, was to hear news of their native land. I was overwhelmed with questions about the situation of various regiments, but above all of the state of France, and the affairs of the Peninsula. I told them all I knew. Several times when I was speaking of our late victories, my voice was drowned by shouts of joy, mingled with expressions of courage, national pride, and vengeance.

All at once, an individual rushed through the crowd, crying out, "It is Guillemard," forced his way to me, and eagerly embraced me. I had some difficulty in recognizing him; it was Ricaud, a sergeant in the 9th regiment, like me, one of the survivors of the action of Ebersdorf. He had no shirt, and wore pantaloons of sail cloth, cut off at the knees, and leaving his legs bare; a piece of a very scanty waistcoat, and shoes made from a collection of soles, tied round the ankle with strings—somewhat like the sandals worn by the ancients—completed his costume.

As soon as I had no more news to tell the circle was broken up, and the crowd dispersed. Ricaud took me by the hand, and led me to a sort of a hut about three feet high, which he occupied along with three others, and invited me to sleep there till I had procured a place for myself.

We took supper in front of the hut; I gave Ricaud and his companions the provisions I had brought, which we partook of along with a part of what they had received. We conversed for a long time; night came on, and we lay down on a small spot of dry grass that formed the floor of our dwelling, into which we could only enter one after another, with great difficulty by creeping on our bellies.

I was very tired, and soon fell into a sound sleep, but it did not last long. Towards midnight, torrents of cold water poured down on my face and body, and made me start up with alarm. A storm prevailed over the island; the thunder rolled without intermission, and a heavy rain, mingled with hail, poured upon us, while a furious hurricane blew over the island. The roof of our hut was made of grass and reeds, and could not hold out long against such an attack; it was soon pierced through in every direction, and the hut itself became a puddle, in which we lay engulfed. The oaths of my companions were soon added to the war of the elements.

To our infinite misfortune, the hut had been made to hold no more than four, and we were now five in number, and could not move without hurting each other. When discontent prevails, any pretext is laid hold of; one of my hosts abused Ricaud, and reproached him for having invited a stranger who had increased the inconvenience of their situation. The latter gave him a sharp reply, and tried to make him hold his tongue. They swore at each other for a while, and would not have stopped there, had they been able; but the hut was not high enough for anyone to rise up, even on his knees, and it was impossible to get out till the man nearest the hole had crept out. After a great deal of noise, it was settled that they were to fight next day. The rain ceased, and we again fell asleep.

Chapter 7

A Prisoner at Cabrera

The sun had just risen, when Ricaud roused me to request I would act as his second. I was not in one of those beds from which, one rises with reluctance. Our dressing arrangements were soon made, and as we had entered our hut the evening before head-foremost, and were unable to turn ourselves, we crawled out one after another, feet-foremost, resting upon our heels and elbows.

After drinking some rum with Ricaud and his antagonist, I tried to bring about a reconciliation; but they told me that it was of no use, and both declared that the thing must be done. I was too well acquainted with military customs to make any attempt at combating a reason so peremptory. Besides I had no great fears of the result of the duel; I presumed that the shadow of a sword, sabre, or pistol, was not to be found in the whole island; and I fancied that these worthies were going to have a game at fistycuffs, in imitation of the ancient Romans, to whom they already bore so much resemblance. But I soon saw that a determined mind will always find means to accomplish its purposes. Before setting out, Ricaud said that as he was the person insulted, he had the choice of weapons, and wished to fight with *scissors.*

"You know," said Lambert, a corporal of a regiment I have forgotten the name of, "that I am unacquainted with the points so that if we wish to fight on equal terms, let us draw *the razor,*"

This sadly puzzled me, for I had no idea of the matter.

Ricaud was determined to have the scissors; Lambert would not give up the razors, so that they were forced to draw lots, when the latter gained his point.

He left us and returned in about a quarter of an hour with a pair of English razors. During his absence Ricaud had instructed me concerning the manner in which they were going to fight, and the kind of duels that daily took place at Cabrera. Sometimes they fixed the halves of razors at the end of long sticks, and used them as swords; at other times they used knife blades, razors, and sometimes even awls and sail-makers needles.

We took two sticks about an inch thick, and three feet long, and prepared to fix the razors on them. But as we had not what was necessary for the purpose, we went to the bazaar to buy some articles. This was the market for the prisoners. It was situated at a spot honoured with the name of the Palais Royal, surrounded by ten or twelve huts, and containing as many stalls, some in the open air, others with a slight covering, with one end fixed to the ground, and the other supported by two poles. Here were sold bread, some salt fish, scraps of cloth, thread, needles, wooden forks and spoons; the various produce of the industry of the prisoners; pepper, twine, and other articles in the smallest quantity, for one could buy a single thread, a scrap of cloth no bigger than one's hand, and even a pinch of snuff, three of which cost a *sous*. I remember a Polish officer who owed nine pinches, and the shop-keeper refused to give him any more credit.

We brought two bits of twine, and after fixing on the weapons, we hastened to the cemetery. It was on a hill about a quarter of an hour's walk from the Palais Royal. Since the arrival of the prisoners at Cabrera, they had uniformly chosen this spot as a place of rest for those who had sank under their misery, or who had fallen by the hands of their companions, it was there that they also met to settle their differences in single combat.

When we reached the ground, I again, for form's sake

spoke about making the matter up. When I saw the were determined on fighting, I told them that as I was the first cause of the quarrel, it was for *me* to uphold it, and take Ricaud's place. Neither he nor his adversary would agree to this, and I saw myself forced at last to give them up the weapons, which I had carried till now.

Ricaud threw off his waistcoat; and as Lambert had nothing but pantaloons on, he was soon ready. They put themselves in a fighting attitude, and both displayed great coolness and courage. Lambert was much the stronger of the two, and my friend required all his skill to parry the thrusts that were aimed at him; the razor flourished round his head and shoulders without intermission, and struck him at last on the chin. He made a furious thrust in return, but fortunately it did not reach its object fully, though it made a pretty scratch on Lambert's nose. We rushed between them, when blood began to flow; we separated them and made them shake hands; as their wounds were not of much consequence, we all returned to breakfast together in front of our hut.

I began to feel a great liking for Ricaud, who had offered me with the most cordial frankness every little service that was in his power; I was desirous of becoming acquainted with the island, which I was probably destined to inhabit for a long space of time; and after breakfast we set out to visit it together.

Cabrera is nothing but a calcareous rock, about a league long, the very irregular coasts of which form two little bays, one situated on the north, the other to the south. .At the entrance of the former was an old dilapidated castle, whose roof had long been destroyed; yet some French officers, who had passed some months at Cabrera, had made some of the rooms fit to be inhabited; and at the period of my arrival a Spanish priest, who was sent by his government to take care of our souls (of which they seemed infinitely more anxious than about our bodies) had fixed himself in it, and said mass every Sunday.

The whole island is covered with rocks and hillocks, and some of those in the centre rise even into considerable hills. It may be well imagined that the vegetation is not very rich: it is like that of all the petty isles in the Mediterranean, The mastick tree, the carob tree, the myrtle and the honeysuckle, occupy the clefts in the rocks; and these, along with the pine trees, which grow wherever there is sufficient depth of soil, are almost the only vegetable substances that shade the earth in this sterile island. There was a pretty handsome pine wood at the east end of the island, but it was daily disappearing, on account of the demand for wood to build huts with.

In other circumstances I should have been delighted at visiting several caves that Ricaud had pointed out to me; one of them contained stalactites of a most singular form; another, called *the honeysuckle cave,* is in a most picturesque situation. But we could not walk a step without meeting with some of the prisoners, and what I saw of their mode of life, which was about to become my own, inspired me with thoughts directed to very different subjects than the views of Cabrera.

I already began to cease replying to Ricaud's conversation, and scarcely listened to his accounts; I walked beside him absorbed in thought, reflecting on the fate of the six thousand Robinson Crusoes before my eyes, thrown upon a desert island, without arms or tools of any kind, and having nothing to look to but their inventive industry, and the native energy of Frenchmen.

I was informed that the whole colony had but one hatchet, and one saw made out of an old iron hoop. The hatchet belonged to a sailor, and the saw to a corporal of a regiment of foot. They hired them out at the rate of three half-pence a day, and a deposit, to those who had occasion for them; and it was by their aid that the greater part of the huts in the island had been constructed.

These huts were placed in the middle of the island, in front of the little port, and those of the soldiers of the same corps were grouped together. In size and shape they all seemed to me to be greatly superior to Ricaud's dwelling. In front of some of them were little gardens enclosed with fences of pine branches, and containing flowers and culinary vegetables. In general, however, I thought that they might have been made a great deal better: I said so to Ricaud at once, and told him that I would begin to show him some proofs next day.

In fact, I hired the hatchet and saw, and assisted by some of my fellow prisoners, I set about constructing a hut, which occupied me eight entire days; but it quite astonished them when completed; one could stand up in it, and the walls were four feet and a half high, and were constructed of a double row of branches, firmly entwined together, with all the interstices filled up with grass and a clayey sort of earth which I had found out in a cave in a distant part of the island; in making the roof, I employed rushes, so well arranged and so firmly bound together, that not a drop of water could penetrate within the hut. By a singular piece of good fortune, I had found on the shore a plank, about three feet long and two broad, quite uninjured, and I resolved to put up a shelf in our hut to hold our provisions. On the south side I made a hole about half a foot in diameter, for the purpose of giving light and air, and when required, it could he stopped up with a handful of grass.

I was obliged to go repeatedly all over the island in search of the objects I was in need of; but in conveying them home I found assistance I had never thought of. An ass had been allowed for the use of the prisoners to convey the provisions of those who were encamped farthest from the shore. Martin, as we called him, wandered and browsed peaceably over the island, and was always ready to lend his back to burdens, sometimes a club. However, he was highly esteemed for his patience and valuable services; and among the six thousand owners of this common property, few would have dared to ill-use him without exciting the anger of their companions; he was of important use to me, and greatly shortened my labour.

On the day that I began my hut, some of the prisoner

had informed me that as I was a non-commissioned officer, I became from the moment of my arrival a member of the council, and they gave me an account of the origin and object of the institution.

When the French prisoners were first sent to Cabrera, they were accompanied by their officers, who preserved all their authority, a very necessary thing among men embittered by misfortune, exasperated by ill usage, quarrelsome, and always on the point of fighting among themselves. But they always preserved the. same deference to their officers, submitted to their decisions, and offered no resistance to the punishments inflicted on them. The officers and non-commissioned officers were soon sent to England. The prisoners were left without control, but were prevailed on by some of their number, who saw the excesses that were daily committed, to choose among themselves a council to judge of their disputes, punish disorders, and provide for everything connected with the good order and harmony of the colony. The sentences pronounced by this sort of court were without appeal, were almost always very severe, and were put in execution as soon as delivered.

Three days after my arrival, I was called upon to take my place in it; the sittings were held in the open air, near the Palais Royal. We were twelve in number, and sat on stones arranged in a circle; an immense crowd waited round us, to hear our decision, and to put our sentence into execution if necessary.

We had to try a soldier, who was accused of stealing a piece of bread from his companion; this was the greatest and most unpardonable crime that could be committed at Cabrera; even betraying anyone attempting to escape, though it excited more horror, did not usually receive a punishment so cruel; nothing could save a bread-stealer, who the moment he was condemned, was stoned to death by the surrounding crowd. We heard the accusers and the accused, the witnesses, and his counsel, for he had one, who, according to custom, endeavoured to prove him as pure as snow. Evidence of the crime was given, and the council were preparing to give their votes, the mode we adopted in all our meetings.

They seemed to me nowise disposed to indulgence, while I thought it very cruel to cut off an unfortunate being for stealing a piece of bread, not weighing two or three ounces. It was in vain that I reflected that everything is relative, and that this theft, so trifling everywhere else, might in our position expose the loser to die of hunger, and therefore deserved an exemplary punishment; I could not bring myself to vote against the culprit. I spoke in favour of the accused, who was very young; I mentioned his good qualities, which his advocate had talked of loud and long, and I concluded by asking, as a personal favour, that the council would incline towards mercy, at this the first time that I took part in their proceedings.

I was so fortunate as to succeed; the criminal was only condemned to be exposed twenty-four hours on the pillory.

The reader, perhaps, remembers that one of the first objects that struck my attention on approaching the island, was a man tied to a pine tree; this was what they called the pillory, the punishment they allotted to all crimes that were not capital. The criminal was tied up on this tree completely naked, left without food, and exposed to the sun and weather for the term of his sentence, which was never less than four hours, nor more than twenty-four.

When I saw the miserable condition of the prisoners on my arrival, I was astonished that more frequent attempts to escape were not made. But I was soon convinced that the almost absolute impossibility of success was the sole cause, and that they had not given up the idea of leaving this wretched spot, till they had seen a series of bold and well-combined attempts fail one after another. This did not prevent me resolving to look out myself for every opportunity of escape, as I was firmly persuaded, that whatever might be the result of my efforts, my lot could not be much worse. I determined to make my escape the constant object of my thoughts, and of all my actions, and to live, in short, only for the attainment of this object.

I soon ascertained that I must give up the idea of attempting it by myself. I thought that too many individuals in the secret would be dangerous, and that it would be quite enough if I opened my mind to three or four of my companions. I had cast my eyes on Ricaud, but I was desirous of seeing more of him before I opened my mind. On the day that the council met, I particularly remarked two young men who were members of it, Darlier of Ollioules, and Chobar of Marseilles. On the following days, I tried to become acquainted with them; I thought from the very first glance, and was soon firmly convinced, that they were the very men I required. They were both sailors, and were likely to be enterprising, firm, and decided, like all their class, and indeed no-one could doubt of this when he saw their open bold look, which at once announced joviality and hardihood. Their similarity of qualities, and the same turn of mind, which led them to make sport of every occurrence, had long made them acquainted, and they were seldom seen apart.

As soon as my hut was finished, I invited them to breakfast, along with Ricaud. It may be easily imagined what sort of delicacy and display our repast presented; but it was not less gay on that account. It was after drinking off the small store of rum which I had kept for this solemn occasion, that I mentioned to my guests the ideas that had occurred to me. They were pretty coldly received at first, even by Darlier and Chobar, who had several times made unsuccessful attempts to escape. They related to me a host of plans of this kind, which had been formed by them or their fellow-prisoners, but which had all failed at the moment of execution.

I omitted to mention, that an English brig, carrying twenty carronades, and two Spanish gun-boats, lay off the port. It was only a short time before, as Chobar informed me, that some French officers, who were then prisoners at Cabrera, formed the plan of boarding the brig, and had swam to it one night during a storm; but the first who reached it were naked, unarmed, and benumbed with cold, and no sooner reached the deck, than they were cut down by the English, whom they expected to surprise. Several attempts of the same kind had been made on the gun-boats, but they were equally unsuccessful. Since then, the strictest discipline was preserved on board these vessels; and at all hours, by night, as well as by day, boats were moving about the port, and sailing round the island.

All these accounts did not lessen my desire of escaping, nor make any change in my resolutions; I made my companions see that it did not follow that a thing was impossible because it was extremely difficult; that at any rate I had no idea of laying down a precise plan of escape, but that we ought to lie on the watch for every opportunity that might present itself, try to make opportunities, and lay hold of them without hesitation. I spoke long, and I believe spoke well, for I brought them round to my opinion.

It was settled at once that we should all four live in the hut I had just constructed; that each of us was to reflect seriously on the means he thought likely to forward the object of our desires; that we should daily communicate our ideas to each other till we had found something satisfactory; that night and day one of our number should be constantly walking on the shore, to see if chance should throw something favourable in our way, and that he should be relieved every four hours. We also agreed that I was to seek acquaintance immediately with the Spanish priest, Damian Estrebrich, the chaplain to the prisoners, and to; endeavour to become intimate with him. We had nothing to hope from him, but I thought this precaution could do us no harm, and might give rise to some circumstance favourable to our cause.

The execution of our plan was begun instantly. Chobar, Darlier and Ricaud brought the few things they had to my hut, and the latter began his round, which we had agreed upon to carry on without one minute's intermission. As for me, I went next day to; hear Señor Estrebrich at mass. He could easily notice me amidst the solitude that reigned in the dilapidated hall, which he had transformed into a church. I could, not help thinking that either this man must be full of an ardent zeal for religion, or in consequence of irregular conduct has been exiled hither by his superiors; but this (thought I) I shall soon learn.

When mass was over I went up to him, and conversed with him as he withdrew, till he came to the spot he had fixed on for his residence. He congratulated me on the manner in which I already began to speak Spanish, asked me how I had been made prisoner, and detained me till he was about to sit down to table, when he signified to me that my presence was inconvenient, but invited me to come and see him sometimes, and to think of my spiritual safety. I left him, determined to visit him again, but perfectly satisfied with what I had seen, Señor Estrebrich was not a priest, but a true Spanish monk, chock full of fanaticism, gluttony, and the most shameful ignorance.

A month elapsed without making any change in our situation; nothing had occurred, we had imagined nothing practicable to get away- Our supply of provisions, which should have been brought us every four days, sometimes did not come for twenty-four hours after; and the greater part of the prisoners were without sustenance, and made fasts not prescribed by Señor Estrebrich, and which were sometimes of three days duration, for several of them eat up their rations during the first two days. They then lived on roots and wild plants, and were conveyed in great number from their huts to the cemetery. Some of the resources they had found, on their arrival in the island, were now almost entirely exhausted.

At the time I came several of them were accustomed to swim in the morning to some of the small isles that are off Cabrera, and examined them so carefully, that they returned back in the evening with a small cargo of oysters and crabs, which they took to the bazaar for sale. Others went in the same way to a small isle that had formerly merited the name of *Rabbit Island*. If they found any traces of rabbits, that had survived the general destruction made of them by the original natives of Cabrera, they watched beside the barrow; and if they were obliged to watch three days, as their prey must either come in or go out, they had the patience to wait and seize upon their victim. At this period a rabbit was an object of high importance, particularly when the Spaniards seemed to have forgotten us. Eatables of all kinds then rose to a shocking price, whilst everything not eatable was considered of no value, I remember seeing a very fine gold watch sold for half a pound of bread. There was no credit given in those times, and it was assuredly not amid such scenes that a debt of fifteen hundred francs had been contracted for a quantity of pieces of bread of an ounce in weight, the vouchers for which I myself saw presented to the council of administration of a particular corps, which paid them without hesitation.

My companions and myself took care to have always more than one day's provisions in advance, and this surplus we endeavoured to increase by every means in our power, so that we might have a supply in case we were so fortunate as to escape; and this hope made our privations less painful.

Meanwhile, everyone was busy at Cabrera; we had tailors, shoemakers, public criers, artisans in hair, bones and tortoise-shell, and some who cut out with their knives little figures of animals in wood; and about two hundred men, the wreck of a dragoon regiment, raised in Auvergne, were quartered in a cave, and made spoons of box-wood. The latter had only one pantaloon and one uniform among the whole corps, and these articles seemed ready to leave them very speedily, and were delivered successively to one of their number appointed to receive their provisions. All the articles I have enumerated were sold at low prices, to the crews of the brig and gun-boats, and to some Spaniards, whom our singular mode of life, or the hope of making a good speculation, attracted to our settlement.

But the most abundant articles with us, were professors of all kinds. One half of the prisoners gave lessons to the other half. Nothing was seen on all sides hut teachers of music, mathematics, languages, drawing, fencing, above all, dancing and singlestick. In fine weather, all these professors gave their lessons at the Palais Royal, quite close to each other, it was quite common to see a poor devil half naked, and who had often not partaken of food for twenty-four hours more, singing a very gay air of a country dance, and interrupting it from time to time, for the purpose of saying, with infinite seriousness of demeanour, to his pupil dressed in the remains of a pair of drawers:

"That's right, keep time with your partner, wheel round, hold yourselves gracefully."

A little farther on, a teacher of singlestick was showing off his acquirements and endeavoured to excite the emulation of his pupil by such phrases as:

"That will do; I am satisfied with you, if you go on with the same success, in less than a fortnight you may show yourself in company."

A scrap of paper, about as large as one's hand, was placed as a sign, and the most eminent of all our professors had no better.

I was also desirous of doing something; but I had no notion of either giving or receiving lessons. After reflecting a great deal, I thought that on account of the want of occupation in which many of the prisoners were placed, a theatre must be eminently successful, and I was astonished that no one had thought of it before. Indeed some scenes had been performed, but it was in the open air, and had not been thought of as an object of speculation. My ideas were quite grand compared to such things. I resolved on being at one and the same time, if necessary, author, actor, director and machinist, and to make my companions partners in my labours and the fruits of it, which were to be employed in accomplishing our favourite object.

I could not think of establishing my theatre in the old castle, which was shut every evening, and where in fact it would not have been allowed by the hypocritical Estrebrich;

I thought of a vast cistern that was falling to pieces, with the pipes long ago broken off, and part of the roof fallen in. I was lowered into it by means of a cord I had bought on purpose, and I found about a foot of water, or rather mud, at the bottom. The first thing to be done was to clear it away, and this was the most troublesome part of the whole business. I wished at first to make a pump, but I soon gave up the idea. I had still sixty francs, and prevailed on Señor Estrebrich to get me four leather buckets from Palma; I made a ladder, hired four prisoners at two *sous* each per day, and got the cistern dry on the third day of our labour.

To season it, I made a huge fire of pine wood, got sand and stones conveyed to it during a whole day, and made an elevation that extended about a third of the cistern, intended for the stage; I procured some ochre and red lead; I daubed the walls yellow, with a red border; hung all round garlands of leaves which I also made use of as a screen between the stage and the spectators, and I finished my labours by writing, not indeed on the curtain, for I had none, but on the bottom of the stage, *castigat ridendo mores.*

I had long before this fixed upon the play with which my troop was to commence their operation. It was the *Philoctète* of Laharpe. I had formerly played the character, and still remembered it, as well as fragments of a variety of plays. I wrote them out as well as I could, and when I forgot the lines, I filled up the vacancy in prose. Darlier engaged to play the character of Ulysses. Chobar that of Pyrrhus, and a pioneer of the line, with a stentorian voice, and no small portion of sense, assumed the character of Hercules. At length, a public crier went through the camp, and gave notice that the same evening *Philoctète* would be performed, with the afterpiece of *Marton et Frontin.* I had transcribed this little piece pretty correctly, and performed it along with Chobar.

About three hundred persons could find room in my cistern, and as I had put the places at two *sous* it was completely crowded; the company descended into it by the ladder I had made; and a confidential man was placed on the first step to receive the money, which he put into a little cloth bag that was tied round his neck. The theatre was lighted up by torches of pine wood, borne at different distances by the attendants of the theatre, and they lighted fresh ones in proportion as the others were consumed. All the allusions to our situation in the tragedy, were noticed, with a tact that would have done honour to the taste of a more brilliant assembly. At the début:

"Nous voici dans Lemnos, dans cette Île sauvage,

Dont jamais nul mortel n'aborda le rivage,"

we were covered with shouts of applause; and I thought they would bring down the roof of the cistern when I pronounced this line:

"Ils m'ont fait tous ces maux; que les dieux le leur rendent."

I was obliged to repeat it, and to stop for some time, to allow the agitation of the audience to be calmed.

Such a successful beginning was well calculated to encourage us; I laboured incessantly, and wrote out several plays that I recollected, and we performed them all in their turn. Our funds increased amazingly, as well as our general comforts. We left half of our profits to the general funds and divided the rest, Ricaud had already procured himself decent clothing. I had already bought a curtain for my theatre; I had obtained ropes, nails, a hammer, and even a hatchet, for which a Spaniard had made me pay a most exorbitant price; all these objects were intended to aid us in our theatrical arrangements, but they could also be of use in our grand project, which we had not lost sight of; every evening we carefully locked them up in our hut. I was very desirous also of obtaining some arms, a sabre at least, for each of us; but I tried in vain, and did not press this matter much, for fear of becoming suspected; so that our tragic heroes were forced to be satisfied with wooden sabres.

The whole colony felt an interest in our dramatic success; for after the second performance, I always allowed twenty of those who had not the means of paying to receive a free admission; but during the month of September a calamity befell the island, which carried off a great number of our fellow prisoners, and suspended for several days work of every kind, lessons and amusements.

The provisions did not arrive on the day they were expected; but this misfortune had occurred so frequently that it did not create much surprise; the next day, at the usual hour, the starving prisoners covered the heights and the shore, expecting every moment to see the long wished for vessel. Their anxiety continued increasing, the day passed over, and night came on, while their hopes became fainter and fainter. There was nothing heard but one universal cry of horror and indignation against the Spaniards, who had resolved, said the multitude, to leave us to die of hunger. On the first day of the scarcity, the small store of provisions in the hands of the shopkeepers had been consumed. On the second night, more than a hundred and fifty persons died of madness or inanition. The third day came, and the prisoners crawled again to the shore; our looks were anxiously directed to the sea; but at twelve o'clock nothing had yet been seen.

The council had assembled, and resolved that a deputation should be sent to Estrebrich, that he might communicate our distress to the English brig and the gun-boats, and that he might find out some means of relieving us. I went to him, along with Ricaud, and found him at dinner, with a dish of meat, and half a stuffed goose that looked very inviting. He heard us without masticating a bit the less, and concluded by offering us a glass of wine, and promising that he would go in a moment and see what could be done.

We carried this intelligence to our companions, and in half an hour, we saw Estrebrich, with his surplice on, his square cap on his head, and a crucifix in his hand, leaving the fort, and advancing towards us chanting the litany to all the saints. He came to persuade us to make a procession with him, to supplicate heaven to have pity on our distress, and to send us the brig with the provisions. Some prisoners yielded to his request, perhaps, in the hope of obtaining from him some little temporal aid; and he was speedily at the head of thirty individuals, who collected the little strength they had remaining, and began to repeat the *ora pro nobis*.

Meanwhile the council assembled a second time; the most violent proposals were first advanced; and we ourselves really began to believe that the Spanish government had condemned us to die of hunger; and we saw no means of escaping the sentence, nor even of prolonging our lives two hours longer. An Italian non-commissioned officer made a proposal that was unanimously rejected with horror. Another member opposed and even succeeded in dispelling the idea of the fate, that we thought reserved for us. He was persuaded, he said, that the provisions had been delayed by some unexpected accident, that we should assuredly receive them next day, and he proposed to make use of the only resource that remained to support the strength and courage of the prisoners till then, by killing our poor ass. Some may doubt the fact, but even in our cruel position Martin had some advocates; his services (it was said) were of the greatest utility to the greater part of the prisoners; and, besides, the share that would fall to the lot of every individual, would be quite inadequate to enable him to wait till next day. It could not possibly do so. Notwithstanding the soundness of these arguments, they were scarcely listened to, and Martin was almost unanimously condemned to die.

The procession was now over, and had brought no relief. Two men were sent off to seek for the victim that was to be sacrificed to our common preservation. Martin was found browsing quietly, at a short distance, and was led into the midst of the crowd, quite unconscious of his approaching fate, and probably thinking of performing his ordinary service. Ten minutes after he was condemned, he was dead, flayed, cut up, and pieces of his flesh were roasting over the coals, or were employed in making soup for those who had somewhat more patience. Two ounces were distributed to every three men, including the bones and intestines.

A misfortune never comes alone. Storms are frequent at

Cabrera; on the night after this disastrous day, a more violent one burst upon us than we had hitherto experienced. For more than an hour, the wind, the rain, and the hail, were so violent that several huts were destroyed. Notwithstanding the strength of our roof, it was pierced through in several places; torrents descended from the heights where the cemetery was placed, hollowed out profound ravines in their course, and carried off in one mass of confusion quantities of earth, shrubs, pieces of dead bodies, and dead bodies entire, which they rolled into the very midst of our camp. At sunrise it was found that about three hundred of our fellow-prisoners had sunk under their sufferings, or had been drowned in their huts, and the collections of water that had been formed round them.

As on the preceding days, we were almost all on the shore by daybreak. This time we at last discovered a sail, and soon recognized it to be the brig; it came to at nine o'clock, and landed us provisions for eight days.

The important cause of the famine we had been exposed to, was nothing less than a dispute which had arisen about the provision accounts, between two contractors, one of whom wished to have the other's place. Military authority was invoked, and the English general who commanded at Palma was very scrupulous in the performance of his duties, and had determined that the dispute should be settled before any more provisions were sent, quite indifferent to the risk in which ten thousand Frenchmen were in, of being starved to death in the interval.

This interruption in the supplies of the colony was the last it was exposed to during my stay. We soon recovered from our privations, began again to lay in a stock of provisions, and recommenced our dramatic performances.

There were amongst us about twenty women, French, Italian and Spanish, who had followed their husbands or lovers after they were made prisoners, and who were almost all sutlers. Some of these modern heroines were young and handsome.

With some trouble I engaged two of them to join our troop, and our performances attracted such crowded audiences that we were constantly forced to refuse entrance to many, and to remove the ladder when the theatre was full.

Meanwhile I had been more than eight months on the island, and we had not the smallest hope of escape; I began to feel discouraged, though we still persevered in our vigilant watching by night and day, as heretofore. Each of us had several times presented plans of escape, more or less hazardous, but we had been obliged to give them up as impracticable.

Chapter 8
Escape

I was one evening performing the *Dissipateur* of Destouches; Chobar was on guard, and did not come to the theatre; I was at the last scene, and looked down towards the prompter to ask his aid, when I saw his place occupied by Chobar: "News" said he in a whisper, and in a very tremulous voice, but his face glowing with joy and impatience.

I do not know how I had the strength to recite on the stage the little that remained for me to say; I ran over it as quickly as possible, hastened out with Darlier and Ricaud, and joined Chobar, who was impatiently waiting for our arrival. He informed us that about nine o'clock, a boat, with three men, had made several tacks between Rabbit Island and Cabrera, that it had at length come to our coast, and had been drawn ashore. Chobar had concealed himself behind a rock, had seen the three men light a fire, take their repast, and lie down under the side of their boat, where they would pass the night, and probably start again at break of day.

Our resolution was soon taken; we agreed upon a plan instantly, and it was put in execution in every particular, with as much exactness and good fortune as if the circumstances had been prepared for us.

So soon as noise had ceased in the camp, we set out, loaded with provisions for more than four days, a keg of water, and ropes of various sizes. We were obliged to go round a long way to avoid passing near the camp, and before we reached the spot to which Chobar conducted us three quarters of an hour elapsed, which seemed to us intolerably long; there was a fresh breeze from the south-west, and if we had had our choice of the thirty-two points of the compass, we could not have pointed out one that was more favourable to our designs.

The night was cold and dark. When we approached, we distinguished through the darkness, the black form of the boat between us and the glimmering light of the horizon; we slackened our pace, and scarcely breathed or touched the sand that creaked under our feet. We moved to leeward of the boat, perceived the three sailors asleep wrapped up in their cloaks. As everything had been settled beforehand, we had only to point out by a motion which of the men each of us was to take charge of; in a few minutes they were gagged with handkerchiefs, bound together, and placed in the bottom of the boat, which we had set afloat, and with which we went to Rabbit Island.

We landed there, and explained to our prisoners that we were determined on escaping, and that we should be forced, for our own safety, to leave them in the position we had put them in, but that they would certainly be extricated in the course of the morning by Frenchmen or Spaniards, who could not fail to perceive them. Without further remarks we took them, one after another, pulled off their cloaks, their thick pantaloons, and Catalonian caps. In exchange for their cloaks, we dressed them in the fragments of our uniforms. We left them some provisions, seventy francs in moneys which was more than the value of their boat, and after wishing them every sort of prosperity, we embarked and gained the open sea.

We fortunately possessed a real treasure, which we had preserved till now more carefully than the apple of our eye—this was a small compass, belonging to Darlier, which he had constantly carried with him till the period we had formed our association. We soon found that as the coasts of the kingdom of Valentia were about fifty leagues to the S. W. and that we were driving towards them with the wind right aft, at the rate of six knots an hour, we could therefore easily join the French army on the following night, provided they occupied the coast. How the latter case might be, we could not say, and this somewhat damped our joy; but at any ate we were firmly resolved to be cut to pieces rather than to be taken back to the horrid desert of Cabrera.

At daybreak we were on the open sea, scarcely able to discover in our rear the heights of the island, which seemed like distant clouds; the wind still blew in the same direction, and with the same force. About four in the afternoon, we thought we could perceive the coast of Spain; in fact, we saw its outlines on the horizon as the sun sunk low, and were soon enabled to distinguish the houses, trees and rocks along the shore. Night came on, and we still moved on with the same rapidity towards a coast that none of us had any knowledge of; we knew only that the whole of this part was full of breakers, so that it was very dangerous to go near the shore.

It was somewhere about eleven at night, when we discovered, about a mile a head of the boat, a range of white houses, lights in various directions, and the masts of several vessels. We thought it must be some small port, and in our uncertainty whether the coast was occupied by our countrymen, we resolved to avoid it.

We therefore tacked a little more to the north, and left it on the larboard side; we also took in a sail, and as many reefs as we could of the other, to slacken our progress, and to enable us to make the land without danger. After half an hour's sailing, we were not more than a cable's length from the shore, and we perceived that good fortune was on our side from beginning to end of our enterprise, for we came to a fine beach of sand and gravel, that presented not the slightest appearance of danger.

After sailing along it for a few minutes, to choose a proper spot, we hoisted our sail, and the boat ran in and grounded so near the shore, that we landed with water only to our knees.

After we had set foot on shore, our first impulse was to embrace each other, and to congratulate ourselves on the good fortune that had hitherto followed our every step. But one engrossing thought soon struck each of us: what were we to do—which way should we go? We thought it right to wait for daylight before determining anything on the subject, with the hope that some unexpected incident might enable us to learn the position of the French army. We therefore walked towards the interior, crossed a high road that ran parallel to the shore, and after wandering some time, discovered a retreat among the rocks, where we could safely pass the night It may be easily imagined that we were worn out with fatigue and want of sleep. After taking some food, we threw ourselves on the sand, (one of our number still keeping watch) determined to end our perils so soon as morning appeared.

I had taken Ricaud's place on guard for more than an hour; it was broad daylight, and I was thinking of awaking my companions, to talk with them on our prospects, when I saw two men on the road conducting seven or eight mules. I left my retreat in a moment, and ran forward so as to get before them; I then came into the road, and advanced carelessly towards them. On my way, I planned what I was to say to them. I spoke the Catalonian dialect pretty well, and it has great resemblance to the Provençal; our boat was also fortunately in the same spot where we had landed, and seemed ready to set sail again. I told them that we had set out two days ago from Palma to go to Trivica, but had been taken by a squall at sea, and forced to drive towards the west, and that the same wind still prevented us continuing our voyage; that we had been driven on the coast the night before, and were quite out of provisions; that my partners had set out for some farmhouse to look for provisions, and that I was waiting for them to set sail again. I concluded by asking them where we were, and what news they had heard.

All that I had said was plausible enough for them to believe it implicitly. They told me that I was about a mile from

Vinaros, a small seaport where we should find whatever we were in want of; this was the village we had seen the evening before. I walked with them for a few minutes, and they spoke of everything but the subject that I cared about. They came to it at last of their own accord. They informed me that *the French demons* were carrying on the siege of Tortosa, a town six leagues from Vinaros, and that it had probably surrendered at the moment we were talking.

I remained with them only a moment longer to ascertain what direction Tortosa lay, and then left them, under the pretext of waiting for my friends, whom I expected every moment.

As soon as I lost sight of the muleteers, I made my way towards the rocks, and having informed my companions of all I had done, we made our way through the fields, towards the N. West, where I was told Tortosa was situated, After a very fatiguing walk for an hour, during which we were several times forced to make our way through hedges and leap over wide ditches, we came to a road that seemed to lead to our destination, and we followed it. How close so ever we *were* to the French army, we were afraid of meeting some of the guerrillas, who would have examined us, and discovered what we were.

This fear was soon dispelled: we perceived a drove of oxen in front of us, conducted to the camp by a French detachment commanded by a sergeant. We made ourselves known to the escort, and continued our route together, About three o'clock in the afternoon, we reached the neighbourhood of the camp, and saw crowds of harbingers and mess-men who came to receive their rations, I examined them all, and soon found out the harbingers of my own battalion.

When I approached them, the harbinger of the grenadier company called out roughly to me, asked what I wanted, and ordered me to go about my business.

"What do I want?" said I to him—"Indeed! I want, like you, nothing more than the provisions of my company."

I was immediately recognized, and nothing was to be heard on all sides, but roars of laughter at my dress, questions about my adventures, and congratulations on my fortunate escape. We returned to the camp together. Another had taken my place; but I was put on the list, and was to obtain the first vacancy.

The next day, I received two months additional pay, and this, with the remainder of the sum I had derived from my theatre, formed a sum that would enable me to be secure from want for a long period.

It was with great joy that I threw into a ditch the clothes of the Spanish sailor, which I had worn for three days, and that I again put on my uniform. I had the honour of being presented to the general who commanded our division; he had the goodness to enquire of me the particulars of my escape, and the manner in which the prisoners were treated at Cabrera. I soon met Ricaud, who had been received back by his regiment as joyfully as I was by mine, and he was immediately employed on duty. The two young sailors received routes to return to France.

What I had suffered at Cabrera had not exactly increased my love for the Spaniards, and I had for a long while past been anxious to show them my mind. I was moreover determined to make up for the time I had lost, and to get up above the rank of harbinger; and I was ardently desirous that the siege should terminate in an assault, or that the garrison would at least have the goodness to make a sortie. Without being too sanguine one might reasonably hope that such wishes would be realized. They were so very speedily.

I arrived at the army on the 25th of December, 1810; on the 30th, our works were advanced as far as the ramparts of Tortosa. It seems that the besieged began to think their situation dangerous; for on the 26th they asked for a capitulation. Our general sent back their flag of truce, without paying any attention to their proposals. They came back several times, and were never even admitted. It was this severity that doubtless enabled us to see the garrison closely. On the morning of the 28th, it feigned a sortie on one point, and at the same moment, bore with almost its whole strength on that part of the camp occupied by our division, which was under arms in less than a minute, and advanced in good order to meet the enemy. I was in the light company, and not being in the front line, I was not obliged to remain by the eagle, the usual post of the harbingers. This purely accidental circumstance gave me an opportunity of seeing my friends, the Spaniards and the English, much closer than I could have done in the ranks.

The light company acted as skirmishers, while the division advanced to charge the enemy. The besieged remained firm for about a quarter of an hour, when they began to give way, and seemed desirous of gaining the ramparts. Our approach soon put their ranks into the utmost confusion; different corps were mingled together, and formed a confused mass, which rolled amidst the dust and smoke, towards the gates of Tortosa. Along with a few light troops I broke through their ranks, but I was almost immediately surrounded, and pressed on all sides by the enemy in their flight, and I found it out of my power to clear my way amidst the crowd, I had lost sight of my companions, who were separated from me, and their return cut off by the runaways.

Meanwhile the balls and cannon-shot from our army made vacancies in the mass, amidst which I still continued to move forward, bayonet in hand. It became thinner and thinner as we approached the town, as everyone moved towards the gate, which he thought he could pass through soonest, and with the least danger.

My ardour increased when I saw the feather of an English officer, who was as anxious as the rest to get to a place of safety. I came up to him, and he acted rightly in instantly telling me, in broken French, that he surrendered; a moment longer he would have been too late.

After receiving his sword, I told him to follow me; he seemed to hesitate, when he saw that I was marching towards the town; but I said two words to him that made him make up his mind; he ought at any rate to have reflected that I was his best security, and that he would have to begin the matter over again with the first Frenchman he met; I therefore made him march beside me, and the desire I had of keeping him secure contributed to delay my progress. But I wanted to make another prisoner; when I approached the gate immediately before me, I came up with a host of runaways, who were rushing towards it; I was now followed by about a dozen of our men who had joined me, and I was quite close to the gate, when a Spanish officer was going to set foot on the drawbridge, when I rushed forward, put my bayonet to his breast, and pushing him towards the parapet, ordered him to give up his sword, which he did without resistance. I ordered him to march before me along with the English officer, who had been a quiet spectator of the scene.

The whole was done in much shorter time than I have occupied in relating it; moreover my first prisoner must have been conscious that I would shoot him the moment he left my side.

I hastened to return to the camp with my two prisoners; several balls from the ramparts fell at our feet, and a shower of others soon followed. I had scarcely moved a few paces before a Spanish officer, pursued by our light troops and running towards the gate, came exactly in front of me: I was in the luck of taking prisoners. As I saw some Frenchmen coming up, whose presence would hold in check the two officers I was leading captive, I levelled my gun in the stranger's face, and called out to him to surrender; he threw down his sword, which I picked up, and made him march back with the other two. Amidst a shower of balls we came up with the division which was returning to the camp, and I had the happiness of presenting to our colonel the three prisoners I had taken, and to deliver him their swords.

After expressing his satisfaction, he ordered me not to leave him. So soon as the regiment had returned to camp, and he had dismounted from his horse, he told me to follow him with my three prisoners. We went to see the Marshal, by whom we were immediately admitted; the colonel presented me to him and told him, in a few words and without any remark, what he had the goodness to call a brave action; he spoke to a man who knew the world. The Marshal reproached the three officers in an ironical manner, and then asked me how I had taken them.

"At one of the gates of Tortosa," I replied.

He said little to me, but what he did say was so flattering, that I was uplifted with pride and satisfaction, and thought myself more than rewarded for the little I had done. He added that he would next day put me in the list of those who were to receive the cross of honour, and concluded by asking me if I had any favour to ask from him.

"Yes, Marshal," said I, unable any longer to keep down the enthusiasm raised by the praise he lavished on me—"Yes, I have a favour to ask of you,"

"What is it?"

"That I be allowed to mount the first to the assault when you storm the town."

"Certainly you may depend upon it, my brave fellow," said he after a momentary pause, during which I thought that he looked at me with some astonishment.

I waited with great impatience and emotion for the moment when we should be ordered to take Tortosa, but I was sorry to see that the garrison did not seem determined to wait for an assault; they made further attempts to obtain terms of capitulation, but they were rejected like the former; and on the 2nd of January, 1811, without any assault being made, a regiment of our division seized one of the gates, and after an action of half an hour's duration penetrated into the town, which was immediately occupied by the French army.

The garrison, consisting of eight thousand men, was treated with a generosity which it certainly had no right to expect, and which it was far from deserving. The men were made prisoners of war, and sent to France with an escort.

The third corps soon gained other advantages, in which I was destined to have no share. A few days after the capture of

Tortosa, I was taken ill with a violent fever, brought on doubtless by my long sufferings at Cabrera; I was sent to the hospital, and was several days between life and death. But I would absolutely come out the day that I learned my decoration had arrived; I received it from the colonel on the parade—it was the most powerful emotion of pleasure I ever felt in my life. Such sensations cannot be experienced twice.

This honour was rarely granted at that period, and was almost a sure guarantee of promotion for those who added some acquirements to their bravery, of which it was the certain characteristic. On the same day I was also made a Sergeant: this rank is the first in the military aristocracy, that leads at once to a commission. How many hopes did not this double favour raise in my breast! I was then very far from thinking that it was the boundary beyond which I was not destined to pass.

Notwithstanding my zeal and sincere desire of justifying, by my future services, the reward I had just obtained, I was forced to return to the hospital; I would not stay in it long; I languished on without getting better, and our chief surgeon declared that the only chance of saving my life was to breathe my native air for some months. Leave of absence for three months was asked for and speedily obtained, as the Marshal felt interested in my fortunes.

On the 18th of February, I set out, along with a detachment of wounded men that were going to the frontiers; and in a month afterward I reached Toulon.

CHAPTER 9

My Native Village

After an absence of four years, I revisited my native village and my family. I had already traversed a considerable part of Europe; I had escaped from several bloody battles, and dangers of innumerable kinds; and I had therefore a great deal to relate, though I told nothing but the simple truth. My family received me with the warmest affection, and my friends and acquaintance with every mark of respect and goodwill. It was known that my stay among them could not be very long, and they accordingly lost no time in welcoming my return, for I was daily the object of their varied and kind attention.

I often recall with pleasure this period of my life, brief though it was, but every moment of it reminds me of scenes of quiet and happiness. Many military men must have felt this charm; after the fatiguing marches and tumult of a campaign, when one has contracted the austere and blunt habits of active service, this absolute quiescence, and these delicate attentions, produce an effect on his mind of which the peaceful and domesticated citizen, unaccustomed to powerful emotions, can form no idea. Nothing, it seems to me, resembles these moments so much as the period of convalescence, during which all that we see or feel seems novel, and we think ourselves entering again into a world whose every sensation presents a charm we never felt till now.

The day after my arrival, I received a visit from M. Bernard, the husband of my first love, of my dear Miette, who came along with him. I had loved her too dearly to see her without emotion; but my heart had been tried by so many violent emotions since my departure, so many troubles and anxious cares, that my love was considerably blunted. The presence of Miette, now become the wife of another, did not affect me so painfully as I should have formerly thought; her presence recalled to my mind the circumstances of my boyhood, and the dreams of happiness which had been dashed away by the conscription.

I involuntarily compared the peaceable life I might have enjoyed with her, with the noisy and dangerous career that was in reserve for me; but after all, these thoughts, though somewhat sad, did not affect me very painfully. Meanwhile I thought she was greatly altered; she had one child, and was on the eve of having a second. Her complexion had lost its brilliancy, her shape was now without grace, and household duties had long before this occupied the time formerly devoted to reading and agreeable accomplishments.

M, Bernard was about six and thirty years of age, and had a situation in the navy victualling board at Toulon. He was one of those individuals who have no characteristic features, of whom we can say neither good nor harm. He was neither handsome nor ugly, was tolerably good-humoured, sometimes aiming at wit and gaiety, though a great calculator, two qualities seldom combined; such was M, Bernard. Upon the whole he did not seem to me the man that would have suited Miette; but this was perhaps the effect of some remains of love and prejudice on my part.

They requested me to go the next day to the country to dine with M. Rymbaud, who was very desirous of seeing me. This worthy man was getting advanced in years; he had never been very nimble, and at this moment, in spite of the skill of M. Ledere, the chief surgeon of the navy, he was kept by palsy in his armchair, and drawn in it to take the air in his garden, thence back to his drawing-room and bedchamber. He could not refrain from crying when he embraced me, I reminded him of his poor Adolphe, my friend, who was killed on board the *Redoutable* at the battle of Trafalgar. During my short stay in the neighbourhood, I frequently revisited this worthy family, whose affection has always been dear to my heart.

I had been at Sixfour about a month, and divided my time between my own family, and frequent visits to Toulon, and the surrounding country, when one evening, while we were at supper, we saw a sailor-looking man come in, deeply sunburnt, and all in rags. He soon went round the table, and was successively embraced by everyone of the family: it was my uncle Eyguier, whom I had not found at my arrival, and who, they told me was a prisoner of war at Malta, whilst I was a prisoner at Cabrera. After being received by every one of us with the kind and open cordiality of our villages, he informed us that he had escaped from Malta on board a Sardinian vessel, whose captain he had formerly known, and that he had been obliged to leave behind all his property. Though the particulars of his escape seemed to me very interesting, I do not think them sufficiently connected with my subject to relate them here; but the reader will not perhaps be sorry to learn the motives which, independent of his love of his country and desire of resuming his profession, had induced him to brave a thousand dangers to effect his escape to France.

About forty officers, of whom my uncle was one, almost all natives of Provence, and belonging to the navy, were prisoners of war at Civita Vecchia, a small town in the centre of Malta. They were destitute of every kind of amusement, received no newspapers, did not visit the inhabitants of the country, and passed their time in the most complete idleness, yet they nevertheless succeeded in finding several means of killing time. The principal of these was the institution of a Masonic Lodge, which they entitled the *Lodge of the Friends in Captivity.* They had received a great many members, and had given frequent dinners; and they were preparing to give a brilliant fête to some English freemasons they had become acquainted with at La Valetta, the capital of the island; but they were ignorant of the fête that was preparing for themselves.

Long before this time, the priests and monks, who form at least a fourth part of the population of Malta, thundered forth their anathemas against these Masonic meetings, to which they ascribed a long drought that afflicted the country, and an epidemic disease that had just appeared. The day of the fete had been designated as the proper period to put an end to these calamities, by setting fire to the hall of the meeting while the members were at dinner, and by murdering those who should attempt to escape. Poignards and faggots, and other instruments of intolerance were prepared; and the peasants of the neighbouring villages were duly convoked, and were to assemble at the spot on the day and at the hour appointed.

Our unfortunate countrymen saw no company, and were not very attentive to their religious duties, so that they suspected nothing, and went on as usual. There are good people everywhere, say the Normans; some charitable soul informed the English governor of what was going on, who gave immediate information of the fact to the freemasons, and forbade them to hold their meeting, which they obeyed accordingly. But the peasants did not like to be called upon for no purpose; they drove in the doors of the lodge, carried all the furniture and ornaments to the principal square, and there burned them with great ceremony, whilst the clergy were making a procession, and purifying, by their ablutions, the house that had been the theatre of the Masonic abominations. The French were hooted at and insulted by the populace, but they had the prudence to keep themselves out of sight for some days.

My uncle Eyguier was known to be the grand master of the lodge, and had been especially marked out for the brutality of the mob, as being the head of the infernal band. From this moment he could never appear without being insulted by the peasants, or even without being exposed to the most imminent dangers. After enduring this treatment patiently for a long time, he determined on making an attempt to leave this abominable country, and he fortunately succeeded.

We could scarcely conceive such ignorance and barbarism to exist among a people so near to the most civilized regions of the globe. But my uncle informed us that education was in this country put exclusively in the hands of ignorant clergymen, and our astonishment was at an end.

A few days after his arrival, he was fit to present himself to the maritime prefect, who gave him the command of a gun-boat. I visited along with him almost all the vessels that formed our Mediterranean fleet, and the sight of them increased my natural pride, and made me attach more value to the name of Frenchman, of which we were then so vainglorious. Nowhere could crews be seen animated with a more determined courage, a body of young officers more skilful or braver than was shown by the squadron of Toulon at that period.

I consider it my duty to add that the excellent state of the fleet I have just noticed was due to the attention, unwearied activity, and unbounded naval skill of Vice Admiral Allemand, from whom however the command had just been withdrawn. His successor received express orders from government never to engage in action with the English vessels that were cruising near the port, and who were in fact continually in sight. Such an order must have naturally disgusted the officers under his command; but they knew their commander too well, and the scrupulous attention he paid to his most trifling duties, to flatter themselves with the hope that an order of this nature would ever be disobeyed.

My father sometimes went with me to Toulon, and I felt a very pleasurable sensation, when I saw him put on an air of importance, when the sentinels, as we passed them, presented arms to me on account of my decoration. It may be easily imagined that I was proud of it; this distinction was then rare, for there were scarcely eight or ten individuals who had it in a whole regiment! I believe there were only three thus honoured in the whole fleet at Toulon, except some admirals and officers of rank; and I was the first who had hitherto appeared at Sixfour. I have found so many since my return, that I have been forced to conclude that the number of men who have distinguished themselves has been greatly increased within the last few years.

As may be imagined, my furlough came rapidly to its close; in fact I scarcely perceived the progress of time. But my health was perfectly restored, and my interest and my duty urged me to depart When the last day came, I went to present my furlough, and ask the commissary for a route. My regiment, which I had scarcely thought of for the last six months, had not been losing its time in the interval. After being engaged in several actions in Catalonia, it left Spain to join the grand army, and was at this moment at Innsbruck in the Tyrol.

On leaving my family and friends, I compared the sensations I now felt with those I had experienced six years before on a similar occasion. My manner of thinking was greatly changed; assuredly I felt regret for those I left behind; but it was very different indeed from what I felt on my first departure. Then deep depression of mind left me no source of consolation, and held out to me no happiness but in my native village and a peaceful life. Now—encouraged by some gleams of success, fascinated by patriotism and the *esprit de corps*, and full of hope and zeal, I rushed towards the future, which seemed to call me and smile upon my anticipations.

As at my first departure, I was accompanied for some leagues by my brother, my uncle Eyguier, and a few friends. The former was desirous of going farther with me, but his father's office, of which he did almost all the business, did not allow him to be absent long. Meanwhile I left my family in prosperous circumstances, and they were able to give me the means of travelling comfortably; but I had become an excellent pedestrian, and determined on going forward on foot.

I went, therefore, for the third time, to see again that Germany, where so many laurels had been gathered by my countrymen. It was said that we were going to have another war with Russia; but though there had never been but one season for our armies since the revolution, it was generally thought that the campaign would not be begun before the ensuing spring, so that I had plenty of time to join my corps. Hence I was in no haste, I stopped several days in different towns on my route, and did not reach my regiment till the month of October. I entered into the company commanded by M. Moutet, who was drawn by the conscription at the same time with me, but who had been more fortunate.

Chapter 10
Russia & Borodino

We spent the winter pretty quietly in the city of Innsbruck, where we were frequently exercised, which seemed to indicate the approach of war. In fact as spring came round, it was reported that war was going to be declared against Russia, and we made long marches and short halts on our approach to the imagined theatre of hostilities. In the month of June, we were on the Vistula, forming part of the fourth corps of the Grand Army, commanded by Prince Eugene (Beauharnois).

At the beginning of July, we learned that war was declared, that the army was crossing the Niemen, that the Emperor's headquarters were at Wilna, and that we were to enter Poland, where the presence of our eagles excited enthusiasm and promised independence.

We entered Lithuania, and were probably the first part of the army who met those hordes of savages called Cossacks, for we drove before us the Russian corps of General Platoff, consisting chiefly of these wandering tribes. The first time their pulks charged us with *houras,* the singularity of their appearance, their strange dress, and a semblance of intrepidity that was greatly aided by the enormous length of their mustachios, surprised us at first; but when we saw them almost instantly turning their backs the moment the first shot was fired and retreating in disorder, we knew what they were worth.

It was thus that we entered Russia, still driving these Cossacks before us like sheep. We then saw the first regular masses of the enemy's troops, and our movements began to be connected with those of the other corps of the French army. We were too far from headquarters to be engaged in the first battle that took place, and had only very partial and unimportant engagements with the Russians, though victory was always purchased by a great loss of blood; but as this was the usual course of business, we paid little attention to it, and looked forward only to the day when, under the Emperor's eye, we should decide the success of the campaign in a great battle. Certain that the result could not escape from our grasp, and that the further the Russians fled before us, the easier our triumph would become, we pushed forward into their deserts with the fullest security. We were accustomed to enter foreign capitals, and already spoke of the Muscovite city, as people who expected to be there without delay; and when we learned the bloody battle of Smolensko, we had no other regret than that we had not been present, but the more important battle of Borodino was not to be fought without our aid.

On the 5th September, we reached, in our pursuit of the enemy, the heights in the neighbourhood of Borodino. On the same day we heard the report of a sharp engagement on our right The fire of musketry and artillery was kept up till ten o'clock at night.

We learned next day, by a Sergeant of the 57th, who had come to see his brother (the adjutant of our regiment) that the Emperor had ordered the division of Compans to attack a redoubt which served as a sort of advanced post to the enemy's line; that the Russians had defended it with the utmost determination, but the 61st had at last entered the redoubt, where the artillerymen had been killed beside their guns; and that this advantage was mainly attributable to the march of the 57th on the enemy's left. The second battalion of this regiment had been terribly cut up; its worthy commander, Colonel Laboulaye, was killed, along with many officers, and more than half the non-commissioned officers and soldiers.

"The Emperor came," (added the sergeant) "to our bivouac this morning at daybreak, and was able to convince himself, by the appearance of the ground round the redoubt, strewed with *green coated corpses* (as he said himself) that the enemy's loss was infinitely greater than ours."

Pleased with having embraced his brother, whom it had been out of his power to see for six years before, and with a slight repast we had prepared for him in a hurry, this brave Sergeant left us to join his eagle.

"The moment approaches," said he to us on leaving, "when we are going to have a skirmish in more numerous company than usual."

In fact, the movements made by both regiments to concentrate their forces gave us reason to believe that a great battle was about to be fought; we were certain of it in the afternoon, when the Emperor himself visited all the Russian outposts, which had fallen back behind the little river Kaluga, and when we saw in the enemy's camp a bishop and all his clergy, making a procession through their ranks.

A little before six o'clock on the seventh, there was read, in the centre of every company, an order of the day, showing that our impatience was known to the Emperor, for it began with these words: "Now comes the battle you have so much desired!"

At six o'clock the cannon on the right gave the signal for action, and the whole army moved forward. The Russians had fortified several points, which it was necessary to carry one after another. Almost in front of us rose that famous redoubt which was so vigorously defended, and the storming of which has been considered as one of the greatest exploits our army ever performed. We were there.

In the afternoon, the French army occupied the field of battle, and all the positions held by the enemy in the morning. At the moment we were about to take up a position, the regiment marched forward again, and we marched in columns along the lines of the army, moving from left to right. We had been moving forward for more than an hour, when a small detachment of lancers came from the direction of the *burned village* (Semenowskoi) and galloped past our right flank.

The regiment halted and put itself in battle array; it was the Emperor. The colonel went up to him, and seemed to be receiving orders, after which Napoleon rode rapidly along the front of the regiment, stopping long enough, however, to express his satisfaction at our conduct in attacking the redoubt, and to make some promotions.

I carried the eagle which the colonel had ordered me to take when the officer in whose hands it was was killed in a charge against the Russians. I lowered it as the Emperor approached, and after saluting it, he cast a glance towards me, reined in his horse, and said to me:

"I have seen you before, Sergeant?"

"Yes, Sire, after the death of Admiral Villeneuve."

"I remember you—where did you obtain your decoration?"

"At Tortosa, for taking three officers from the enemy"

"He is an ensign," said he to the colonel, who followed him, and he rode on.

The regiment again moved forward; the officers of the nearest companies came to congratulate me on my promotion, and the colonel said to me as he passed on:

"Ensign, you will be appointed this evening."

Thus I had finished my career as a non-commissioned officer, and was about to begin one of a quite different nature.

We marched towards those points where we still heard the firing of cannon. The battle was over; but the Russians made a last effort along their whole line to cover their retreat, perhaps also with the design of keeping possession of some of the heights, and of covering the high road to Moscow. The colonel doubtless followed the orders he had received in hurrying us forward, along very difficult ground that had been cut up already by the movements of thousands of soldiers.

When he saw the same sort of ground along our whole line, he thought fit to move much more to the left, so that he might gain the direction he wished by making a circuit. While we were executing this movement, a Russian corps, which had remained firm till then, was driven back by the divisions on the left, and came exactly in front of us. They thought we had come to cut off their retreat, and in fact we ourselves thought at first that this was the colonel's object, hut the disparity of numbers was too great to keep us long in error.

We instantly thought of cutting our way through this corps, while the Russians could not retreat, except by passing through our ranks. The engagement began on both sides at the same moment by firing in platoons. A number of our men and the colonel himself were killed. The major, who took the command, made us rush forward to charge the Russians with the bayonet. Amidst the confusion, embarrassed by the fall of the men around me, and wounded by two thrusts of a bayonet, I fell, but made a violent effort to prevent the eagle falling into the hands of the enemy who rushed on me, and threw it over the heads of several ranks of them to a group of our soldiers, who had already cut their way through. This was all I could do. Crushed under the feet of the Russians, overwhelmed by numbers, unable to draw my sabre, I could not get up, but was borne along by them in their retreat, whilst the remains of our regiment rallied in their rear.

The heat of the action had entirely absorbed my mind, and I had thought of nothing but of doing my duty. It was not till I approached the Russian bivouac that my misfortune all at once presented itself in full to my mind. At the moment I had just been appointed an officer, but before taking possession of my rank, at the close of a great victory, thus to lose all the fruits held out to me by a decisive campaign!—Overwhelmed by numbers, and crushed to the earth, I had found it out of my power to die like a brave soldier, yet I had scarcely received a wound! These ideas tormented me during the night.

At daylight, the Russians joined the corps of Kutosoff, and gave up their prisoners to the Cossacks, who stripped us without mercy. We were sent back to the rear of the army, and three days afterward entered Moscow, almost stripped to the skin.

The governor of the city ordered the most indispensable part of our clothing to be restored to us, and after giving us the most violent abuse in presence of the populace (by one of his officers who spoke French) because we had left our own country to ravage his for no cause whatever, he sent us to a barrack that served us for a prison.

As far as I could judge, in traversing the city with a soldier's indifference, Moscow was larger than Lyons, and had several streets filled with palaces. It was adorned with a host of churches and public monuments. The approach of the French army must have necessarily called to the Russian camp every man capable of bearing arms, and forced the greater part of the remainder to retire from the city, for profound silence reigned everywhere, and nothing was to be seen but a thin and miserable population moving about.

We were sad enough on taking possession of the barracks assigned us; but we had scarcely been there twenty-four hours before we were assembled in great haste, and Cossacks drove us before them out of the city, and marched us towards Wladimir. Their precipitation seemed to us a good omen, for it indicated, as we thought, the arrival of the French, and gave us hopes of a speedy deliverance.

Meanwhile we continued our march, and moving farther into the country, we heard no more about the victories of the French army. The march of the Russians was somewhat singular, for all the corps we met for two or three days were evidently in full retreat, which gradually disappeared the farther they went from Moscow. But after the first three days march, we met with nothing but troops going down towards the city.

We concluded from this that a great assemblage of troops was taking place in the neighbourhood, and that a decisive battle would be fought. Although we were prisoners, we formed the plan of conveying some useful information of the enemy's disposition to the Emperor's headquarters. We held counsel on our march, and resolved that twenty of our number, chosen by lot, should make an attempt to escape that very evening.

They took advantage of the time when our guards were putting us into the ferry-boat to cross the river Kliasma, near the village of Bunkovaia; and at a fixed signal, they ran off to the fields with all the speed they could muster. Several Cossacks rode off to pursue them, and pierced the least active with their spears; but the rest gained a neighbouring wood where the Cossacks could not follow them. I never learned whether any of these brave men ever reached his destination. This act of self-devotion was considered by the Russians to be a revolt, and they treated us with more severity during the remainder of our journey from Moscow to Wladimir.

I confess that I was so wholly occupied with thinking of the situation of the French army, and the hope of a speedy deliverance, that I scarcely paid any attention during the first part of our journey to the countries that we travelled through; but in fact they were little different from the country we had marched over for two months before. Thick forests in the distance; sandy heaths along the road; everywhere rough and fatiguing plains, furrowed by profound ravines—such was the country we passed through; it was like Lithuania, Poland, and three-fourths of Upper Germany, a wretched country where everything yet remains to be done to bring the soil under cultivation, and after all it will never be worth the soil of the poorest department in France.

But my indifference ended when we had marched five days and travelled forty leagues; and when I perceived that we should not in all likelihood be restored to liberty for a long period, and that we were going to be banished to some of the distant provinces, I no longer believed, like the rest of the prisoners, that peace would soon be made, and preparing for the worst, I endeavoured but fruitlessly to learn where they were taking us to.

On the sixth day after we left Moscow we arrived at Wladimir, Almost all the inhabitants of the place came out to meet us, and received us with cries of joy, which, as may well be imagined, were not altogether agreeable to the prisoners; but none of us became the victims of their joy, as so frequently happened in Spain.

Wladimir presents a very remarkable prospect: the city is situated along several little hills, the summits of which are occupied by churches. Gardens innumerable embellish the city in a most picturesque manner; and all round the present walls rise the ruins of the ancient city in an immense plain that spreads out to the west, and along a surface of more than three leagues. It was amidst these ruins that our conductors enclosed us during two nights, the coldness of which made us suffer greatly; but on the second day, the sun rose in a cloudless sky and soon heated us with his rays, so that we recovered strength to resume our journey.

We left the banks of the Kliasma, and entered upon a detestable road that leads to Kasimof on the Oka. When I say a detestable road, no idea can be formed in France of the sort of road in question. The highways in Russia, in proportion as one enters into the interior, are not formed, as in the rest of Europe, of beaten, solid earth, either paved or raised into a causeway. The people have neither had the time, the means, nor the materials necessary for accomplishing such a work, in a country which is almost under water; and in making their roads, they have made use of the forests of firs that cover the country, and through which indeed the greater part of them have been made by the aid of fire. Wooden piles are driven into the earth at each side of the intended highway. On these piles are thrown beams of wood, across which is placed a floor of trees rolled close together, and with their bark still on.

It is on these rough roads that the foot traveller fatigues himself to death, and that he who risks going over them in a carriage is so terribly jolted as to cause him to spit blood. Besides this, these log-roads are kept in such bad order, that the traveller is often exposed to the risk of remaining whole days in the marshy spots, where the beams have become rotten, or have been broken by wagons.

The country between Wladimir and Kasimof is sandy, and difficult to travel in. There is nothing remarkable in it but the village of Constantinovo, wholly occupied by potters. From this spot to Kasimof the country is broken by barren hills.

Our journey was not regulated by settled distances, and we did not every evening find a village, in which we could pass the night. In fact, the Cossacks who conducted us, knew no more of the geography of the places, than simply to follow the road before them, and fall in with the hamlets that they met on their way; they never knew the name of any place, and I believe this was what made some of our men say on their return, that the greater part of the Russian villages had no names.

However this may be, we had marched so diligently, that we reached Kasimof six days after leaving Wladimir. We again became the objects of popular curiosity, but the eagerness to see us was not so great as it had been farther back. The population of Kasimof is commercial; the city was formerly called Gorodizets, and contains more than three thousand shopkeepers; its situation on the Oka is very remarkable. In various parts of it are seen the ruins of mosques built of bricks of enormous size, to which the inhabitants attach a host of superstitious feelings. I could enlarge upon the remarkable things to be seen in this almost Tartar place, were I not afraid of appearing tiresome to the greater part of my readers.

We remained three days at Kasimof. In the evening of the third day, we were divided into two detachments. The one consisting of about a thousand men, was sent towards the south; it was to ascend the Sua, as far as the plains where that river approaches within a few leagues of the Choper, which falls into the Don. the detachment was to remain in the immense region inhabited by the Cossacks. The other consisted of about nine hundred men, and was ordered to descend the

Oka as far as Nig-Novogorod, and thence, to follow the Volga to Rozan. I was in the latter detachment, and was not without anxiety concerning the place of our final destination.

Before we were separated from our companions, to guard whom was sent the whole band of Cossacks who had escorted as to Kasimof, I endeavoured to obtain from them some intelligence of our future prospects. They pointed out the north to me, and said *Sibir,* a word I could make little of; but by frequently talking to them on the subject I got something more explicit, for they said *Sibiry* to me; and I thereby understood that we were condemned to the Russian galleys, to Siberia, in a word.

As soon as my companions learned the news, and the best informed had told the rest what sort of a place the war prison of the Russians was, they became completely discouraged. They all talked of the labours of the mines, and the sufferings of those condemned to work in them, for they thought that this was to be their lot. I remembered perfectly all the most remarkable circumstances contained in various books of travels through Russia, and related them to my companions, imagining with a foolish simplicity I have often laughed at afterwards, that we should see assembled on one spot all the curiosities they describe.

Meanwhile, after the first impression of sorrow, which we felt on learning that we were going to Siberia, speedily succeeded thoughtlessness of our situation, and even gaiety, the never failing companion of our countrymen. We continued our journey with less trouble or fatigue, for our mode of travelling now became very convenient; we were embarked on a kind of rafts, under the charge of some very good hearted Russians, and we rapidly descended the Oka, a river as large as the Rhone, which flows between high banks of calcareous stone, above which wave forests of birch and pine.

We had fires on board; provisions were abundant; and we scarcely perceived the cold that had lately set in, when on the sixth or seventh day after leaving Kasimof, we arrived

Nig-Novogorod. We had thus taken an immense turn to the south, for the purpose of avoiding the log-made roads that lie between Wladimir and Novogorod, which were then impassable, and likewise to give more facility to the escorts that were to go with us, and to allow the return of the Cossacks to their own country.

All the prisoners taken at the battle of Borodino, amounting, as I have already mentioned, to about two thousand men not wounded, had been sent to Kasimof. Among them were a great many officers belonging to the different corps, who were more plundered by the Cossacks than the rest, on account of their epaulets and decorations, and their rank was not acknowledged till we went into the interior, and by the French alone. The Russians had had no time to pay attention to them, and they would have remained confounded in the ranks, had we not belonged to the best disciplined Army in the world.

Their rank was acknowledged, and they preserved all the authority they could still exercise in a state of captivity; and amongst men whom the absence of every competent judge might easily tempt to the assumption of rank and authority, there was but one man who attempted to abuse the confidence of his companions. His name was Aillaud, and he was a private in a regiment of horse-chasseurs. He took advantage of the education be had received, and the forced disguise to which we were all condemned in our turn by the rapacity of the Cossacks, and the munificence of Rostopchin, and gave out that he was a captain; but in about eight days time, while we were at Wladimir, he was recognised by one of his old companions, a prisoner like the rest of us, and so laughed at, that I never saw from that day a more docile or obedient soldier. For myself I told how I had been made an ensign by the Emperor, and no doubt rose of the truth of my recital The respect of the soldiers I saw during my captivity, were the only advantages I ever derived from the rank I had momentarily attained.

During the first days of our journey, whilst we were trying to ascertain to what corps we each of us belonged, and endeavouring to form friendships with our fellow prisoners, I had for a considerable time marched beside a young man whom I soon recognised to be an officer of rank. It was Colonel Laplane, who had been one of the first to enter the redoubt with General Montbrun's cuirassiers, and had unfortunately charged the Russians at the moment they were falling back on Kutusoff's corps, and had been taken prisoner. He was immediately taken before the Russian commander-in-chief, by whom he was brutally treated; and the Cossacks, imitating the conduct of their leader, stripped him as soon as Kutusoff had turned his back. Colonel Laplane was the proposer of the attempt, made by twenty of our companions, to inform the Emperor of the concentration of the Russian army towards Moscow, He had been scarcely acknowledged in his proper rank before he exerted a salutary influence over the prisoners, and this influence was gradually extended even over the escort itself.

As I was one of the first who had sought his conversation, and aided in making his rank be acknowledged, he showed me a great deal of attachment, and we became extremely intimate. But we were always afraid of being separate reckoning that in proportion as we advanced farther into the country, the prisoners would be divided into detachments smaller and smaller. The colonel knew how to turn this danger aside. On my side I made every effort to remain in the same detachment with him.

It was not without difficulty that, at Nig-Novogorod, where our party was divided into three detachments of about three hundred men each, ordered in different directions, we succeeded in getting ourselves included in the one that was going to Kazan; the other two, before they descended towards the south, received orders to set out without delay; though the season was far advanced, and the north winds blew without intermission.

For ourselves our quarters were pretty good for prisoners, and we remained six weeks at Nig-Novogorod, tiring with our questions everyone that came near us, for we were eagerly desirous of learning some news of the French army; but we could learn nothing, and were always ready to console ourselves with the saying, "No news, is good news." During our stay in this place winter began. The sky had been invariably clear till about the 10th of October, when it became dark and foggy; the snow fell in immense quantities, and when it ceased, intense frost set in and in a few days stopped the course of the streams and rivers.

In about twenty days time, the weather became serene again; the cold, though sharp, was not so painful as it had been at first, and we were told that winter had set in. We were then informed that as soon as the sledges were ready, we were to set out for Kazan, under the charge of a small body of men, who had brought down the iron of the imperial foundries to Novogorod by water, and would take advantage of the first favourable moment to return, The horses which had been employed in remounting the sledges on the Volga, had been frost-shoed, and were to pull the prisoners and their escort over the snow as well as a great quantity of goods.

We left Nig-Novogorod on the 25th of November. None of us had ever witnessed such a sight. We all forgot that we were prisoners, to enjoy ourselves as travellers in sledges. This was no longer a sort of journey such as those I had taken at the castle of Wishendorf, on the shores of the Baltic, but an immense concourse of pilgrims moving through deserts of snow. I shall not detain the reader by describing this mode of travelling, which proved as agreeable to us as the log-made roads were detestable. We were huddled together without distinction in those carriages with skates, which the Russians call *kibick*, and we followed out the beaten path, which was sometimes on the banks of the Volga, and at other times in the very middle of the bed of the river. It was not, however, till towards the end of our journey, that we travelled upon the

Volga, for the ice and snow that covered it had not till then acquired a suitable degree of firmness. At night we entered the villages, where we were quartered in large caravanserais. Taking everything into consideration, we were not very ill off, and were only unhappy through our anxiety to learn where our strange journeys were to end.

At length, on the 5th of December, after crossing a very flat country, which seemed to me, however, to be agreeable, because it was sprinkled with clumps of trees, we arrived at Kazan, the appearance of which was altogether a novelty to us.

When I perceived it, I remembered that it was formerly considered to be beyond the limits that separate Europe from Asia. It has preserved a truly Oriental aspect. Its inhabitants are a mixture of Armenians, Mohammedans and Tartars. We only stopped at Kazan a few days, when our party was again divided. About one hundred and fifty were ordered to Oremburg and Osa, towards the south, and the remainder to Perm and Ekaterinburg to the north east. I was counted over among the latter, for it may be well imagined that we were not called over by name. Colonel Laplane was likewise one of the number. We continued our journey in sledges. Our numbers were again reduced at Perm, and we amounted to no more than seventy on setting out for Ekaterinburg.

Perm is the last town in Europe that is to be met with in that direction. It is situated in a mountainous country, which already forms a part of the Ural mountains, which are more celebrated than their lowness of elevation would make one suppose, but they form the real divisional line between Europe and Asia.

After climbing for a day and a half the easy ridges that cover the surface of the country, we descended towards Ekaterinburg. It is a very fine town, with the houses covered with iron plates, a mint, and a government office, for the general direction of the mines of Perm, Kasan, Oremburg, and Siberia.

Here, in consequence of an agreement entered into by the crown agent, and the agent of M, Demidoff, one of the richest men in Russia, we were for the last time separated from each other, and formed into little detachments of about ten men each, which were sent to each of the mines of that powerful iron-master.

Colonel Laplane had become the leader of us all, and his authority had been acknowledged by the Russians themselves, who had at length shown him a part of the respect due to his rank. He learned at Ekaterinburg that the forge of Nishnei Taguil, about ten leagues to the north, was conducted by a Frenchman, and requested to be sent thither with nine men, among whom he included me; and his request was granted without hesitation.

We set out for Nishnei Taguil, which we reached on the 31st of December- This was the termination of our journey, which had thus continued from the river Mosqua, and deducting the time we spent at Nig-Novogorod, had lasted two months and a half, during which we had travelled five hundred leagues—and France, Paris, and Sixfour were still six hundred leagues beyond our point of departure! What an immense space separated us from our homes! When could we undertake to go over the distance again? Who in the wide world could feel an interest in our fortunes, and come to seek us in such a remote region? Should we be forgotten, like the exiles of Kamtschatka or Tartary, who during the whole period of their banishment received no order from the Russian government, but the one that drives them back a thousand leagues from the court?

Still were we certain that the French armies were victorious, we should feel some consolation among the painful labours to which we had no doubt we should be condemned!—But at Kasan, we were told that the French had been completely defeated at Moscow, which they had seized by surprise, and burned on their retreat; and at Ekaterinburg nobody thought of the war at all, but considered it settled long ago.

The news we had heard at Kasan gave us great uneasiness; but the Emperor and the grand army could not be defeated, we said, at the very moment they took possession of the Russian capital; and we would not believe the rest of the story. We were more vexed and impatient at the indifference of the people of Ekaterinburg than we were with the erroneous notions of the people of Kasan.

Alas, for a very long and melancholy period, we were destined to hear no news either of our companions or of our native soil!

Chapter 11

Siberia

On our arrival at Nishnei-Taguil, we were received by one of the foremen of the forge, who gave us a house, where we were to wait for the orders of his masters.

The next morning we were agreeably surprised by the entrance of M. Mazin, a Frenchman, the sub-director of the works, who had arrived during the night from a journey in the neighbouring country, and could not rest a moment quiet, since he learned that ten Frenchmen had been sent to work under his command.

He gave us all a most pleasing reception, asked us what province we belonged to, and said something to each about his district or native town. He had been long resident in the province of Colonel Laplane, knew several members of his family intimately, and had even received favours from them. It may be easily imagined that on this occasion, so far from France, he seized with avidity the opportunity of displaying his gratitude. He presented the colonel, whom I accompanied to the head manager of all the works, and obtained unrestricted liberty for us, and all the comforts that could be procured at a forge, where, in fact, everything was in the utmost abundance. A Russian servant was ordered to wait on us, and M, Mazin gave us a very pretty little house, well warmed, and immediately adjoining the church.

Our eight companions were put into the least fatiguing workshops belonging to the forge, with orders to make them as comfortable as possible. Their situation was as happy as it could be in Siberia, and they were soon at the head of various departments of the works- They were private soldiers; it never came in to their head that it was improper for the colonel and me to be exempt from labour, and in fact they would have thought themselves disgraced had we been forced to work- Everything was therefore as fortunate as we could expect.

Nishnei-Taguil(which means *Lower Taguil,* to distinguish it from Verknei-Tagnil, or *Upper Taguil)* is an iron-work on the river Taguil, which flows, after changing its name, in different parts of its course, into the great river Ob. It belongs to M. Demidoff, along with nine other forges or foundries situated near it, where the ore is melted that is brought from the Ural mountains. Nishnei-Taguil is the centre of M. Demidoff's establishments, and the most productive counting-house and iron-work belonging to the Ural mountains which are in the hands of private individuals. Orders emanate from it to the forges of Seldinskii, Vouiskii, Nishnei, &c. &c.

The river Taguil is dammed up in this place, and spreads out into a pond over the surface of the plain, by whose waters the machinery of the works is moved, and all kinds of articles in iron manufactured, such as bells, tools of every kind, iron pots, &c. &c. The water rushes from the top of the dam, and sets in motion innumerable hammers and wheels along the long line of factories.

On each side of the workshops rise the houses that form the *zavode,* to use the language of the country; for the crowd of houses round iron works is not called a town *(gorod)* but keeps the name of the forge *(zavode)*, our present residence contained nine thousand inhabitants, all employed directly or indirectly in the works. On the most prominent spot was a fine house, kept for the use of the proprietor, M. Demidoff, when he came to visit the establishment The church is built on the top of the highest hill among which the forge is situated. Like all the churches in Russia, it is divided into two parts, one for summer and another for winter, and is covered with sheets of iron. A number of gardens are scattered among the houses; and though they are not kept in very good order, they give the village a most agreeable aspect, particularly at the approach of spring, when the cherry trees, with which they are planted, are loaded with fruit. In the lower part of the village, is the bazaar, a sort of Oriental fair, where all the shops of the place are collected on one spot.

This population of smiths presents a peculiar aspect, which cannot be adequately conceived by those who have not seen Saint Etienne-en-Forez in France. The prospect is very remarkable in the evening, when along the two long rows of buildings all the fires are lighted, all the hammers beating, all the wheels in motion, and thousands of individuals, blackened with smoke, are moving about the furnaces that pour forth daily many thousand weight of cast-iron. The immense proceeds of these forges are conveyed in sledges to the river Tehoussovaia. whence they descend to the Volga, which they again ascend to a great distance north, for the purpose of being sent all over Russia in Europe, or to be exported to England.

M. Mazin had considerable authority in the forge. He had been lately appointed director of the works for the preparation of the ore, instead of an ignorant Russian, (who had himself succeeded another Frenchman M. F———, whose merit and virtues were warmly remembered at Nishnei,) and had encountered many difficulties in bringing back the establishment to the prosperity and splendour it had formerly enjoyed. The late incidents of the war had been too rapid in their course, and Siberia was too far distant to allow the precautionary measures adopted against Frenchmen resident in Russia to be extended to him, He was highly esteemed and beloved, and through his influence, we remained nothing more than prisoners on parole.

We were very desirous of learning something from him concerning the events of the war, but he knew little of what was going on; hence, we were obliged to wait, as we would not believe the ridiculous reports, as we called them, that were in circulation about the entire destruction of the French army in Russia.

We passed the winter at Nishnei-Taguil: it was towards the close of it that the news of the defeat of the Emperor Napoleon were confirmed. We were forced to believe it at last, when we learned that a certain number of prisoners was quartered in most of the establishments in Siberia.

We knew not how long our exile was to last. To send some intelligence to our families, the colonel and I had taken advantage of the winter parties of travellers that descend towards Europe, and had written letters, though with slender hopes of their reaching their destination. We became every day more intimate, and he generously shared with me all the comforts, and means of enjoyment and pleasure that M. Mazin could procure him.

We went several times to the winter races, which the Russians of all classes are passionately fond of, and to the fishing that takes place on the lakes when the ice is at the strongest, and the fish in a state of the most complete numbness. This fishery sometimes produces several hundred quintals of fish, and is always a grand holiday, to which the people from the surrounding country come in their sledges: they drive over the ice, and furrow it in every direction, while a little lower down, under the horses' feet, the net is introduced by a hole in the ice, and by means of a succession of holes, through which long poles are put, it is pushed to the other end of the lake, and then dragged back with a shoal of fish, which are hauled out upon the shore. The fish are motionless in the water, but become animated by the effect of the air, and struggle violently. The different kinds and sizes are picked out and left exposed to the air, and next day, when they become completely solid from the frost, they are packed up. Salmon, pikes and tench are sent in this state to the centre of Asia, to Petersburg and all parts of Russia. After remaining frozen for three or four months, they are exposed to a proper temperature, and are restored to a similar state to that which they were in an hour before being taken.

Though winter be the gay season of the Siberians, they see the return of spring with the same pleasure as the natives of other climates; and it is apparently to show their joy at its approaching arrival, that they have a sort of amusement during Easter-week—at least, the only object of it which I can fancy is to celebrate the end of winter. Everywhere throughout Russia swings are put up in the houses, gardens, and public squares, and the whole nation devotes itself for eight days to the pleasure of swinging in the air. The sport becomes quite a mania, and you may see grown up people who never leave the swing except to take their meals; and, of course, the young people are not behind hand, After some holidays have been thus spent, they leave till next year the pleasures of enjoying this singular amusement, the origin or object of which I am completely unacquainted with.

Spring does not come gradually in Siberia, as it does with us; like winter it comes all at once. The evening before we feel as if under the arctic circle; the next day, we breathe the air of spring. The snow suddenly disappears, and the earth, as if by enchantment, appears enamelled with flowers, which seem to have burst forth amidst the frost. This unexpected prospect engaged our warmest curiosity.

When the fine weather had set in, M. Mazin told us that the attention he had shown *to* us began to excite ill-will, and he was desirous that we should go to pass some time at another forge, where he had the same authority he possessed at Nishnei, and which was not more than three leagues distant; he had prepared at this place everything we could need, and we should be quite in the country. We joyfully accepted an offer that gave us an opportunity of seeing more of the country, and of leaving the nine thousand smiths of Nishnei-Taguil.

Two days afterwards we set out for Tchornaia-Zavode, our new residence. This forge is situated on the banks of lake Tchornaia, which takes its name from the river Tchornaia-Reka, whose waters flow over a marshy soil before they enter into the lake, and thence discharge themselves into the Taguil. The road that leads to it is monotonous enough; but after travelling along the full-flowing torrent of Tchornaia, crossing a bottom, and ascending the barren ridges of the Ural mountains and the Lipovaia Gora (or mountain of linden-trees, which are in flower at this season,) we breathe a purer air, and enjoy a more varied prospect. Before us was the lake stretching towards the south-west, at the very spot where the Ural mountains are divided into two branches. There are several agreeable islands on its surface, and farther down towards the west, rise two steep mountains, on whose summit the clouds collect in the rainy season.

We were lodged in an *isbas,* or wooden house, built on the island nearest to the dam of the lake, and as soon as we had taken possession, we took no farther interest in the labours of the smiths of the work at Tchornaia. Our time was divided between the pleasures of hunting and fishing, and walks into the neighbouring country, in which a very thin and scattered population is wholly engaged in working the mines on the forges.

The long chain of the Ural mountains, at the foot of whose eastern declivity we were placed, is generally of small elevation, and the views are uninteresting, Masses of dark green rocks are seen on the brink of the ravines; and forests of white cedar, birch, and pine, cover a fertile soil, still fresh and uncultivated, but often marshy. Here and there are found vast heaths, covered with high grass, mingled with sainfoin and trefoil, and making an excellent turf. Nobody is to be met with in the interior of these forests but miners and the charcoal burner belonging to the forges; cultivation is only attended to when the forges allow time to labour, and the soil is miserably neglected, because it belongs to emigrant workmen, who are moved about from one village to another at the order of their lord, and change their country and their climate without any hope of ever returning, or any means of disposing of the improvements they may have made.

The Emperor Alexander has endeavoured to restrain this power of the lords over their serfs, by the establishment of judges in feudal matters, that are appointed by himself; but this first attempt to weaken feudal power remains without effect in the distant provinces, where the lord has always law on his side, and where the judge prefers to be the friend of the lord, who buys justice, rather than of the slave, who has nothing to give. Moreover, though the labour required be severe, the peasants mode of life is not very painful; everyone resides with his own family in the village belonging to the forge. He usually possesses a cow, a horse, some sheep, and a spot of ground, where he raises some cabbages and grain.

As the work done at the forges is not gratuitous, everyone strives to add to his little store of money, that he may one day be enabled to purchase his liberty. Though a serf, the Siberian knows too well the advantage to be derived from saving all he can of his salary, to agree to work for nothing. He leaves his work the moment he is not paid regularly. In 1809. there was a large assemblage of the workmen belonging to M. Demidoff's establishment, and in fact a sort of insurrection, because there was a deficiency of money to pay the men. This embarrassment might have led to serious results, if the men had formed a plan and had leaders; it was very disastrous to some of them, who were severely punished. Since that time, the canteen-keepers have been ordered to keep farther off from some of the forges, though they could not approach within a certain distance before, and were only allowed to open their stores on the Sunday.

The natural magistrates of these men are their lord, and his agents on the establishment; but the workmen also obey one of their own race, who derives his authority from the influence of age and tradition. This is the *starost,* or elder. They usually belong to families in easy circumstances, and there are some very rich ones in the establishments in Siberia. It is easy to ascertain their wealth by looking at the dress of the women on Sundays and holidays. Their costume is very convenient for the display of ornament, and this they know marvellously well. Over a light coloured silk or muslin gown, with wide flowing sleeves, they put a dress of darker silk that covers their bosoms, and is joined on the shoulders by two strips, which are clasped on the middle of the back, along with the belt. The gown shows off the shape in perfection, and is closed before by a long tow of metal buttons. The belt is formed of rich materials, and is tied on the left side; the two ends are adorned with tassels, often of great value, that hang down to the ground, A diadem forms the head-dress of the young girls. Above another sort of diadem, the married women wear a kind of glory, in metal or gilt paper, covered with richly embroidered silk, and tied behind with a large knot of ribbons, whence flows a long veil.

The men are not so luxurious in their dress: they wear a wide caftan or gown, with a silk sash, a fur cap in winter, and a hat with a wide brim in summer, no cravat, but almost always boots.

The nobles and wealthy people shave in the European manner, but the free traders, and peasants, allow their beards to grow. There is another difference between the nobles and serfs; the latter address everyone in the second person singular, while the former disfigure the Russian, language, and never thus address any of their equals. Here, as in other countries, the nobility are the earliest civilized of all classes—though they may one day do their utmost to make their countrymen retrograde to the habits of past ages.

On leaving the forges, and advancing into the country which rises towards the Taguil, we meet with some Mohammedan villages, which are colonies of Kirguises, who during summer plunge with their flocks into the remote steppes, and encamp in huts made of bark. At every short distance, the appearance of the inhabitants is totally different, and we see that Europe contends with Asia for the superiority, and the north with the south.

From this very point flow those rivers that bear their waters to the Frozen Ocean and the Caspian Sea, which pass through Asia and European Russia, and between which very little trouble is required to open a communication, which is now carried on solely by the sledges in winter. How many resources might new means of communication lay open to industry and commerce in such an extensive region as this, if a more enlightened government introduced liberty and property among a nation of serfs? Winter, however, comes annually to shorten the distances, and communication is thus easily opened with the most distant countries. Thus we were at one and the same time on the road to Kamschatka, on the road towards Europe through Kazan, and in the vicinity of Tobolsk, which is about one hundred leagues distant.

In this singular country, there are no other sorts of antiquities than earthen mounds, pretty solidly built, and galleries hollowed out in the sides of the mountains. As they are very different from the attempts at mining made by the Kirguises and Tartars, they are attributed to a people long ago extinct, called the Tchouds, nothing but whose name has come down to us: but they prove that the mines in the Ural mountains have been known and wrought in ancient times, by nations far advanced in refinement, and that hostile and warlike nations have overrun this almost inaccessible country, which is separated from India by the Altai mountains, a border of deserts, and the lofty mountains of Taurus.

CHAPTER 12

Wassili and Daria

I have already mentioned that we lived in a small island not far from the dam of Tchornaia-Zavode. In the morning the colonel and I usually went out together, and crossing the pond, took a walk among the hills at the foot of Beloi-Kamen, towards the south, or went to visit the mines.

We returned before mid-day. After dinner, we sometimes read some books, which M. Mazin had lent us, or we cultivated our little garden; but I got tired of these occupations, and to dissipate my ennui I again got to the other side of the lake, and plunged into the woods, whence I returned in the evening more melancholy than ever.

On landing not far from the dam, I was one day surprised at seeing a young Russian girl crying beside a clump of trees; she seemed pretty, and I approached; she saw me not, but continued to give vent to her tears. I stopped to examine her appearance; her black hair, arranged in the fashion of the country, flowed from under the diadem usually worn by the Siberian girls, and formed a striking contrast, by its jet black colour, with the fairness of her skin.

Whilst I was looking at her she turned her head, and perceiving me, rose in great embarrassment, wiped off her tears, and said to me:

"Pardon me, father—but I am *very* unfortunate."

"I wish," said I, "that it were in my power to give you any consolation."

"I expect no consolation," she replied, "it is out of your power to give me any."

"But why are you crying?" She was silent, and her sobs alone intimated that she was deeply afflicted. "Can you have committed any fault," said I, "that has roused your fathers anger against you?"

"He is angry with me, it is true; but is it my fault, if I cannot love his Aphanassi?"

The subject now began to be interesting; for as Chateaubriand says, there were love and tears at the bottom of this story. I felt peculiarly interested in the narrative.

I asked the young Siberian girl who this Aphanassi was whom she could not love. She became more composed, and with enchanting grace, and almost French volubility, she informed me, that the summer before a Baskir family had travelled further to the north than these tribes arc accustomed to do, and had brought their flocks into the neighbourhood of the zavode of Tchornaia; they came from time to time to the village to buy things, and to sell the gowns called *doubas,* which their wives dye of a yellow colour with the bark of the birch tree.

Now her father, the respectable Michael, was a shopkeeper, and constant communications began to be established between the Baskir and the Hussian family. This connection became more close, when it was discovered that both families were of that sect which pretends to have preserved its religion free from all pollution or mixture, and gives its members the name of *Stareobratzi*. The head of the Baskir family, Aphanassi, soon fell in love with young Daria , and asked her in marriage from her father; but though wealthy, Aphanassi had a rough and repulsive look, and Daria could not bear him; she had, therefore, given him an absolute refusal.

Her father doted on her, and had not pressed the matter farther, though he was desirous of forming an alliance so advantageous to his trade; and the Baskir had returned to his own country in the month of August, to gather the crops of hemp and rye. But winter passed away, and the heats of June had scarcely been felt before Aphanassi had again appeared, with an immense quantity of bales of rich *doubas,* Chinese belts, and kaftans, and a herd of more than five hundred horses; he came, in fact, surrounded with all his splendour, and renewed again his offers and his entreaties. Old Michael was nearly gained by his offers, and Daria was in despair, for she was about to be sacrificed to gain, and she detested Aphanassi more than she had done the year before.

While Daria was giving me this narrative, I examined the play of her features, and found them soft and melancholy. Her skin was of that soft vellum white which distinguishes the Caucasian races; and all her gestures were indicative of languor and voluptuousness.

I listened to her with strong emotion, pitied her sorrows, which had so easily procured me her confidence, and when she left me, she was less afflicted than before. The next day I returned to the spot where I had seen her, and found her again; she received me with an enchanting smile. Aphanassi had not come that morning, and Daria, probably thinking that I would come back to the spot, had come to ask me what she ought to reply to him, as well as to her father. I gave her my advice with a strong feeling of interest, and convinced that pity would henceforward open to me the road to her heart, I tried to become acquainted with her family. The same evening I bought some things from old Michael, and flattering him on his judgment and experience, endeavoured to lay the foundation of intimacy.

During several days I went regularly to the same spot, and almost always found Daria, as if we had appointed a meeting. Her melancholy increased; every time she saw me she asked for further advice, and although she showed me nothing but confidence, yet the habit of seeing her, of deploring her situation, of having near me a young and beautiful woman, after hearing for many, many months, no other voices than the rough ones of officers, soldiers, and smiths—all these circumstances affected my heart with unusual emotion, The sight of Daria reminded me of the circumstances of my first love; and these recollections, in their turn, embellished Daria with all their charms.

One day she said to me, "You have seen Aphanassi this morning at my father's; don't you think he is very rough, and has an ugly, ill-natured countenance?"

"Yes," I replied.

"Well! I will show you whom I prefer to him."

She smiled in saying this, and I was powerfully affected, as if she had been about to say, "You are the man." She then threw back the gauze veil that flowed from her headdress, and instantly, at a certain signal, a young man sprung from behind the trees, and cried out to me:

"Thank you, Frenchman, for your good advice! I am Wassili, the friend of Daria!" This sight perfectly confounded me. So close to love; and to be nothing but a confidant after all! I blushed for shame, but Daria soon dispelled this impulse of ill-humour. She said to me:

"Wassili, whom I have never mentioned to you, is my friend; I was desirous of making you acquainted with him. But he was jealous, because you gave me consolation, and I wished him to remain concealed from you, that he might be convinced, by your language, of the purity of your sentiments. Wassili will love you as I do; stranger, still give us your advice!"

The words of Daria calmed my trouble; and I felt happy that, at a thousand leagues from my native land, in the bosom of an enemy's country, I was bound by no tie to a foreign soil, but could still afford consolation to two beings in misfortune.

Wassili was handsome and amiable; he was also wealthy; but Aphanassi was much more so, and old Michael, though formerly flattered with the attentions of Wassili to his daughter, now rejected them with disdain. We agreed upon a plan of attack against the Baskir; I talked to Michael several times on the subject, and tried to arrange their differences; but it was of no avail.

Meanwhile took place the feast of St. John, the patron saint of Tchornaia, which assembled all the inhabitants of the neighbouring villages. Early in the morning of the-holiday, the whole of the inhabitants, dressed in their finest clothes, get into a number of little narrow boats, made of a single tree, like the canoes of the South Sea savages. A man is placed in, the middle, with one oar in his hands, and strikes the water first on one side and then on the other, and makes the boat move forward with great velocity. These frail skiffs are all in a line, race against each other, and perform a variety of evolutions on the lake. The women are placed at the bow and stem, and sing national songs, while the men are engaged in a variety of exercises and amusements on the shore.

A large barge, carrying the heads of the village, and the most distinguished inhabitants, contains a band of music, whose harmony contrasts with the songs that are heard from the other boats. Beautiful weather usually prevails at this season, and the day closes with dances and suppers in the open air: and the lake of Tchornaia, naturally of a solitary aspect, becomes all at once full of life and animation, and presents an enchanting prospect.

Wassili had got several boats ready, which were filled with musicians, who attracted general attention, and were soon followed by almost all the skiffs, in the same way as the gondolas, in the Venetian lagoons, follow the musical amateurs who sing during the night. Wassili knew that Michael would be flattered to hear an account of the success he had obtained; but Aphanassi bad also come to the festival. As soon as he learned that the musicians of Wassili were followed by the crowd, and that his rival's name was in every one's mouth, he collected twenty of his finest horses, covered them with rich stuffs, and as soon as the sports on the lake were over began by the sound of Tartar music, a series of races on the shore, which was a novel sight in the summer season, and was generally admired. His triumph was complete, and at Tchornaia nothing was talked of for several days but the races on the shore of the lake, and the Baskir's influence with Michael increased considerably.

The grief of Daria made her father suspect that she met Wassili out of the house, and he confined her at home. I saw none but the young man, whose communications were far from being so pleasing to me as those of Daria. Towards the end of July, he informed me that Aphanassi had made another attempt to get her from her father; but that the old man was so overcome with her despair, that he had only agreed that the marriage should take place the ensuing summer, delaying the matter under the pretext of getting her portion ready, but in truth, to give her time to make up her mind to follow the Baskir.

He therefore set out. About this period Wassili was sent by M. Demidof's agent, at the head of a body of workmen, to the centre of the Ural Mountains, to cut down trees, and burn them into charcoal. He was not to return till the middle of September. During his absence I saw Daria almost daily; she had lost the brilliancy of her look, but it seemed to me that her beauty was increased, her countenance had assumed such an expression of melancholy.

I had gradually obtained the good will of Michael, and dispelled, as far as lay in my power, the sorrows of his daughter. I was a foreigner, a prisoner, little to be feared, and pretty well off in regard to money, so that Michael felt no alarm at seeing me, and neglected no opportunity of showing me his good will. I received a strong proof of this about the middle of August. He brought the Colonel (to whom I had told all Wassili's story), and me, to a family festival that takes place at the gathering of the cabbage, and to which women only are usually admitted; it is in fact their vintage season.

On the day that a family is to gather in their cabbage, which they salt and lay up for the winter season, the women invite female friends and neighbours to come and assist them. On the evening before, they cut the cabbages from the stem, and pull off the outside leaves and earth that may be adhering to them. On the grand day, at the house where the cabbages are collected, the women assemble, dressed in their most brilliant manner, and armed with a sort of cleaver, with a handle in the centre, more or less ornamented, according to the person's rank. They-place themselves round a kind of trough containing the cabbages. The old women give the signal for action; two of the youngest girls take their places in the middle of the room, and begin to dance a kind of *allemande*, while the rest of the women sing national songs, and keep time in driving their knives into the trough. When the girls are tired with dancing, two more take their place, always eager to surpass the former by the grace with which they make their voluptuous movements. The songs continue without intermission, and the cabbages are thus cut up in the midst of a ball, which lasts from morning till night. Meanwhile the married women carry on the work, salt the cabbages and carefully pack them in barrels. In the evening the whole party sit down to supper, after which only the men are admitted, but even then they remain apart from the women. Glasses of wine and punch go round; dancing begins in a more general manner, and they withdraw at a late hour to begin the same amusement at another neighbour's, till all the harvest is finished.

Undoubtedly the lively pleasures of the vintage in Italy and, the south of France are not to he found in these northern festivals; but sports and holidays are so rare occurrence in Siberia, and everything bears such an aspect of immobility, that a festival wholly presided over by women, and to which I was admitted by an exception in my favour, must naturally have seemed to me delicious.

Amidst all these young girls Daria always seemed to me the most amiable; she danced when called upon by her mother; her motions expressed satisfaction, and her eyes, scarcely refraining from tears, turned towards the stranger, who alone knew her real situation, though amidst so many indifferent people, who called themselves her friends.

Towards the end of September, Wassili returned from the woods. Daria had a prospect of several months before her before the return of Aphanassi, if ever he should return at all; and she gave herself up to her love with pleasing improvidence.

At this period there came to Tchornaia two Russian officers, with several Sergeants, who were much more like Cossacks than regular soldiers. Their appearance was the signal of universal mourning—they came to recruit. They proclaimed, in the emperor's name, that on a certain day all the men in the district, whatever their age might be, were to assemble in the public square, there to be inspected. At the appointed day everyone was on the spot; but it was easy to see by their looks that it was with the utmost repugnance that they had obeyed. All the women were placed on the other side, and anxiously waited for the result of the inspection; and some of them were crying bitterly. We were present at this scene.

The officers placed the men in two rows, and passed along the ranks very slowly. Now and then they touched a man, and he was immediately taken to a little group that was formed in the centre of the square. When they had run over the two rows, they again inspected the men that had been set apart, made them walk and strip, *verified* them, in a word, such as our recruiting *councils* did in our departments for many years. When a man was examined, he was allowed to go, and then the crowd raised a shout of joy; or he was immediately put in irons, in presence of his family, who raised cries of despair—this man was fit for service.

These unfortunate beings, thus chained up, were kept out of view till the very moment of their departure. No claims were valid against the recruiting officer; age, marriage, the duties required to be paid to an infirm parent, were all of no avail; sometimes indeed it happened, and that but rarely, that a secret arrangement with the officer, for a sum of money, saved a young man, a husband, or a father, from his caprice, for he was bound by no rule; it often happened also, that he marked out for the army a young man whose wife or mistress was coveted by the neighbouring lord, or whom injustice had irritated and rendered suspected.

Such is the mode of recruiting in Russia! To finish this description, which has made me leave my friends out of view, at a very melancholy period, I shall add a few more particulars. Wassili, as I said before, was at the review; the recruiting officer thought he would make a handsome dragoon, or a soldier of the guard, and having looked at him from top to toe, he declared him fit for the army. Whilst his family were deploring his fate, and preparing to make every sacrifice to obtain his discharge, someone cried out that the officer would allow him to get off because he was wealthy, but that the poor must march. The Russian heard this, and. perhaps on the point of making a bargain, felt irritated, and would listen to no sort of arrangement, as a scoundrel always does whom you have been on the point of buying. Wassili was put in irons, and destined to unlimited service, that is, to an eternal exile, for the Russian soldier is never allowed to return to his home. Daria nearly fell a victim to her grief, and only recovered some portion of vigour when the recruits were to set out.

On that day the recruiting party gorge them with meat and brandy, till they are nearly dead drunk. They are then thrown into the sledges, and carried off, still loaded with irons. A most heart-rending scene now takes place; every family follows them with their cries, and chants the prayers for the dead and the dying, while the unfortunate conscripts themselves, besotted with liquor, remain stupid and indifferent, burst into roars of laughter, or answer their friends with oaths and imprecations.

Notwithstanding the force that had been shown to him, Wassili had drank nothing, and preserved his judgment unclouded; he stretched out his arms towards Daria, towards his friends, and towards me, and bade us *adieu* with many tears. Amidst the mournful sounds that struck upon her ears, the young girl followed him rapidly, and had time to throw herself into his arms before the sledge set out; but the moment he was beyond her reach, she fell backward with violence on the ice. No-one paid the least attention to her; they all rushed forward and followed the sledges of the recruiting party, which soon galloped out of sight.

I lifted Daria up; I did not attempt to restrain her grief, but took her back to her father's, where she was paid every attention her situation required, in about a month's time she was able to resume her usual occupations, but she seemed to have recovered only a portion of her former self.

We had endeavoured to learn from the recruiting party, if there were any news from France. They knew nothing certain. They had orders from Moscow to march from Kazan, and all that they had heard was, that the war was still going on on the right bank of the Rhine, This recruiting seemed to indicate that the government of Russia did not think the war near its close, and from this we concluded that France, in spite of some reverses, still commanded Europe.

We gave these officers other letters for our country. We had not omitted a single opportunity of sending letters to France, but we had received no answer. M. Mazin, who came to see us sometimes, and whom we often visited when we went to see our fellow prisoners, had at various periods engaged to send our letters by the couriers of the house of Demidof. We should, therefore, have received letters from France, and the communications should have been open, if peace was made; hence we were forced to wait still more; but French valour and the genius of the Emperor made its hope for a speedy and glorious peace, and all our companions were of the same opinion, for in Siberia, as on board the English guard-ships, confidence in the nation, and its chief, never for a moment failed to cheer the prisoner's heart.

Winter had again set in. We had left our residence in the island, and had taken a more convenient house in the village of Tchornaia. Time passed slowly along, and we languished in this forgotten spot, with our thoughts constantly directed towards France.

I often saw Daria, either at her father's house, or when she walked out on purpose to meet me, which her father allowed, in the hope of dissipating her sorrows. How the poor girl was altered since the departure of Wassili! How many sad things the young Siberian told me when our sledges glided together along the surface of the lake! What melancholy there was in her language, and superstition in her belief!

I attempted to dissipate her sombre thoughts; but I soon perceived that everything brought them back to her mind, and that the sight of this savage nature, whose solitude affected my own thoughts with sorrow, contributed to increase her melancholy. Within her own dwelling she was less agitated, but more depressed; her fever was then languid, and her beautiful face despoiled of that expression, full of agreeable recollections, that animated her in our private conversation. These walks could only make her worse, and I endeavoured to avoid them. She understood my meaning: "Go," said she, "kind Frenchman, you are taking fruitless care; Wassili has taken my life away with him; it cannot return any more than he can."

I still continued to see her frequently. Old Michael was unhappy because she wept on hearing even the name of Aphanassi; he foresaw that it would be out of his power to have this wealthy man for his son-in-law, for his promises had gained his heart long ago. However this may be, he made his preparations in secret, bought fine silks, and ordered a magnificent diadem to be made for his daughter. She guessed his object, and once said to me: "My father is preparing a handsome ornament for me; it is intended for the last time I shall be at church; let him make haste, for Daria won't keep him waiting."

About the middle of June, Aphanassi returned, more in love and more eager than ever, and as soon as he appeared, the daughter of Michael was attacked by a burning fever that never left her. In a few days she was at the gates of death. All the care bestowed upon her was of no avail, and she died pronouncing the name of Wassili.

Full of profound grief, I followed her body to the church of the Starcobratzi, at Nishnei-Taguil. It had been dressed in her finest clothing, and she was placed in the coffin with her face uncovered. The relations, friends, and members of the same church, were present.

The men were ranged on one side, and the women on the other. After a funeral hymn, in the language of the country, the priest, who was bareheaded, pronounced the eulogium of the defunct. His grey hair, long beard, Asiatic gown, and loud sobs, gave his discourse a peculiar solemnity. When it was finished, everyone came forward silently to bid farewell to Daria, and kiss her hand.

I went like the rest; like them I went alone towards the coffin, took-hold of the hand I had so often pressed, and gave it the last farewell kiss. But here I must leave this melancholy scene.

CHAPTER 13

Return to France

The painful impression left on my mind by the scenes I had lately witnessed, and my sad recollection of the last moments of the young Siberian, greatly increased the sorrow I felt at the want of intelligence from home; and I eagerly seized the Colonel's invitation to return and pass the end of summer at Nishnei-Taguil, where M. Mazin had recovered so much authority as to allow him to show attention to his countrymen without incurring blame.

Our fellow-prisoners lived very pleasantly in the village, and the house they had built was one of the most remarkable in the whole place for order and neatness. They had planted a little garden, which, at the commencement of the second season, was far superior to the gardens of the Siberians around them. Their labour, moreover, was quite of a different nature from that of our unfortunate fellow-prisoners, who had been sent more into the interior, where they were directly employed in working the mines.

In the month of July, an agent of M. Demidof, who was sent to inspect his establishments in the province of Verchoturié, informed us, that according to the reports that were in circulation when he left Nig-Novogorod, peace must by this time have been concluded between France and Russia.

We remained in a state of incessant anxiety during two long months; at length a courier arrived at the end of September, and brought letters to Colonel Laplane, and a letter of credit on the counting-house at Nishnei-Taguil. I was surprised that he said nothing to me about the contents of his letters, nor of the news he had received from France; but reflecting that his silence, I might say his chagrin, might arise from some information he had received from his family, I asked no questions; perhaps his old father, his brothers and sisters, and mine too, who knew what had become of them in such a long interval?

The Colonel went next day to visit our eight fellow-prisoners; he gave them some money, and promised them a very speedy deliverance; then turning towards me, he said:

"Robert, I was desirous of ascertaining how our companions were situated; they want for nothing, are exposed to no inconveniences, and I have no reason to fear leaving them exposed to want; we may therefore depart. Tomorrow, at daybreak, we shall leave the *zavode*, and return to France."

Surprise and joy occupied my mind.

"Guillemard," said the Colonel to me, with an air of satisfaction, "I have sent our servant Fedor out of the way; let us prepare whatever is necessary for our journey: it is of great importance that our departure be not known. As soon as the peace was concluded my family hastened to send me a passport, signed by the Russian ambassador, for two persons, as they naturally concluded I would not attempt such a long journey alone. It is to be feared, that if we remain a day longer, the news of the peace will be confirmed, and we shall be detained to command some detachments of prisoners returning to France, which would be a delay too painful to both of us; we have sufficient regret in being obliged to leave our companions behind us."

I instantly set to work. M. Mazin came to bid us *adieu*; and the next day (the 2nd of October) though the snow had only been settled four or five days on the ground, we set out in a sledge.

The moment we lost sight of Nishnet-Taguil, and the distant peaks of the Ural mountains began to disappear on our right, I said to the Colonel, who seemed melancholy, though he had such a just subject of satisfaction:

"Colonel, to you shall I be indebted for the pleasure of seeing the soil of France sooner than I could have done by my own means; how can I ever show my gratitude for all the kindness you have shown me during our captivity?"

"By your friendship, Guillemard."

"It is yours forever," said I; "but, Colonel, I am sorry to see you depressed at the moment you are about to resume your career, and to return to the standard of the Emperor."

"Guillemard," said Colonel Laplane to me, "there is no Emperor now."

"Is he dead?" said I sorrowfully.

"No—but he has quitted France."

"Why so?"

"Because he was beat by the Russians and English."

"Beat—he—it cannot be,"

"Robert, he did not fall without a struggle."

"Hence, we are now again become a Republic?"

"Quite the contrary—the king has returned."

"The king!—whom do you say? Did he not die during the Revolution?"

"To be sure he did; but his brother is returned, and now governs France; after an exile of twenty years, he has ascended the throne held by his ancestors for many generations."

I put several questions to the Colonel, but he gave me no answer. The little he had said had completely confounded me. I reflected on the intelligence he had given me while we were driving over the ice, "The emperor is alive," said I to myself, "and is not in France! He has been succeeded by another. But what has become of his son, that young child who was the hope of the army when it set out full of vigour and glory for the deserts of Russia? What has become of the daughter of the Emperor of Austria? What has become of the Emperor's brothers? Has all this large family of kings allowed Napoleon to lose his throne and another to seize it? This cannot be; the

Colonel is assuredly misled—the whole story is too improbable to have taken place. There is something extraordinary in the whole of it which I cannot account for. The Colonel is too melancholy to give me any circumstantial account; perhaps, after all, the general facts have only been pointed out to him, and he would be greatly embarrassed in explaining them. Wait till time clears up this singular mystery."

As we changed horses at every village we met with, we soon crossed the Ural mountains, and the vast plains that extend between Ekaterinburg, Kazan, and Nig-Novogorod, for we did not go by Kasimof, as we did on coming into the country. On the 28th of October we arrived at Moscow. On our route from Wladimir we had learned numerous particulars about the burning of that city in 1812. A great number of houses were building; but we thought that this capital would never again display the splendour we had seen it possess.

We passed rapidly through Russia proper, where two years before we had marched as soldiers and prisoners. The fields seemed to have been cultivated, and the villages were rebuilt. We scarcely recognised under the snow the spot where the battle of Borodino, so important to us, had been fought. We passed over the bloody fields of Smolensko without perceiving them; but as we harassed with our questions all the post-masters and peasants whom we met, we learned, on approaching the Beresina, that the greatest disaster of the French army had taken place at the very spot where we were. Nothing could then overcome the sadness that oppressed us; we thought we were still in 1812 with our unfortunate brothers in arms, struggling with the elements, and falling under the attacks of the enemy.

Amidst the snow that surrounded us, we could easily judge of the disasters of that terrible day. I felt an extraordinary oppression of heart. We alighted for a moment to honour the memory of our companions. Upon a bush which had caught my cloak, I perceived a leather sword-belt hanging, almost worn away, but still retaining a plate of copper with an eagle on it. This sight powerfully affected me, but seemed to have still more influence over the Colonel's mind. His gaiety did not return, even after we had left the banks of the Beresina far behind us. His disposition, usually extremely open and frank, seemed to change more and more as we approached nearer France. It is true that nothing pointed it out to our impatience. We had traversed Poland, where we left our sledges, Prussia, and a part of the German states, without finding either the dress or the language of a Frenchman in a single village. It seemed that a century had elapsed since the beginning of 1813, when all Europe was French, and the end of 1814.

We travelled nine hundred leagues without meeting with a single French uniform; and now we were on the Rhine without hearing the challenge of a single sentinel, or hearing the *good day* of a single citizen. For my own part, the joy of seeing my country again was neutralized by my painful surprise at having become a total stranger to the immense countries we had just traversed.

Under our Tartar fur-cloaks we wore none but plain clothes; but we were often betrayed by an old soldier-look, which did not always procure us the goodwill of the inhabitants, This feeling of dislike to us seemed to become stronger as we came nearer to the end of our journey. It had all the characteristics of hatred in the south of Prussia, where we were exposed to many insults. I was ignorant of the peculiar jargon of the country, and could not make out very clearly what they said to us, but the whole seemed to me a very bad omen.

The Colonel had become extremely reserved; but once, on hearing some insolent language from a few Prussian officers, tears came into his eyes, and he said to me:

"The cowards! They insult misfortune!——They believe that it will last forever; but they are mistaken; Napoleon has had reverses, it is true; but on leaving France, he did not leave it captive. The time is not far distant when we shall make them repent their momentary triumph. We shall only be the stronger after so many trials."

When we entered the Duchy of Wurtemburg, I several times heard people say, that after three unfortunate campaigns, the Emperor had retired to the island of Elba, and that a new reign had commenced; but I had not taken into account the changes that had taken place since that time; I thought that everything but the head of the government remained the same, and that even that head must still be an emperor.

At length we reached the Rhine.

When we perceived France from the right bank of the river we involuntarily shed tears. We had so often thought that we had lost it forever! Before we entered the village of Kehl, which is situated on the banks of the Rhine, opposite Strasburg, the Colonel said to me:

"Guillemard, we shall find a great many changes in France. We must be prudent and respect the opinions of everyone."

These words were still a kind of enigma to me, notwithstanding all I had learned about the new situation in which France was placed; and the tone in which they were uttered was not fitted to make them more intelligible. I had never heard the word *opinion* in the Colonel's mouth before this moment.

I was very desirous of obtaining a fuller explanation of its meaning; but wholly occupied with the happiness of seeing France again, and certain of being able in a few minutes to ascertain, by my own inquiries, all the subjects Colonel Laplane left me to ruminate upon, what need had I to fatigue him with questions which all seemed to afflict him? I therefore held my tongue; we passed the river in silence, and on the 29th of November, at mid-day, we entered the city of Strasburg.

It is impossible to express in words the feelings that rushed upon my soul, when, after such a long captivity, I set foot on my native soil. I was struck at once with a multitude of things. Above all, the language, which I so long fruitlessly expected to hear, went to the heart with a most singular impression. It seemed that after a painful period of deafness, I had all at once recovered my hearing. Everyone feels an inexpressible restraint, which is very improperly omitted among the misfortunes attendant on captivity, when he never hears the accents of his native land. For my own part, I listened to everyone I heard talking; and I confess that the accent of Alsace that day seemed to me as soft as that of the inhabitants of Blois and Orleans.

Although Strasburg is a fortified place, there were scarcely any soldiers in it, which seemed to me a strange piece of inconsistency. Whilst the Colonel was enjoying some repose, having put off till next day his visits to the different people in power with whom his rank brought him into contact, I wished to show my presence on the soil of France, to see my fellow-countrymen—in a word, to find somebody to talk to.

At this very moment, the innkeeper at whose house we had alighted, was talking at the door to one of his neighbours, and it was evident that they were talking about us.

"You are going to visit the city," said he to me; " after such a long absence it is very natural you should do so; but if you like, we can accompany you."

I wished for nothing better than to have some talk with these good souls.

"With pleasure," I replied, and we all three sallied forth into the public promenade.

"You have come from a great distance, Sir?" said the fat innkeeper to me, for the purpose of entering into conversation.

"From the extremity of Siberia?"

"You must have been a long time on the road?"

"Two months; and yet we travelled very quick."

"I imagine you must have been in great haste; you must have often thought that you would never return to France; but the moment the king returned, he thought of the prisoners of war."

The king! It is impossible to conceive with what satisfaction I heard this word pronounced; I saw that it would give me an opportunity of talking of many things that had excited my warmest curiosity for two months before.

"The king," said I hastily, "had doubtless made an arrangement with the Emperor Napoleon on the subject."

"With Napoleon Bonaparte?" said the innkeeper; "how could that be—could they have anything to do with each other?"

"Bonaparte truly paid great attention to the unfortunate," said the neighbour, with a tone of authority. "But scarcely had the king returned, before he in fact made an arrangement with the allied powers, for the mutual restitution of prisoners of war."

"Very well," said I, though irritated at the disrespectful way in which Napoleon was mentioned; "everyone will therefore resume his service in the army?"

"No doubt of it?" said the innkeeper.

"Not at all," cried out the neighbour in the same breath; "are the sailors who returned from England entered again into the navy? No; there was no mode of managing people who would have cost us a great deal, and whose imprudence, excited by their remembrance of the guard-ships, might perhaps have compromised our close union with England. As for those who come from Russia, it is a different matter; they will perhaps be admitted into their corps."

"Perhaps!" exclaimed I; "have we deserved any blame from France?"

"I do not say so," replied the neighbour; "but prudence requires, in my opinion, that you ought also to be set aside to avoid any rupture with Russia."

"If this be the case," said I, "why not set *every* French soldier aside? There is not one of them who has not assisted in conquering some nation or other in Europe."

"It would be very wise policy," said the neighbour, "and we should thus be secure from military despotism."

"You are more suspicious than our king," said the innkeeper to his neighbour; "you know that he has adopted, and, on his arrival, claimed the aid of the marshals. He acknowledges all past services; he loves the army, and has assumed their uniform, and wishes to associate himself with their glory."

"That may do very well for the past; but he will stop this inundation of military spirit, and will reduce the army to a size that suits a peaceful people. These colossal armies, instruments of oppression...."

"Gentlemen," said I, interrupting the neighbour in the midst of his harangue, and greatly surprised that after eagerly seizing the first word in conversation that I thought would bring him round to the subject I wished to hear of, I could comprehend nothing of the dispute that had arisen: "Gentlemen, I cannot make out a word of what you have been telling me; explain to me...."

"It is very plain, however," said the innkeeper.

"Yes, when one has not been absent for two years," I replied.

"Let us go a little farther back," said the neighbour.

"First of all," said I, "inform me what has taken place in France since the beginning of the retreat from Russia; then satisfy me concerning the safety of the Emperor and his family, and inform me who the new king is, where he comes from, how he mounted the throne, what things remain the same, what things are changed from what they were two years ago."

"Mercy on us!" said the innkeeper; "who could tell you all these things in less than a fortnight?"

"I," said the neighbour, "and in less than half an hour, too."

"Distrust what this worthy fellow tells you," said the innkeeper to me; "he is a violent enthusiast in politics. He is going to tell you a parcel of stories, and make you hate your old general, Napoleon."

"Don't be afraid," replied I, "he won't impose on me; I have seen the Emperor in battle and in the bivouac, and know what to think of him."

I listened with distrust to the stranger's narrative; I know not whether I did right, but the reader can judge for himself. He informed me that after the retreat from Russia, Napoleon had experienced one defeat after another, and had at last fallen in the plains of Champagne, less (as he said) from the efforts of twelve hundred thousand foreigners, than from the attempts of a party roused by the persecutions it was exposed to, and from the Emperor's ill-luck.

His abdication had given France up to the allied powers, who out of their desire for peace had granted it the return of its ancient royal family, which was loudly called for by the voice of the nation. These princes had been received with enthusiasm; they had wisely terminated the struggles of the revolution by effacing from our history all the years that had elapsed since their departure, and preserving nothing but the glory that had been acquired.

The reign of Napoleon was forgotten by some and execrated by others; safe under the shelter of the legitimate throne, France would again flourish and resume its proper rank among the nations. It was true that some obstacles were still in the way of its prosperity; concessions unfortunately made to the revolutionary spirit, the recognition of the new nobility, and of the sales of national property; but a short time would speedily destroy the usurpations of liberalism, crush the new by the firm consolidation of the ancient nobility, and indemnify the emigrants for all their losses.

During this long harangue, of which I only caught some straggling ideas amidst the mass of vagueness and confusion, the innkeeper was agitated with the strongest impatience; his features became contracted with eagerness, and he coughed loudly; but he could restrain himself no longer, and cried out:

"Neighbour, you are calumniating the king. The *charte*, which he has given us, guarantees all the institutions of the Revolution, and he has sworn to maintain the charter."

"But, Gentlemen, what do you mean by charter?"

"An ordinance of reform," said the neighbour.

"The constitution of the state," said the innkeeper.

As the stranger perceived, by my question, (which the reader will, perhaps, think misplaced enough), that I did not understand him, he began to ask me a variety of questions; and after a two hours' debate, I felt a most violent headache; his words sounded in my ears like n painful murmur, and my brain was completely confounded with all the nonsense I had heard.

I returned to the inn, and took some repose, which somewhat calmed my mental confusion; I then endeavoured to resume our conversation, but found it not so easy as I thought; I succeeded, however, in obtaining some certain facts on the subject. I found that France had undergone a great change in the space of two years, and that I must not forget the Colonel's advice about *opinion*, nor hurry my political education too fast, for it would be gradually formed by the progress of time. Meanwhile I resolved to form no opinion on any subject before I had examined it minutely. As affairs had gone on at a rapid rate during my absence, those who had followed their movement must judge of them in a different manner from me, and believe in the realization of very different prospects from those I formed in my own mind. Hence it was necessary for me to gain, by forced marches, the time I had lost, to put myself on a level with the ideas of the day.

The subject that chiefly occupied my mind at this moment was to join my corps, and assume at last my rank as an officer. The day after my arrival I went with the Colonel to visit the commandant, by whom I was informed that my regiment had changed its number and was now at Valence in Dauphiny. I requested him to give me an officer's route for that town, when he enquired the date of my commission, and I informed him of the particular manner in which I had been made an ensign by the Emperor. He observed that, as the Colonel of my regiment had been killed at Borodino, before giving me the rank I had been promoted to, and my companions had doubtless thought I was killed, it was not probable my appointment had been confirmed; that he could not, therefore, give me any other route than in my old capacity of a sergeant He concluded by urging me to present my claims as soon as I reached my regiment, and seemed to believe they would not be unsuccessful. I felt no doubt of success, and easily resigned myself to my temporary disappointment.

Next day we left Strasburg; the Colonel was going to Normandy, his native province, to see his family, and I to join *my* regiment at Valence. I also intended to go on as far as Provence, to see my family also; but I wished to have my prospects settled beforehand, and to appear with an epaulet on my shoulder.

At the gates of the town Colonel Laplane said to me:

"Guillemard, we are now about to part; I am going to Paris on my way to see my relations. If Marshal Ney remembers what he said to me at the beginning of the battle of Borodino, I shall resume the command of my regiment. I shall request the minister of war to get you into it, and shall speak to him in your favour; I hope that my rank will enable me to show you the friendship with which you have inspired me; and you may be assured that I shall make use of every opportunity to do you service."

I was most sincerely attached to him. It is well known how misfortune and captivity bring all ranks of society into contact. He had long inspired me with the same feeling of attachment one feels towards one's dearest companion, though I had never, on any occasion, forgotten the deference due to his excellent heart, and the rank that he held. After a farewell, very affecting for military men, we parted; he entered the *diligence* at the gates, and I, with the funds with which his friendship had supplied me, got into a kind of *calash*, and travelled on towards the south.

Since the day of our separation a variety of events have taken place, and have prevented me from renewing my connection with Colonel Laplane; I have been informed, however, that he fought like a hero at the battle of Waterloo, and that he was afterwards struck off the army list; the newspapers, in 1817, said that he had gone to America, in consequence of some political intrigue, in which he was said to be compromised.

I travelled towards the south as fast as my *calash* would carry me; but after a few hours' journey, the noise, which prevented me from speaking or hearing, and the driver's stupidity, who had no idea that I wanted to talk with my new-found countrymen, made me resolve to pursue my journey on foot, and see the country more minutely. I had traversed the deserts of Russia, the sands of Poland, and the plains of Germany; but I hated the very thought of them when I looked at the picturesque soil of France. Nothing is so beautiful as one's native land: nothing presents so fine a prospect as France in the autumnal season.

The lively emotions I had felt on first bearing the sounds of my native language were very soon blunted; but the happiness of treading my native soil was constantly renewed, for each day presented me with new prospects, and I was daily approaching nearer to the province in which I was born,

I had travelled through Franche-Comté several times since I was in the army, and had been always struck with the soft and pacific habits of the inhabitants. But, on this occasion, I was strangely surprised at seeing them in a warlike garb, and displaying a roughness of manner I had never seen them show till now.

I made some inquiries, with the timidity of one who is afraid of giving offence, or of being compromised. I was told of the events at Bourg-en-Bresse and Lons-le-Saunier, and I found out the secret cause of their enthusiasm. With the tribute of praise which I paid to their courage, and the regrets which I felt on not having along with my brethren in arms, shared their heroic efforts in the campaign in France, I dared not blame the affection they still preserved for a state of things which was no more; and I must confess that, like other old soldiers. I was tempted to partake of their feelings.

The more I advanced towards Lyons, I found the inhabitants less restless and enthusiastic; but their hatred against their foreign conquerors was equally violent. I heard everyone talking about treason; and the term was more frequently used when I came near to the Maison Blanche, and farther on, when I approached the Isere, where a bridge had been recently burned down. People in misfortune always think themselves betrayed

Chapter 14
Campaign in the South

I reached Valence in the month of December, 1814, The colonel who had been appointed to command our regiment, instead of the one who was killed at my side at Borodino, had left it in 1813, with the rank of general attached to the Emperor's staff, and had been killed at the battle of Montereau, to the success of which his skill and gallantry had powerfully contributed. Another old campaigner had taken the command at Bautzen, and during the Saxon campaign, besides fighting gloriously in the campaign of Paris, He had been lately superseded by the.Marquis de ——, who had been in the army of Condé, and a staff officer in the service of the Emperor Alexander.

I presented myself to him; he asked me many questions about my captivity, and advised me to be extremely circumspect in any accounts I might give of it to my companions. He was completely embarrassed when I explained the peculiar circumstances in which I was placed; for all the officers that could have borne evidence to the truth had perished in the retreat from Russia, and I could scarcely find a single soldier in the regiment who had known me, He urged me, however, to send the minister of war an account of the facts, with a petition, which he promised to support to the utmost of his power. He declared to me that in the meantime I ought to do my military duty as a sergeant.

To this I had nothing to object, and in fact I ought to

have been prepared for it; but till this moment it never had occurred to my mind that any difficulty could possibly arise about my rank. I now saw, but not till now, that I had to recommence all my labours to obtain it, and the thought of this almost overwhelmed me; but I made up my mind to resume my duty as a non-commissioned officer, in hopes that full justice would speedily be rendered to me. I, therefore, entered a company as a sergeant, and found the ensign to be a man who had been my corporal; so that the disappointment of not receiving a confirmation of my real rank was still more aggravated by the thought of having lost three campaigns, the consequences of which were so favourable to many, and would have been of incalculable service to me.

I immediately got my papers and petitions prepared, and sent on to the War Office, and anxiously expected an answer, which unfortunately for me the affairs of the time were not well fitted to hasten.

I resumed, but not without disgust, my services as in former times. At this period the soldiers had nothing to do, associated too much with the inhabitants, talked of politics, and in the evening had their private parties, where they had strange discussions about their future prospects. The serious tone with which these honest souls who shouldered the musket talked of the grossest absurdities and most ridiculous tales, did not altogether deceive me, and I foresaw a crisis approaching. I was gradually acquiring experience, and at the close of winter I believe that I knew as well as many others the actual state of affairs.

I had written to my family the moment I set foot in France, and received an answer on my arrival at Valence. My father informed me that I had the misfortune to lose my dear mother three months before. Worn out with domestic cares, and the dreadful thought that I had fallen in the Russian campaign, she had fallen into a sort of helplessness that brought her to the grave after much suffering. This part of my father's letter was the only one that struck me at first, and it was not till after paying the tribute of some tears at this painful loss, that I could attend to the joy that was expressed at my return, and the news that were sent me about my relations. My father was desirous of enjoying some rest in his old days, and had just given up his business to my brother. His fortune had become embarrassed. The rest of the letter informed me of a variety of deaths and marriages, and of the birth of a third child of Miette.

I wrote again and again to the War Office, but received no answer. I began to think that no attention would be paid to my claims till the mass of business with which the government offices were overwhelmed, was considerably diminished. I became every day more restless and uneasy, and often desired that a new war would put it in my power to merit a second time the rank I had once obtained, but which I now found it so difficult to get restored to me. A garrison life was insupportable in 1814, for we were tormented by recollections of too recent a date, and, as old Montagne expresses it: *idleness ate us up.*

We were, therefore, all very tired of Valence, but endeavoured to find some consolation when we saw the approach of spring, which was to restore the brilliant vegetation of the majestic banks of the Rhone, when we were suddenly awakened from these rural dreams by a strange piece of news—the landing of Napoleon. What effect it produced on the inhabitants I do not well know—the blow was terrible upon our regiment. The colonel became taciturn; the officers restless and reserved. After two days anxiety, and, as it would appear, without having received any orders of the kind, the colonel put the regiment on board some barges he had collected, and we went down the river to Beaucaire, which we reached the same evening, *viz*, the 9th March.

Our battalions were quartered between Beaucaire and Tarascon, which are on opposite sides of the river. The colonel sent for me, and told me I was to go along with him to Nimes, where we accordingly arrived on the 10th. I have afterwards thought that I was indebted for his preference of me to my absence from France during the revolution of 1814. He had long conferences with the magistrates, and several of the most eminent citizens, whom the imminency of the danger and the confidence of the public had put all at once on a level with those who .were invested with authority, and who seemed themselves to share with pleasure a responsibility of which they felt all the difficulty and danger.

Several days were spent in going backward and forward. In the meanwhile I had often heard people say to the colonel that he had done well to bring his regiment away from the contagion, and to quarter them among a faithful population. The aspect of Nimes and the surrounding country was terrible; in the evening I heard people singing political songs, the real sense of which I could not make out till after many inquiries; they cursed Bonaparte and all his party, which was intelligible enough; but they called out also for the lives of the Protestants, and this I could not understand. I inquired who these Protestants were, whom, judging from the menaces levelled at them, I considered to be at any rate conspirators legally condemned.

I learned, however, that they were a class of respectable, quiet, and industrious citizens, who worshipped God according to their conscience; for I held of no account the intentions they were said to possess, since nothing could hitherto be laid to their charge but their mode of worship. In all this I saw nothing but the effects of old deep-rooted quarrels, and the innumerable evils that follow in their train. The population, however, seemed to be unanimous in their desire to resist the progress of Napoleon. They took up arms precipitantly and tumultuously; but still they took up arms.

The Duke of Angouleme arrived; I was extremely desirous of seeing one of the new French princes. This desire I had no difficulty in satisfying, for never was any prince more easy of access. During his stay in the south the urgent wants of every moment placed him in contact with every class of citizens, whom his presence roused to enthusiasm, and who called out to be led against the enemy. These cries and tumults, through which, in spite of their agreement on one point, old quarrels and discords showed themselves, inspired me with anxiety and strong doubts of the result.

I was alarmed at the sight of so many passions roused to action, and could not help pitying the prince who was exposed to them. Though a crowd of distinguished officers had joined him, and his staff was composed of more than twenty lieutenant-generals, (amongst whom were the Duc de Guiche, the Vicomte d'Escars, the Vicomte de Levi, the Baron de Damas, Generals d'Aultaume, Perreymond, Ernouf, Mounier, Pastonneaux, Merle, &c-). I saw no chance of success in the tumultuous and undisciplined army that followed them.

The elements of success are, in my opinion, coolness and reflection, and nothing of this kind existed round the prince, even among the men of talent in whom he seemed to place the greatest confidence. I was constantly called upon by the colonel to write letters for him; I was considered by him as converted (that was the term he used,) by Russia, which he loved somewhat more than I did, and had constant opportunities of hearing the conversation of the greater part of the individuals whose names are connected with the history of this period.

I saw the doubts of old soldiers giving way, or kept concealed, on account of the mere assertions of a courtier; I recognised the headstrong will of the Marquis de Riviere, so distinguished for his unbounded and uncompromising loyalty. I was astonished at the overwhelming activity of M. de Vitrolles, the almost heroic coolness with which young Damas prepared for possible reverses—the obstinacy with which some men opposed the observations of General Gilly, who was desirous of calming the inhabitants before he began offensive operations.

It is not necessary for me to describe the movements of the army in the south. A corps was sent from Marseilles to

Grenoble, and was seen to march with great spirit against the enemy, but it arrived too late; thought that it was betrayed, and dispersed without doing any thing. The corps that marched along the mountains of the Lozere and the upper Loire, found nothing to do, and returned peaceably to their homes. The centre column, which the prince animated by his presence, left the Pont-Saint-Esprit, and advanced towards a district where the inhabitants were not fully aware of the advantages of legitimacy, but they did not, however, offer any resistance to the troops. No obstacles were found till the second day, and even to surmount these, all that the prince wanted was good luck.

Near Montelimart, a little skirmish took place, which was produced by a half-pay officer of the chasseurs of the guard. As soon as the report of Napoleon's arrival at Lyons was spread, he had imagined that his old general was restored to the throne, had instantly taken up arms, had collected some peasants and young men, and lay in wait to surprise us on our march. He received us with a well supported fire, which threw some of our young soldiers into confusion; but the tenth regiment soon cleared the hill, and the officer in question moved off to take up a position farther on.

Our officers had not yet met with the imperial troops, and were quite alarmed lest General Debelle, who had received the Emperor's orders before the Prince's, and, therefore, obeyed the orders of the former, should retreat rapidly before our army. They therefore moved forward, with the intention of crossing the Drôme as speedily as possible. They might have reached Lyons in four days more, but some scattered troops and a few hundred partisans had posted themselves along the avenues of the bridge. Our troops advanced with too little precaution. The head of our column was assailed by a well directed fire, which instantly threw the royal volunteers into confusion; but a battalion of our regiment formed in front of them, and gave them time to rally.

Whilst this was going on, the tenth regiment made a well

timed movement, and rushed rapidly on the enemy's battery. The firing ceased in a moment, and the tenth entered the battery, and threw the guns and the gunners into the Drôme. It has been said, indeed, that that regiment had acted treacherously towards the Imperialists by coming forward with cries of *Vive l'Empereur*, which had induced them to refrain from firing, and allowed them to enter into their battery; but I never heard anything of this at the time the action took place.

Our battalion manoeuvred beside the prince; I saw the Duke in front of the officers marching towards the bridge, without seeming to notice the heavy fire of musketry which was pouring upon him from the top of the road. Old general officers several times attempted to persuade him not to expose himself so much; but he paid no attention to them, still moving forward carelessly in the midst of the fire. It was with strong interest that I saw, for the first time, a prince, little known to the army, exposed to fire, and undertaking to contend with Napoleon. We are always sure of finding bravery in a French warrior; but this quality seems to me to be infinitely more attractive when possessed by those who are near the throne. On this occasion. I was perfectly delighted; a soldier, I must naturally be on the side of a brave man; and though Napoleon was before us, I did not from that moment feel any regret that I was in the hostile ranks.

The action at the bridge of the Drôme made us occupy Valence the same day, and our advanced posts were placed on the banks of the Isere, a deep and rapid river, whose magnificent bridge had been burned down in the retreat of 1814, and beyond which we ought instantly to have taken up our positions, to keep the road open to Lyons. The next day it was too late to do so; the opposite bank was defended by two or three battalions of the national guard, who were soon joined by a regiment of light infantry and a squadron of cavalry under the command of General Piré. These troops were from the very first strong enough to prevent us crossing, and they were soon enabled to cross the river themselves. To prevent them, the bridge of Romans was destroyed; but they built another in twenty-four hours; we had now no longer any means of acting on the offensive, and retreat was resolved on.

The most inauspicious reports then began to circulate in our ranks. The Emperor, it was said, was at Paris; the army had declared in his favour; the king and royal family had withdrawn from France, and General Grouchy was marching against us with superior forces, and our rear was not protected. These reports completely discouraged the volunteers. Our soldiers had marched against the Imperialists with some repugnance, but they were determined to do their duty, and it was not till now that they began to look wistfully towards their eagles.

The Prince's staff became wonderfully thinned in the space of a few days. Things were in this state when we learned that a part of the south had declared for the Emperor, and that we were menaced on all sides. Everyone knows the capitulation of La Palud, and its consequences: and none could be worse situated than I was to say anything new upon the subject, for my duties as a non-commissioned officer were never so incessant as at this period, and in fact, I am afraid that I have already committed some inaccuracies in noticing the events of this chapter. I was taken by surprise by the events that had occurred, and felt almost indifferent about the result, because I had not, like the greater part of my companions, long arrears of revenge and humiliation to satisfy.

Yet, I will confess that it was with the most powerful emotions that I heard the Emperor's first proclamations after his return; I knew that voice which had gone to my heart on the day of the battle of Borodino. The recollections of ten years, my disappointed hopes were all roused at the sight of our eagles, and I joyfully entered into a new regiment. My former regiment had been disbanded, and I now felt assured of being speedily restored to my real rank. This was an additional reason for me to double my zeal; besides, *the circumstances of the time were important,* and if I did not recover the commission gained at Borodino, I should soon acquire another. But

I found it necessary to show my new companions, in order to recover their good opinions, that the chevron I wore was not obtained in the array of Condé. Some of them could find no excuse for an old soldier being at Nimes instead of Lyons, and for having served in the prince's army. They had no idea of those feelings of self-denial that constitute true patriotism, and they held nothing to be correct but the party of the great man who had been restored to them.

During the hundred days, my regiment marched towards Lyons, and formed part of the corps of Marshal Suchet. "The period of reverses," we said to one another, "has gone by, the triumphal march of the Emperor through France was a sure token of it. We were about to renew the wonders of Austerlitz and Wagram; and after three months of victory, should obtain repose in an honourable and wished for peace"

Such were our hopes; and the joyful shouts with which a part of the nation had hailed Napoleon at his return, were well calculated to strengthen them: but as soon as the campaign began, it was easily seen that discontent had assumed the place of enthusiasm. Yet the national guard was called together, and came to join us. They felt the necessity of preserving the soil of France from a second invasion, and the soldiers burned with the desire of avenging their past injuries.

The campaign began in the midst of a solemn and ominous silence, which was suddenly broken by the thunderbolt of Waterloo. Our corps then retreated towards Lyons, which was not intimidated by that great disaster, but actively carried on its preparations for defence. We manoeuvred from one position to another for about a fortnight, till a capitulation, pretty nearly the same as the one concluded at Paris, settled that we were to withdraw behind the Loire with the rest of the army.

CHAPTER 15

Lyons

On the 13th of July, the day that the capitulation was signed, I was sent by the colonel to Lyons to take charge of some clothing and shoes belonging to the regiment. The city presented a singular appearance; a large and handsome *tête de pont,* placed on the left bank of the Rhone, at the end of *Pont* Mozand, had just been dismantled; all the batteries formed on the quays had also been destroyed, and the redoubts made on the heights of Pierre-Seise and Fourvieres had been abandoned. But it was evident to anyone who considers the people's wish of any value, that they had not of their own accord given up the idea of defending their city. The inhabitants of the suburb La Guillotiere left, their houses with shouts of *Vive l'Empereur* and prepared to set them on fire as the enemy advanced.

A sad but proud enthusiasm animated the inhabitants. If they had listened to nothing but their patriotic feelings,, perhaps the second invasion would have been defeated on the banks of the Rhone; if one single man had come forward in those decisive moments when the inhabitants knew not what to do—if one single man had had boldness enough to call them to battle, he would have been followed by the great mass of the inhabitants, and would have renewed the contest that had been put an end to by the capitulation of Paris.

The measure would have been perfectly easy, for the inhabitants thought themselves betrayed, and had great suspicion of their magistrates and officers, because they had published no account of what had been done at Paris. They did not know that the magistrates themselves received no intelligence from the capital, and that from the 5th to the 15th of July, Lyons was left to its own resources, and to its own management.

Meanwhile the generals and chief magistrates saw their communications cut off with Paris, three times more of the enemy round them than they had soldiers, and that disproportion becoming greater and greater every day; they, therefore, determined on signing a capitulation, and it was settled that the allies were to enter the city on the 18th. Doubtless, those who commanded Lyons at that period could not think of risking the safety of the city; they would not accomplish the intention of our foreign allies, who perhaps wished Lyons to offer resistance, that they might have an opportunity of ruining our greatest manufacturing city; and those even who had no future prospects but in the imperial government, generously agreed to its fall for the safety of all.

On the 12th, at the moment I entered the town-hall, an Austrian flag of truce likewise entered. I had an opportunity of seeing the bearer, and of talking to him, whilst he was waiting for an answer to the despatches he had brought. He was surprised that he was addressed by magistrates and citizens, and not by military officers. When he had received the despatch he was to take it to his general, and his eyes had been bound; he was put into a *post-chaise* to convey him away, but a great crowd was perceived on the quays and seemed to fill every street.

The agitation of the mob, and the shouts they made, made the magistrates feel uneasy about the safety of the officer with the flag of truce. To save the citizens from the effects of their own imprudence, they persuaded General Puthod to get into the carriage with the young officer, and to go with him as far as the barriers. When they came out of the town-hall, and moved forward among the crowd as fast as their horses could carry them, shouts of "*Vive l'Empereur! Vive la Liberté!"* burst forth on every side- Assuredly on hearing himself thus assailed by the formidable cries of a whole people, the young Austrian could not have fancied that all this scene had been prepared to deceive him as to the public spirit of the inhabitants. It is said that he reached the barriers overwhelmed with terror.

The army was in full retreat. On the 13th, a grand park of artillery entered Lyons, and was stationed in the Place Bellecour. The city was crowded with soldiers, and as their opinions agreed with those of the great mass of the inhabitants, they were very friendly towards each other. Enthusiasm seemed to increase every moment.

About two o'clock in the afternoon, crowds of people ran through the streets and sang the *Marseilloise* and the *Chant du depart.*

Some Austrian officers had been desirous of enjoying the advantages of the capitulation before the time appointed, and had entered the city; the soldiers and the mob followed their carriage in a menacing attitude, but they reached the Place Bellecour, and sought shelter in the governor's house. It was said that some ladies had waved their white handkerchiefs to them from a balcony. The house was attacked, and some transparencies prepared for the day the Austrians were to enter the city, and containing some of the royalists' insignia, were said to have been found in it.

The fury of the mob now became unbounded; the house was gutted in a moment, and the furniture piled up together and burned to ashes. The enthusiasm of the soldiers and the populace was at its height. The forty pieces of cannon that had been placed in the Place Bellecour in the morning were in their power. They shouted "V*ive l'Empereur!* We are betrayed—we must defend ourselves; let us go and attack the enemy."

Whilst a company of the young guard, accompanied by an organized body of the populace, was crossing the bridges to violate the capitulation, and that prudent men were running after them to restrain their fury, General Mouton Duvernet, who had just been appointed commandant by the provisional government, M. Jars, the mayor, M. Pons, the prefect, General Puthod, and M. Teste, lieutenant of police, rushed among the people to call them back to their duty. General Puthod was abused; General Mouton Duvemet lost his hat in the struggle, and was driven back to his hotel; and Pons and Jars, though universally beloved, could produce no effect.

The lieutenant of police, M. Teste, was the only one who succeeded in getting these mistaken men to listen to him, and in disarming their furious zeal by the fascination of his eloquence. I listened to his truly popular harangue with infinite pleasure. At the very moment, I saw, unnoticed among the crowd, the conventionalist Thibaudeau, formerly prefect of the Bouches du Rhone, who had just been making such a singular figure in the Chamber of Peers, He was accompanied by his son; I had seen them both at Marseilles at a former period. I thought on seeing them there, that things must be very forward indeed at Paris, since one of the most prominent members of the vanquished party was already a fugitive at Lyons.

All the shops had been shut up, and amidst this tumult, Lyons looked like a city about to be subjected to the utmost disorder and confusion. However the national guard had assembled, and marched in every direction where violence was feared. It was fortunately commanded by a man who, after having voted in the council against the capitulation, and urged the defence of the city at the risk of his private property, had seen the necessity of avoiding the dishonour attached to the violation of a formal agreement. M. de Corcelles zealously aided the respectable citizens who exerted themselves to maintain good order. Weis, the actor, at the moment the mob were about to break into the house of royalist, who was his personal enemy, rushed forward to the door, and defended it at the risk of his life. After many exertions, he succeeded in dispersing the mob.

At night, a battalion of the national guard kept the Place Bellecour, and another, the town hall. About eleven o'clock, I went thither to obtain an order, which I had been unable to get during the confusion of the day. I was coming away when I heard some shouts; the national guard on duty at the town hall, ran to their arms to defend it against an unexpected assault; the Place des Terraux was blocked up by the crowd, who advanced by torch-light, and seemed determined to force the guard; men of all ranks were seen in the crowd, and even directing it.

The lieutenant of police, Teste, who had remained at the town hall, now rushed forward among the crowd, and made his way through with a serene look. I followed involuntarily the steps of the man whose genius had fascinated me in the morning, and almost at the same time with him got up upon a stone seat. He asked, in a commanding voice, what they wanted, and why they troubled the quiet of a great city in the middle of the night?

Confused cries were heard in reply. "We are betrayed—they wish to deliver us unarmed to the enemy."

"You are betrayed!" said Teste—"and by whom, and for what purpose? Have not we done our duty so as to draw upon ourselves the hatred of all who do not love their country? What have we done to rouse your suspicion?" At these words, which were pronounced with an energy that overawes evil passions, the crowd ceased to murmur. Teste continued: "What can be the pretext of this armed multitude?"

"A shameful capitulation," cried out one of the mob.

"A shameful capitulation," said Teste; "and no foreigner has yet entered our walls! We have retained our colours, and no contribution has been imposed on the city. Could we oppose forces ten times more numerous than ours? A shameful capitulation! Let those who enjoy your confidence come forward. If I do not prove to them that it is wholly to the glory of the army and to the advantage of the city, I give myself up to your vengeance." A murmur of applause rose among the multitude. "Citizens and soldiers," continued Teste, "if a report was spread through France that Lyons had been the scene of disastrous confusion—if it was said that the army of the Duke of Albufera had aided in troubling public order, and in spreading terror among the peaceable inhabitants, which of you would dare to say, '*I defended France under the walls of Lyons*'? Friends, let it be proclaimed without fear of contradiction, 'If the army and the people of Lyons, roused by unfounded alarms, were desirous of punishing those by whom they thought they were betrayed, the confidence they placed in their magistrates and the love of order had instantly tranquillised them.' No—inhabitants of Lyons, you have not been betrayed. By whom could you be betrayed? By Marshal Suchet? The army knows that, like the Chevalier Bayard, he is without fear and without reproach. Could it be by your magistrates? All France know that they have more danger to encounter by submitting to foreigners than by fighting against them. No—you have not been betrayed! Wait but a moment longer and those brave officers whom I see amongst you, will bear testimony to the truth of my assertion. But if my efforts cannot disarm you, remember that you will find me the defender of your victims, posted in front of every house you may menace, I have already told you, your enemies will not reach you till they have passed over my body; I tell you also that you will not reach the men you falsely accuse, except by treading me under foot. Soldiers and inhabitants, distinguish yourselves by your moderation; it is the never failing companion of strength and justice."

The more this extraordinary man spoke, the crowd became more attentive, and tranquillity began to spread in the minds of all, while his sonorous voice was heard all over the Place des Terraux. The moment he ceased, a profound silence ensued, for the crowd still listened. All at once a loud murmur, not at all of a hostile kind, burst from the crowd, and they hailed the speaker with shouts of applause. The most mutinous came up to him, and shook him by the hand, in token of agreement The crowd then dispersed, the torches were extinguished, and the noise gradually died away; and by a quarter past twelve, ten thousand men, who had assembled together through fury and despair, had returned quietly to their own homes, disarmed by the voice of a single individual.

I had never conceived anything at all similar to the scene I had just witnessed; but what struck me most was the self-denial and heroic courage that distinguished the orator in these solemn moments—feelings that are the true means of acting powerfully on great bodies of men, and suddenly pacifying popular seditions. But such a victory strikes only at the moment and the remembrance of it seldom survives the danger. This was exemplified in the case of M. Teste; I have been informed that he was rewarded by a series of cruel persecutions for the honour of having preserved the second city in France.

At two o'clock in the morning I joined my regiment on the quay, and we set out on our march behind the Loire, along with the main body of the army. The distribution of shoes, which I had come to settle, was instantly made, and without taking up quarters for the night, we marched forward without a moment's delay.

A detachment was ordered to escort the property I had brought to Lyons as far as the depot, and I obtained permission to join it. Though I naturally felt a strong desire to see my native place, after such a long absence I did not return to the south without anxiety. I knew that our uniform was not looked upon favourably since the violent convulsions that had lately taken place, and of these I had been informed by a townsman who related to me the particulars of what had taken place at Marseilles, on the 25th and 26th of June. There was no doubt that the neighbourhood of Toulon had also been the theatre of disastrous tumults, that blood had been shed, and that my relations and friends at Sixfour, Ollioules or La Seyne, had suffered in the general confusion. I wished and yet feared to learn their situation.

On the 14th, our detachment received notice that a barge

was to descend the Rhone next day, and we were all sent on board, under the command of a lieutenant, exceedingly glad that we were not forced to witness the entrance of the Austrians into Lyons.

No orders nor news had been received from government on the morning of the 15th, yet the king had entered Paris on the 8th. How is it possible to account for the inexplicable silence the government maintained towards the second city in France? We soon passed slowly under the beautiful bridge of Tislsitt, and descended the Saone till we got below the hills. We then entered the Rhone, which carried us rapidly forward. We then got a view of Lyons for a few moments, but speedily lost sight of the bridge of La Guillotiere.

Assuredly, I must be a very foolish politician, for I drew most erroneous conclusions concerning the scenes I witnessed on both sides of the Rhone. I should have wagered any sum that a civil war was raging in France; and who would not have thought so? Lyons belonged to the Emperor; Vienne to the Piedmontese soldiers and the white flag; Coudrieux had a tri-coloured flag, while Tain and Tournon were neutral; the tri-coloured flag was of an enormous size at Valence, while the white reigned at LaVoutte; at Rochemaure, the three colours waved in the breeze, and the white at Bourg-Saint Andeol; the tri-coloured flag was at Pont-Saint-Esprit, while the white waved at Avignon, and indeed commanded all the rest of the course of the Rhone. This strange mixture of colours was also to be seen in the country villages, as far as the eye could reach. Everywhere, in fact, the people were in arms, nothing but furious cries, and hateful passions prevailed. After all this tumult, this diversity of opinion soon disappeared, and in a few days but one single colour prevailed.

While we were moving forward, the manner in which each of my companions talked of the scenes I have just mentioned, discovered to me a fact I never knew till now; that in intestine troubles discord marches with giant steps, even among the soldiers who are following the same career, and bound to fight under the same banners. I already saw some hesitation in our ranks, and they all seemed to be afraid of civil war. I know not who threw this terrible word into our ranks, but it instantly destroyed the confidence and discipline of the army. Some few, indeed, would hear of no submission to the events around them, kissed their cockade, and said with tears in their eyes:

"We ought to have died in Russia, Prussia, or Champagne. How miserable we are to have survived!"

During our whole voyage, we had sailed past royalist towns with the tri-coloured flag waving; but when we approached Avignon, the lieutenant told ns that our duty was not to support any particular opinion, but to join the majority of our fellow citizens; and that we ought therefore to abandon our customary badge. Some murmured, but everyone was convinced of the danger of obstinacy, and the soldiers abandoned now and for ever those colours which they had so nobly and unfortunately worn for three months before.

The same evening a high wind rose, and forced us to stop at Comps, a village a little higher up than Beaucaire. It was occupied by a post of volunteers of the royal army, whose headquarters were at Beaucaire. The commandant came with two or three peasants armed with fowling pieces to examine our boat on our arrival. and seemed greatly surprised when he saw it occupied by five and twenty soldiers.

He harassed our officer with a host of questions, told him that we could not continue our voyage on the Rhone, and that so he had an precise orders to give us he could not send us to Beaucaire, where the popular effervescence would expose us to danger, nor keep us at Comps, where the troops he could dispose of were too few to watch over us. He thought that the best thing we could do was, to go on to Nismes. Our officer showed his order of march; but the volunteer commander would have nothing to do with it, and informed us that if we persisted, he would instantly send a messenger to headquarters.

This phrase seemed to indicate that some centre of authority was near at hand; we knew that there were troops at Nismes, and thinking it might be better for us to approach a military force, we resolved on marching to that city, consequently set out next morning. The whole road was covered with men armed with fowling pieces, adorned with white ribbon, and marching in the greatest tumult and disorder; they seemed all to be in pursuit of some important object. They talked with vivacity, disputed, ran over the road and cultivated fields, and collected in troops on the hills.

The first whom we came up to, told us this was their way of maintaining the good order of their district, and of making head against the Bonapartists. We wore the same cockade as they did, and they received us tolerably well. Farther on, we saw the hills covered with guns, and four armed men came down, with some municipal officers, to *reason* with us, and would not allow us to pass till they found they would have some difficulty in detaining us.

Near Saint Vincent, while we were delayed by the same pretences, the whole band that had collected round us, dispersed the moment a shout rose from the other extremity of the village—"A robber! A robber!"—We saw the mob rushing towards the spot whence the shout had come, climbing up the hills and pursuing with ferocious cries a man who seemed to be somewhat ahead of them all. The pursuers fired several shots without effect.

"This brigand," said I to an old man whom I met, "is no doubt a highway robber?"

"No, Sir," said he, "he is a rich gentleman in the village, who never took anything away from any one."

"How is he a brigand then"

"Because he is a Bonapartist."

Several of my companions began to took grim at this, and put their hands to their cartridge boxes, asking him with a tone of irony:

"Did he ever do harm to anyone?"

"No, but he wished to do if...."

"He wished," said I with astonishment, "and how do you know that he is a Bonapartist!"

"There can be no doubt of it—he is a Protestant."

Three months before I had heard the menaces uttered against the Protestants, and I was not surprised that they were now realized. My companions could not understand this matter at all, and were enraged that the Bonapartists should be hunted down like wolves. Our lieutenant had great difficulty in restraining their violence; however, we arrived at Nismes, in no very good temper of mind, on the 17th July.

CHAPTER 16

After the One Hundred Days

The suburb through which we entered the town was silent and almost deserted; a few people were hurrying through the streets, and some shots were heard in the interior of the town. Some women perceived us first, and rushed towards us in the greatest disorder, clapping their hands above their heads, and shouting as loud as they could "*Vive le Roi*". We gave the same shout, and they retired with an air of satisfaction and astonishment, that formed a singular contrast with the violent agitation they seemed to be in a moment before. The men whom we saw were not less animated than the women; however, we reached the town-hall without obstruction, and were immediately ordered to the barracks, in the north-eastern part of the city. Here we found some companies of the 13th and 79th regiments of the line (I believe I have given the right numbers) who had withdrawn hither, as people retire to their homes on the approach of a storm.

On the 15th July, the garrison of Nismes had quitted the place, and left only a few companies. On the 16th, these companies, along with the national guard had proclaimed the restoration of the king's government; and on the 17th, the day of our arrival, the national guard with white ribbons, and dragging along some pieces of cannon, from which were hanging and trailing along the ground some tri-coloured flags, which seemed stained with blood.

In the evening, a few men, among whom were some soldiers of this army (but who certainly acted without orders) came to our barracks to ask for the pieces of cannon that had been left there. The officers refused to give them up, unless they received an order from the commandant of the place, and a strong dispute took place, at the end of which several shots were fired. We hastily shut the gates of the barracks, and the officers and non-commissioned officers were immediately called together to deliberate on what was to be done.

The square in front of the barracks was covered with people, and hostile cries and threats were heard. They talked, and disputed, but came to no decision, and I was astonished that among so many men who would have acted bravely in the field of battle, not one was able to decide in a case of difficulty. Meanwhile General Maulmont, who commanded us, sent to the town-hall to learn if the band who had demanded our arms was authorized to do so. The mayor came to us, but was scarcely listened to by the furious mob whom he wished to restrain.

At the same moment an officer of gendarmerie came to the gate of the barracks, and ask leave to come in. His presence stopped the firing for a few minutes; he came in the name of the people, to propose to us to surrender our arms. Unfortunately he refused the general's proposal, though it was very moderate; we offered to give up immediately all the artillery we had, and to withdraw to any town pointed out, with our guns and ammunition; we even went farther, and offered to give up our guns, at a league from Nismes.

These conditions were not accepted, and the negotiation still went on during a part of the night. From nine till twelve o'clock at night the tocsin was sounded in all the churches in the city, and collected the most violent portion of the country people. It was evident that we were threatened with the most imminent danger. In the council, which continued sitting till morning.

I proposed that we should wait silently till the middle of the night, and then march out hastily but in good order, without beat of drum, and march towards some neighbouring town, after leaving a large fire in the middle of the court, which would engage the attention of the inhabitants more than our departure. My proposal was scarcely listened to; yet it would have saved us all.

At daybreak the firing began again. We were forced at length to return it, and a *very* sharp firing began on both sides. Our numbers were small, and we were shut up in a large edifice open on all sides, without provisions, and almost without ammunition, hemmed in by an innumerable and furious mob. I again proposed to hold out till evening, and then to attempt to leave the city. My opinion was now more favourably received. Whilst our men were deliberating, the plenipotentiary with the white scarf came again to our gates, and asked for admission; the firing ceased, and he was admitted. After going backward and forward several times, it was agreed that we were to give up our cannon, that we were even to surrender our guns, and were to be sent to Uzés.

This capitulation was wholly verbal. Our officers much terrified by the important circumstances they were placed in, and too confident of the honour of the assailants, and were therefore satisfied with the officer's word of honour, and the apparent acquiescence of the crowd.

We opened our gates and began to evacuate the barracks. Our men had not all come out before innumerable shots were fired at us by the surrounding mob. Several of our men fell, and our ranks were thrown into disorder. An unarmed soldier is no longer a soldier; we fled in various directions; some entered the city, others rushed to the right, and got beyond the walls. I ran with some of my companions along a long street that goes up to the fort, but we were all pursued; two of our men fell beside me, when I rushed into some narrow streets, and the moment I saw no-one behind me, slackened my pace, and reflected on what I ought to do, I still heard firing at a distance.

I perceived a woman with tears in her eyes at the window of a small house, and said to her with strong emotion:

"Which way can I go to save my life?"

"Come in," she replied. She came down and opened the door. "It is not possible for you," said the good woman to me, "to get to Uzès, nor to hide yourself in the country; remain here. I am a poor woman, but I have some bread to give you. My husband is in safety; I can keep you here for two or three days, and you can then escape during the night."

I accepted her offer. My preserver lodged me in a garret, whence I could get into a stable that looked into a garden, the walls of which were low and easily to be climbed over. She soon went out, and came back to inform me that a great number of my companions had been kilted, and that the mob were pursuing the remainder. Some bands of partisans had posted themselves on the heights that command the road to Uzés, and fired down on my companions who had gone that way. An artillery officer was massacred, at the moment he thought himself in safety; a colonel was wounded, and our little corps annihilated in a few hours.

I could not imagine for what reason we were the victims of such fury, of such brutal violation of every right human and divine; but when I asked my preserver, she replied:

"It is because you are a *grieur*?"

"But what is a *grieur*?" I asked.

"A protestant."

I was going to say, "I am not one." but I confess that I was afraid of diminishing my hostess's good will towards me, and held my tongue. "How," said I, "the Catholic mob have no other object in all their ferocious violence than to exterminate the Protestants; and perhaps if the latter had the upper hand...."

"We triumphed during the last three months," said the good woman with an air of sorrow, "but we did not treat them in this way."

The neighbours of Susan Delon (that was the worthy creature's name) were soon informed that I was concealed in her house: but I had nothing to fear, for they were all of the same side as Susan, as I felt myself also to be at that moment, without being able to say no, time and circumstance have such influence over men's minds.

All these women brought me articles of clothing, to enable me to appear in plain clothes instead of my military dress, which was privately burned. I heard them every evening relating all the horrible scenes that had taken place during the day, and mentioning the names of the persons who had been killed in the streets or in the fields, and the houses that had been plundered in the city or burned down in the country; but their accounts were accompanied by furious outcries, and seemed disgusting by their exaggeration—I could not have believed any portion of their narratives had I not been myself a witness of many scenes of horror.

The day after I had sought shelter in the house of Madame Delon, she was talking at the door with one of her neighbours, when another woman came up to her in great sorrow, and said:

"Claudine, they say your man has been killed."

" Killed," screamed the other, where?"

"At your vineyard, near Saint Cesaire."

"Can it be so?" said the unfortunate woman, with a shriek of grief.

"Stop," said her neighbour, "here is your sister-in-law, the wife of poor Imbert Laplume, who was killed along with him, and she saw them both lying dead in your vineyard."

Cries of grief now burst forth on all sides.

In the morning of the 18th, Antoine Clot had been killed at Nismes, near his own house, by an assassin already notorious, and whose deeds I should like to hold up to public infamy, had he not been declared innocent by the verdict of a court, so that he might now prosecute me for a libel. On the same day, Chivas, the husband of Claudine, and Laplume, both brothers-in-law of Clot, were massacred in the country. A single family thus saw in one day three of their principal members cut off in the flower of their age.

As the bodies were usually mutilated, and left in the fields to feed birds and beasts of prey, Claudine Berinargue, after her first burst of grief had subsided, resolved to save her husband's body from this brutal usage; she hired some labourers, and having obtained permission to go beyond the barriers (a permission extremely difficult to obtain at that time) she went herself to inter her husband, and returned in the evening overwhelmed with grief.

Three days had elapsed, when someone came and informed Claudine that her husband was not buried, but that his body was lying in his own field above ground. She would not believe the account at first; hut she was convinced at last by the evidence of several persons, who came to relate the circumstance to her with an ironical pity and affected eagerness, and she determined to go and bury the body a second time- But she could not find a soul who would assist her in the work; some considered it as impious, and others as too dangerous. She then put a spade on her shoulders and went to the town-hall, to obtain permission to leave the city. She told what her object was, and obtained permission to go to her fields *to dig up a tree,* a pretext that was thought more prudent to justify the use of her spade, than the acknowledgment of a murder that was never inquired into. I am not the only person who has seen this singular permission.

Claudine went to the vineyard, dug a grave beside the disfigured body of her husband, put it in, and covered it over with earth and stones, to prevent it being pulled up a second time. Whilst she was doing this, some women appeared at the corner of her field, and burst into shouts of derision. However, the strong hearted widow fulfilled her pious duty, and returned towards Nismes. She found a mob of people collected at the barriers, by whom she was insulted; but she held down her head, and marched silently towards her own house, hoping when she reached it that she would be safe from the fury, not of her enemies, for she had none, but of the fanatics, who pursued her with insults and contemptuous outcries.

When she came near her house, she heard the mob behind her raising shouts of joy, and raising her head to see what had produced it, she saw her furniture piled up before her door, and all in a blaze- They had taken advantage of her absence to plunder her dwelling; and the cannibals who had met her at the gates of the city, had, by a diabolical species of cruelty hitherto unknown in multitudes, restrained their joy during her whole way from the gates to her own house, that they might keep this horrible surprise in reserve for her, and procure themselves a demoniacal satisfaction.

The moment Claudine Berinargue saw the scene before her, she made her way through the crowd without complaint, without uttering a single word, her eyes fixed in vacancy, and hurried along by the mental alienation that supported her under her load of misery. No-one followed her. The mob of marauders dispersed, for they had satiated their vengeance, and did not plunder the adjoining houses, as might have been expected.

I kept myself concealed in my garret under some hay, and expected they would set fire to our house which was opposite the unfortunate widow's, in which case I was prepared to rush into the country, or perhaps into the crowd, armed with a large cutlass, which was the only-sort of weapon I could find in the house.

Of the scene I have just mentioned, I saw only the concluding part, the plunder of the house; and that alone affected me at the moment. But I learned all the rest of the particulars, a few hours afterwards; and was terrified at such a diabolical accumulation of horrors. It seemed to me, that such crimes were about to become general, and Nismes on the eve of being sacked; I could not endure the idea of witnessing such scenes, and resolved to set out the same evening.

My hostess was overwhelmed with the fears and tumultuous emotions of the day, and did not endeavour to detain me.

I tried to arrange my dress, so as to look like a man of those scenes and times, and assumed a large cockade; and about nine o'clock I thanked the kind Delon for her services, went to the barrier, where I was asked no questions, but I did not pass through without lively apprehension.

CHAPTER 17

Helping a Fugitive

I immediately took the road to Ados, through the sandy district of Bellegarde. At day-break, I was near Fourques; I went carefully round that village, and to avoid the guards on the bridge, was preparing to swim over a little arm of the Rhone, a quarter of a league lower down. At the moment I was about to enter the water, four men armed with muskets, rushed out from behind a small hut, and presenting their guns, cried out "your papers"—As their hats were adorned with white cockades, at least six inches in diameter, I supposed they were gallant royalists, who had been sent to guard the banks of the Rhone; and as I had no desire of entering into discussion with them, after the polite manner they had began, nor of running the risk of being taken for a Protestant and treated as one, inasmuch as I had no passport to show, I did not wish to wait till they came a step closer, and jumped into the water.

They had levelled their muskets, at me at first; but now like inexperienced fellows as they were, they raised them up and ran towards the bank.—I followed the current, and whilst they were getting to the bank, and wasting their time in fruitless menaces, I got into the middle of the stream, and dived so as to avoid their shots. They fired at the moment I rose above water, and their balls whizzed round me and struck the water. One of them had loaded with small shot, and some of the grains entered my arm; I had no need of this stimulus to urge me forward, and before they had loaded again, I was nearly beyond their reach. Two of them, however, still discharged their guns, but it was of no avail.

Although I was quite breathless when I got to the left bank of the Rhone, I did not take time to look behind me, but ran as fast as I could to a small wood that I saw at some distance. On coming up to it, I perceived that it was large enough to afford me concealment, and prevent me being taken by surprise. Hence I stopped and began to dry my clothes in the sun. The good Delon would absolutely fill my pockets with provisions before I set out; and I breakfasted with a piece of bread, well steeped in the Rhone during my passage; and this meal, though frugal enough, soon restored me to my former strength and vigour. In half an hour, the burning sun of the field dried my clothes, and I resumed my journey, with eye and ear intent on every sight and sound, and not a shadow waved in the breeze, but I thought I saw an enemy.

I passed along the Camargue, following the left bank of the river, which I thought I should be able to cross by the first boat I met moored on the shore. About mid-day, I took some refreshment in a farmhouse, and continued my journey. The Rhone became wider and wider; I met with no boat, and began to get alarmed, when I saw a *felucca* loaded with wood coming down behind me pretty rapidly, and approaching the bank where I was. I hailed it; when I learned that it was bound for Toulon, I asked the master if he would take me on board, and after asking who I was, he found that he would be doing a service to an old soldier, and sent his boat for me.

We entered the open sea the same evening, and having fortunately caught a S.W. wind near the coast, we set sail for Toulon. The next day, the 24th July, at daybreak I discovered Bandol and the roads of Brusc on the north; on the west, right ahead of us, the *Deux Frères,* Cape Sepet, and the hill of Sixfour, which was lost among the vales of Ollioules. We heard salutes of cannon fired on the shore; but knew not what was the cause of it! I learned on reaching the shore, that it was in honour of the white flag being hoisted in the place, in consequence of the treaty signed by Marshal Brune and the royalists.

We soon landed at La Seyne, in the road of Toulon, and nobody thought of examining our vessel. I went immediately to Sixfour, where I was received by my family, with all the affection they had so often shown me in times past. I found a cruel void at home, and my return renewed the grief of the family for a loss that had occurred a considerable time back, but which was every day felt more sensibly; yet it was with melancholy satisfaction that I found the memory of my excellent mother still fresh in the hearts of all the members of my family.

My father was still mayor of the village. On the day of my arrival, I expected to receive, as I had done in my former journey, the visits and congratulations of our neighbours; but not a soul came. I inquired the cause, and learned that there was the greatest contrariety in people's opinions, and that my father, who had been formerly accused of moderation, was now accused of liberalism by the very same individuals.

Next day I perceived that those whom I met, looked at me suspiciously, and those I spoke to, replied with an air of constraint. I thought that my presence could only increase the difficulties of my family, and two days after my arrival, set out again for Toulon, with the intention of getting a marching order to join the depot of my regiment; but I found that town in such a state of alarm and confusion, that I prolonged my stay, thinking always that I was on the eve of seeing some important event. At any rate it would not have been easy for me to get an order of departure, for nobody was at his post; and I knew not whether to apply to the old or new authorities.

I resumed the uniform I had been obliged to abandon at Nismes, and had not been two days at Toulon before I fell in with several of my old acquaintances, who like myself, had escaped from our late political disasters. We communicated our melancholy reflections on the dissentions we had witnessed. The white flag had been a few days before hoisted in the public buildings, the forts, and the government vessels in the roads; hut a great many soldiers, after putting aside the tri-coloured cockade, hesitated to assume that of the existing government. The garrison, full of the recollections of the empire, and irritated by the massacres which had taken place at Marseilles, had, it was said, declared to Marshal Brune their desire of burying themselves under the ruins of the town, rather than to give up their eagles.

Admiral Gantheaume, though loved and venerated throughout Provence, had yet encountered the greatest danger in calling upon his countrymen to return to their duty; and when Marshal Brune agreed to submit to the king's government, before hoisting the white flag, it was thought necessary to send off to the forts, the most violent troops in the town, among whom were the half-pay soldiers of the Isère, a sacred battalion, and two battalions of grenadiers of the department of Var. The last mentioned corps was disbanded and disarmed on the Place d'Armes at Toulon, on the very day of my arrival. I knew some men who had belonged to it; their discontent was at its height, and their language was not very circumspect. However, Toulon did not become a scene of bloodshed; it is true that an officer of the 16th regiment of the line was assassinated in a public square, in the middle of the day; but can this solitary fact be put into comparison with the horrible atrocities that were perpetrated at Marseilles, Nismes, Montpellier, and all the other towns in the South?

On the day of my arrival, I met in the harbour M. Don—, who had first served in the navy, then in the army, when he was present at the battle of Wagram, after which I had an opportunity of seeing him; he had again returned to the navy, and had reached the rank of master; he seemed exceedingly happy to see me after such a long separation, and the numerous dangers we had both encountered. I met with him several times afterwards, and latterly saw his mind harassed with some important care, but I did not like to ask him any questions.

About eight o'clock one evening (I believe it was the 21st of August) I was walking by myself in the Champ de Bataille (a square at Toulon) and reflecting on a variety of subjects, (and in truth I had quite enough to reflect on,) when this officer came up to me, and said:

"Guillemard, you are known to be a man that can be depended on, will you assist in an undertaking that requires courage and generosity?—Follow me."

"Captain," said I, "I am ready to follow you anywhere; I have seen you at Wagram and other places; but in the situation in which things are placed, I will not do it till you give me a formal order, well assured that whatever the consequence be, you will never deny the transaction."

"Very well," said he, "I order you—follow me"

We then walked towards the gate of Italy, and left Toulon. We climbed over the hill of La Malque, and reached a spot where we found a boat moored on the shore; M. Don— entered it, examined it for a moment, came out, walked up and down the shore, and looked every now and then in the direction by which we had come down. In about half an hour, when it had become quite dark, we heard the steps of some persons coming towards us. My officer listened for a moment, got upon a rock, and said:

"Is it you, Ang—?"

"Yes," replied an officer I had not yet seen, and who arrived quite out of breath. "He is coming this moment" he continued, "is that your non-commissioned officer?"

"Yes," said M. Don— and you may depend upon him. "Let us get everything ready."

He made me a signal to come into the boat, and came in after me, while M. Ang— walked up and down on the shore, and seemed to examine everything round him. We hoisted the sail, prepared the oars, and put into a box some provisions they had no doubt brought here beforehand.

After waiting some time, during which we remained in the deepest silence, M. Ang— said "Are you ready?—here he comes."

We got upon one of the seats of the boat, and looked in the direction pointed out by M. Ang—, and heard the steps of several men, M. Ang— moved quickly out of the way, and knelt down as if to conceal himself; we did the same, and soon saw a body of men going along the shore, and marching towards the big tower. They were doubtless fishermen, who passed by us without noticing us. M. Ang— returned, and we walked up and down the shore, and waited in silence till daybreak.

By the frequent and rapid movements of both officers, it was very evident that they were burning with impatience. For myself, I had for some time witnessed so many strange and unaccountable events, and had felt so many powerful emotions, that nothing could henceforth astonish me, and I remained almost indifferent about every event that took place round me. I imagined that the service required was to save some naval officer of rank, who was proscribed by the government of the moment, from the captivity that awaited him, and to put him on board a merchant vessel.

When we heard the cannon that announced the opening of the gates of Toulon, one of the officers said to the other, "Something extraordinary must have taken place. Let us haul down the yard; go into the country, and see what can be the cause of this delay, and I shall return to Toulon with the sergeant; you know where to find me, and if there are no new orders, we meet this evening at the usual hour."

As we were on our way to Toulon, my companion said to me:

"Guillemard, I must give you some explanation of the present circumstance; our object is to save an officer of rank, who has fought more campaigns than you and me put together; he is pursued, and we wish to put him on board of a vessel that is waiting for him, and the moment our object is accomplished, we shall return to the shore. We have thought we might rely safely on your discretion and goodwill, when our object was to save the life of a brave man."

"You are not mistaken, Captain," said I.

"Well," said he, "we meet this evening at eight o'clock at the *Trois Oranges,* behind the Champ de Mars. I am going to hasten forward that I may enter Toulon alone."

We separated; I made a long circuit, and going round the lines, walked towards the gate of France.

I reflected on what I had just heard, and recalled to mind the names of all those who were exposed to danger by the late political events, and involuntarily stopped at the name of General Brune, whom his violent opposition to the new government seemed likely to expose to many dangers. It is true that a report of his death had been in circulation for some days; but the manner in which it was told necessarily raised doubts of its truth in the mind of every reasonable man. In fact, I could not possibly imagine that peaceful citizens, who knew nothing of that warrior but his glory, could assassinate him in cool blood, and thought that the report had been spread on purpose to favour his flight, and that he was still concealed in the neighbourhood, *If, indeed, it be necessary to save him,* (I thought) *I may be safely relied on. I care not what his opinions are; but I cannot forget that I have served under his command, and that he must be in misfortune.*

I had got thus far with my reflections, when I saw about fifty or sixty persons coming forward in the direction of La Valette, most of them dressed in remnants of uniforms of the national guard, and four or five of them with epaulets. They were all covered with dust, and their looks presented an appearance of terror and alarm. They marched in great disorder, and formed rather a crowd than a company. When they came up to me, their commanding officer, M——, son of the general of that name, clapped me on the shoulder, and said roughly:

"Where do you come from so early in the morning?"

I was not prepared to answer this question, but I was angry at the tone in which it was made, and replied, "It is not earlier for me than for you, where do you come from yourselves?"

"I have no answer to give you."

"Nor I either I hope?"

A loud clamour burst from the fellows who followed him; those who wore epaulets surrounded me, and asked me if I did not know what their rank was.

"How the devil should I be able to recognise you? Did I ever see you along with the army?"

"We are officers."

"So much the better for you," I replied.

The cries and clamour began anew, and they seemed on the point of attacking me. Fortunately some soldiers who were passing by, saw one of their men among this tumultuous band, and rushed forward. The moment they saw them, the gallant fellows who surrounded me began to clear off, and said to each other:

"Come along, come along, he is a fine fellow, let us move on,"

We each of us resumed our march to the town. *Are, these,* I thought to myself, *the people destined to supersede our brave officers, whose birth is not sufficiently ancient? It cannot be! They would not surely go and seek out that baker who can scarcely read—that ugly confectioner—that mean smith—that bankrupt broker with the villainous countenance, and all these fellows that strut away with epaulets! No—these are not the nobles to whom military commands are reserved; they look more like fellows who would rob on the highway, I have no objection to see lords of high birth and distinguished education at the head of our troops; but these are fellows that have been drawn up from the mud for a moment during a political crisis, and cannot be fitted to command us.*

I returned to Toulon. I do not know how it was, but the day seemed tedious to me. I was at the *Trois Oranges* at eight o'clock. M. Don— came immediately after me, and seemed depressed. After drinking a bottle of beer together, we walked towards the spot where we had left the boat, which we found in the same state as before. We waited several hours. The night was very dark, and we walked quietly up and down the shore, listening to every noise we heard; at length, about half past eleven, we heard some footsteps, and saw four persons coming forward with great precaution. M. Don .... made a signal, which they answered, and immediately came forward.

"Is everything ready?" said M. Ang—whom I then recognised.

"Yes," we replied.

"Come, Prince, let us embark," said he to a person who was wrapped up in a large cloak.

"But who are these men?" said he, in a tone of alarm, and pointing to us.

"Friends."

"But—Do you know the coast well?"

"It's of no consequence. We run the same danger as you do."

"Very well, let us go."

He then turned towards a little thin man who held his arm, and said to him:

"*Adieu*, generous Mar—, whether fortune be favourable to me or otherwise, I shall never forget your conduct." And he embraced him,

"Prince," replied the latter with emotion, "I have only done my duty; I wish it were in my power to do as much for every member of your family, for all in misfortune."

As he said these words on retiring, the person to whom they were addressed, put one foot on the gunwale of the boat. He was a man of high stature, and majestic aspect. He seemed to hesitate for a moment, but M. Ang— took hold of his arm, and said:

"Come on, everything is settled; let us depart," and he entered the boat along with him.

We pushed off from the shore without a moment's delay, and sailed with great caution to avoid being hailed by the boats cruising off the harbour, and at dawn of day found ourselves beyond Cape Cepet. Our passenger was seated in the stern, took no share in the management of the boat, and had not yet uttered a single word. So much mystery made me very desirous of learning who he was, and I saw the approach of daylight with pleasure; but his cloak was crossed over his shoulder, and completely concealed his face, leaving nothing to be seen but the tassels and a part of his velvet cap.

We moved about till sunrise. He then rose up all at once, and cast his cloak back to look at the horizon around us. The oar I had fell from my hands, I rose almost involuntarily, and put my hand to my forehead, to give him the usual military salute. It was the King of Naples. Without noticing my astonishment, he said with an air of satisfaction:

"We ore now out of reach. But you surely do not mean to go with this boat to Corsica?"

"No, Sire," replied one of the officers; "we are going to beat about, without going far from the entrance of the roads. In a few hours, the schooner that conveys the mail from Toulon to Corsica will come out; our intention is to put your majesty on board; and the captain will be forced to sail to any port you point out to him: this has seemed to us the safest plan; but whatever plan you may adopt, we are ready to obey your orders; and to sacrifice our lives, if necessary, in your defence; but the captain shall obey you."

"I shall not ask him to do anything," replied the King, "but to continue his voyage; I shall find plenty of opportunities in Corsica to go to Trieste or elsewhere."

We made several tacks, but still kept sight of the entrance of the roads. The packet did not appear, though the hour of its sailing was past. We resolved to wait for it a while longer, and to avoid the suspicions of the custom-house-officers, whose attention might have been roused by the sight of our boat, we pretended to be fishing; but towards evening, we felt full of anxiety, and determined to move out into the open sea, to avoid being taken by surprise, in case we had excited suspicion on shore.

During the greater part of the day, the king and one of the officers lay upon one of the seats, to conceal the numbers of our little crew. We had taken some refreshment in the morning, but for some reason or other, the king seemed afraid of taking anything. Our officers wished not to eat till after he was served, on account of his rank, but they could not persuade him to take anything. He would not take any food till towards evening, and then he wished us, like jovial travelling companions, to take our meal along with him. This was the first time, and will probably be the last, that I dined, I do not say at a king's table, but with a king in person. But in truth, we required to take some nourishment; we were very far from the shore, and as the wind had changed and freshened considerably, we were threatened with a very disagreeable night. We lowered our sail, and took every precaution in our power against the bad weather that was lowering over us.

Chapter 18

Murat at Toulon

We began to despair of meeting with the packet, but still continued sailing about, so as to get as near her route as possible. We were fatigued and worn out, the king, on the contrary, seemed to resume his accustomed energy the more distant he got from the coasts of France. He doubtless felt anxious to reanimate us, and several times renewed the conversation when it became languid.

"You did not tell me," said he to Don—, "how Bon— was detained, and was unable to come along with us"

"You know, Sire, that he became suspected after the sailing of your suite; at the moment you were to have set out, it was settled between us that to avoid the active persecution of your enemies, he was to go towards the mountain, as if he had gone to prepare for your journey by land. The suspicions of your enemies must have been turned in that direction, and by leaving the coast, he has assisted you to escape."

"I am happy that he has adopted such a step. Otherwise it would have been another brave man who had risked his life for my sake. I return you my thanks, gentlemen," said he afterwards, addressing himself to us, "for your perseverance in risking everything for my sake; I hope that you will be able to return to Toulon in a few hours. For myself, wherever I may be, I shall never forget the important service you have rendered me."

Thus went on the conversation, and while we felt the

strongest anxiety, the king spoke to us with a smile about the dangers he had encountered for the last month.

He had first withdrawn to Plaisance, a beautiful country seat in the neighbourhood of Toulon, but he had been obliged to leave it hastily at the time of the tumults at Marseilles. He had then sought shelter in another country house much more secluded, and more than a league and a half from the town.

The first thing he did on his arrival was to write to the new government officers, to notify to them that "he had nothing to do with the internal quarrels of the country, but requested that the asylum he had sought in France might be respected." At the same period he sent several persons to Paris, one after another, to negotiate in his name with the allied powers. He felt assured that he had lost forever the kingdom of Naples, and merely asked an asylum from England or Austria, where he might live as a private individual. Dangers of every kind crowded round him whilst he was waiting for the answer of the allies; armed bands had orders to seek him out, and it was even said that a reward was offered for his head.

It was then only that he thought of leaving Provence, where he could not hope to escape much longer from the assassins, who had not respected the rank and character of Marshal Brune. He made an attempt to go by the mountains to Lyons, where he could have more tranquilly waited for the decision of the allied powers: but whilst (according to the plan of his aid-de camp, General Rossetti) M. Blan—, one of our number, had prepared everything for the journey, he received news that the Duke of Rocca-Romana had taken his passage on board a vessel bound to Havre de Grace. He resolved to adopt this way in preference to any other. It was agreed that to prevent detainment or surprise, the king was not to embark at Toulon, but was to get into a boat the day the vessel left the harbour, and join it at sea.

The king was on the shore at the appointed time; but by some strange mistake there was no boat waiting for him. He was, therefore, obliged to get into a boat with two sailors and his nephew Murat, a captain in the navy. The vessel had got far from the coast, and they had scarcely left it, when a high wind drove them on shore. They landed again, soaked with rain and the seas the boat had shipped.

The king passed the remainder of the night on the shore. At daybreak, he saw the vessel sailing out into the open sea, and lost all hopes of getting up with it. He was then obliged to conceal himself in the mountains, to escape from the search that was made after him, for he judged rightly that the vessel's sailing without him had been produced by the suspicions the police had formed of his projects. In fact, he learned afterwards that they had constantly watched the movements of the vessel till it was out of sight. Joachim Napoleon was obliged to dry his clothes in the sun, and to eat a piece of coarse bread in a solitary farmhouse, while his valet Leblanc left him on some slight pretext, and ran away with his master's money.

In this state two days were passed. He was without a roof to cover him, and almost without food, when at last pressed by want, he resolved on entering a small house, where he thought he should not be known; he found an old woman in it, and told her that he belonged to the garrison. Whilst she was preparing some food he had asked her for, the master of the country house came in. His situation was embarrassing. The King of Naples' countenance was too remarkable not to be instantly recognized by any one who knew the political events of the day, or who was at all acquainted with the history of our military glory. Hence M. Mar—, the master of the house, saluted Joachim respectfully the moment he perceived him, and assured him that he would do everything in his power to secure his asylum from the researches of his enemies.

It was here that the king waited some days longer for the answer of the allied powers to the proposal he had made; but notwithstanding his multiplied despatches, he received no answer. Seeing his hopes dashed away by being neglected so utterly, while his life was every moment in jeopardy, he resolved at last to accept the offer of some enterprising and faithful young men, who engaged to put him on board the packet that conveys the mail to Corsica, at the moment the vessel got to sea. By means of the gardener of the chateau of Plaisance, in whose house he had one night sought shelter, he had opened a correspondence with M. Blan—.

M. Don and M. Ang were then presented to him; it was the latter who conceived the plan of putting the king on board a vessel, and offered to put it into execution. They bought a boat and prepared everything for the attempt. Before leaving the French territory, the king wrote Fouché a letter giving an account of his misfortunes and the danger he was constantly exposed to; and he informed him that he was going to Corsica to wait for the decision of the allied sovereigns.

However, it has been already seen that M. Bon— was sent towards the mountains for the purpose of concealing his escape. A few hours before they were to set off, the officers who were to convey the king felt the necessity of getting another associate in place of M. Bon—, if he did not return before they sailed. Whilst one of them went on to inform the king that everything was ready, the other entered Toulon, where among the military men whom he met, I was the first whom he thought fit to confide in.

But whilst we were waiting on the shore, and Murat was about to leave his retreat to join us, an unexpected incident came in the way. The old servant perceived a light at a little distance moving towards the house, and suspecting some people were looking out for the king, she gave him instant notice. He had scarcely time to leap into a ditch covered over with furze, taking his poignard and two pair of pistols with him, before the house was surrounded by a band of sixty men, who searched into every corner. They then examined the garden, and several times passed quite close to the bush which concealed the king; but the lantern, which had given notice of their approach, and which they absurdly carried with them on such an enterprise, increased the obscurity around them, and actually hid the very object of their search. Once, however, they thought they had got him; a voice was heard; and they all rushed back in various directions. They rallied again, when they found that it was nothing but a dog beginning to bark, taking them no doubt for robbers.

At this moment the king had a great mind to get out of the ditch and rush upon them. There is no doubt that if he had done so, he might easily have put his pursuers to flight, for they could not have thought that he would singly dare to attack sixty men. But he was restrained by the fear of exposing his host to future risk; and our sixty gallant fellows soon left the house, shouting forth their curses against him. As it was probable they would still haunt the neighbourhood (which in fact was the case, for it was these very fellows whom I met on my return to the town early in the morning) the king resolved to put off his departure till next day.

It may be easily imagined how great the prince's anxiety was during the whole night, for he thought he would lose the last opportunity that presented itself of leaving Provence. However, when he saw some of his officers arrive next morning, he recovered his serenity; and in the evening, without waiting for M. Bon—, who was expected every moment, he left his last asylum, followed by Mar—, who would not leave him till he knew that he was in safety.

I have thus briefly noted the subjects that were talked of during the greater part of the night. I have omitted a multitude of particulars, which seemed full of spirit and energy when told by the king, but which I should be afraid of describing very adequately. In his narrative there prevailed a tone of irony and carelessness that formed a singular contrast with the dangers he had encountered. However, he assumed a solemn and almost melancholy expression when he said:

"Why am I hunted down with such animosity? A fugitive, I have asked for nothing but the rites of hospitality; unconnected with the political events of the time, I have refused during the last crisis to resume any authority. What have I done to the French to be so hated by them, I who would still give my life for France?"

He was frequently interrupted by the necessary changing of our sails and ropes, but this became every moment more difficult. We were often obliged to let go the sheet to avoid being overset, and each time we shipped large seas. Had it not been for these accidents the king's conversation would no doubt have informed me of many more particulars; but it was soon out of our power to think of anything else than our safety.

A wave dashed over the side, and extinguished the lamp at our compass, which we were unable to light again; we had no tinder box, and indeed it was not surprising that we had forgotten it, considering the precipitate manner in which our voyage had been begun. We were out of our reckoning in a moment, and could only distinguish the way we were going by the direction of the waves, which still flowed upon us from the open sea, so that we were evidently driving towards land. We were constantly occupied in throwing out the water with our hats; and this feeble resource would have been unavailing had not the wind fallen all at once just as day began to dawn.

A few moments afterwards, the king first perceived a brig coming from the west, and sailing in the same direction as ourselves; we exerted ourselves to come up with it, and when we were within hearing, hailed it, and learned that it was the *Santa-Maria-di-Pieta*, Captain Benvenuto. By the king's order, we offered the captain a considerable sum if he would take us to Corsica, for now it was out of our power to return to Toulon so soon as we expected. The sum offered, perhaps, roused his suspicions; and it must be admitted that the sight of five armed men in a boat such as ours was not well fitted to tranquillise him. He must have taken us for pirates, for he not only refused to grant our request, but at the moment we least expected it, he turned his helm and sailed right down upon us. It was only by the skill and promptness with which we put our boat about that we escaped being run down.

In his first burst of anger, the king seemed desirous of boarding the brig and seizing it; we all felt the same desire, and for my own part, I wished I was already rushing on sword in hand. But the king no doubt reflected that it did not suit his situation to commit an act of aggression against whomsoever it might be; he stopped our impetuous feelings, and we let the brig continue its voyage. Our boat was much damaged by the brig; but fortunately the sea became calmer, and we soon felt certain, that if the wind did not rise again, we might wait some hours longer for the packet, or for any favourable circumstance that might occur to extricate us from our very critical situation.

Whilst we remained in this painful situation, the king was still unmoved as before, and paid no attention to anything hut our hardships; he felt deeply the misery and danger into which we had been involved through our zeal for his service, and he endeavoured to alleviate our melancholy situation by conversing on those subjects that were personally interesting to us all.

He several times told us, in the most explicit manner, how desirous he was that circumstances would put it in his power to show his gratitude in an adequate manner. He asked my companions if in case fortune or favourable circumstances restored him to power, he could cherish the hope that they would enter into his service. They returned the king thanks for his kindness, but firmly expressed their intention of never serving under any flag than that of France. Our officers then flattered themselves with the hope of retaining their rank in the navy.

It now came to my turn. The king asked me where I had served, what battles I had been present at, and if I had seen him along with the army? I answered very briefly at first; but he smiled occasionally at my narrative, particularly when I mentioned the circumstances that had deprived me of the promotion I had gained. He heard my story with great attention. I gradually forgot that I was speaking to a crowned. head, and expatiated very fully upon my services and the reward I had obtained. He interrupted me several times to ask some questions about the engagements I spoke of, some of which he had been personally engaged in, I mentioned a few particulars concerning the battle of Trafalgar, and my voyage with Admiral Villeneuve.

The account I gave of his death struck him forcibly. He wished to learn all the particulars, and the inquiries that had been made of me by Napoleon on the subject. He expressed his regret at the non-fulfilment of the emperor's order to give me a commission, and at the moment I alluded to it, made me the same offer he had already made to my companions; but I must confess that I was not patriotic enough to make the same reply. I had been the victim of too much neglect and injustice, and my prospects were too uncertain not to take advantage of the opportunity that now came in my way to leave at last that subaltern rank in which I had vegetated so long. I joyfully accepted the offer. The king then said to me:

"As a reward for your past services to France, which shall ever be dear to me, and for the generous proof of zeal you are showing me at this moment, Ensign Guillemard, I appoint you a captain. Whether I remain in private life, or be called again to power, from this moment your appointment will run, and you may wear the epaulet of the rank you have obtained."

Well, I got the long wished for epaulet at last, and lost nothing by waiting so long. My newly acquired rank increased my dislike to the position we were in, and I burned with impatience to get out of it, and see how my appointment would be realized. I was entering upon a new career, and had just made my first step forward. *Who knows* (I vainly thought) *what prospects may be in reserve for me?* I had attained a time of life at which an individual has acquired experience enough to take advantage of favourable circumstances, and these might occur in great numbers. The chances of adverse fortune had disappeared; unforeseen prospects opened upon me, and these seemed of infinite value, because I bound my hopes to the fortune of an illustrious individual, who could not long remain in obscurity.

On the morning of the 25th, three days after our departure, we perceived the post office packet to the south-east of the cape, and sailing towards us. We clewed up our sail to wait for it, and to engage the notice of the crew hoisted upon the end of our yard a cashmere shawl, which the king wore as a sash. In about half an hour's time, the vessel was only a few cables length from We rowed up to it and were hailed: but without giving any reply, we ran alongside and mounted on board.

We had at first intended to return to Toulon, after putting the king on board this vessel, but we had seen for some time that this was quite out of the question. The damage our boat had sustained from the brig, and the effects of the gale, rendered it quite unfit to make the passage. At any rate, after what I had seen of Captain Benvenuto's conduct, I was afraid the master of the packet might wish to force us to return to Toulon in our own boat, so I took hold of an iron bar, put it under one of the ribs of the boat, and the moment the king put his foot on the ladder of the packet, I raised the bar, and pulled up a piece of one of the planks below the level of the water, which soon filled the boat, and it went down in less than a quarter of an hour after we left it.

We told the captain of the packet, when we went on board, that we had gone to take a pleasure excursion the evening before, but that the wind had driven us out to sea; and as we could not go back to Toulon, we should go with him to Corsica, and return with the next packet. He believed us, or seemed to do so.

The king had scarcely entered the vessel before he was recognised by some of the passengers, and we vainly tried to treat him on a footing of equality. The captain now came up to him, and asked him respectfully to go down to the cabin, where he ordered refreshments to be got ready.

We remained on deck the whole morning, while the king enjoyed some repose; but he called us down in the afternoon, and we partook of his dinner. He was dull and silent, and seemed embarrassed by the captain's presence; but, after the latter had gone on deck, after telling the king that he had the sole disposal of the cabin, Joachim resumed his gaiety, and began to talk very fully about our voyage, and then reverted to the dangers he had previously encountered.

What seemed to affect him most painfully was the conduct of M. R—; however, the tone of his voice, which was harsh at first, gradually softened down, and tears fell from his eyes when he spoke to us of his friends. It was, perhaps, through fear of having wounded our feelings that he added:

"Yes, gentlemen, these were real friends; and you alone can occupy their place."

Blan— hastily observed, " Sire, I never knew any of your suite but General Rossetti; and if the rest are equally zealous and loyal, you may flatter yourself with having preserved in your adversity friends capable of any sacrifice."

"I know it," replied the king, "they would have risked their lives at all times—they are gallant fellows. The Marquis de Giuliano is a young man whom I trained up myself; he distinguished himself in the Russian campaign, and is sincerely devoted to me. The Duke of Rocca Romana, my master of the horse, is equally fascinating by his handsome person and dignified manners. I hesitated a long while before I attached him to my person, but I was wrong; for ever since he has been in my service, he has constantly shown me the most distinguished proofs of his attachment. This worthy man has always been equally loyal; be saw his only son killed at Tolentino, and desired to follow me in my exile. I shall never forget this noble proof of his loyalty. The brave General Rossetti was my friend: it took some time before I could accustom myself to his rough and blunt disposition;

but circumstances show the value of men, and the queen very justly styled him the *imperturbable*. In fact, gentlemen, had I followed his advice, I should have avoided many misfortunes, and we should not have been here."

Whilst he was talking in this way, he seemed to be in a state of continual emotion. About ten o'clock at night the captain came into the cabin for something belonging to the vessel, when Joachim remarked that we must all be worn out with fatigue, and desired us to go and take some rest.

CHAPTER 19

The King Of Naples

The packet reached Bastia in safety on the 26th. We remained here only one day, during which it may be easily imagined that I did not forget to put on my epaulets, and have a sword by my side; and we then marched to Vescovato, a village about fifteen leagues south of Bastia. Here we found Colonel Franceschetti, who had long and frequent conferences with the king.

Several days passed over, and my fellow travellers were already preparing to return to France, when we were informed by some Corsican peasants that the garrison of Bastia was about to march to seize the king.

This report had been spread through the mountains, where everyone knew that he was living among them; and we saw multitudes of armed people flocking to us to offer their services, maintaining that the inhabitants freely offered him a safe asylum, which they would not permit to be violated.

The secluded life which Joachim led seemed likely to allow him to remain unmolested, and it was not without indignation that we heard of this first attempt upon his peace.

He received no news of any kind from France, and seemed completely forgotten by the allied powers, whom he had asked for asylum. His patience was worn out by three months of painful expectation and constant alarm. Those around him became enthusiastic in his cause, and raised frequent shouts of *Viva Gioachino;* and some hot-headed people even went so far as to talk of making him king of Corsica.

These things were reported to him, and perhaps without reflection, he mentioned them to the naval officers who had come with him from Toulon, with that warmth with which his imagination always seized strange and romantic ideas.

"Sire," one of those young men replied to him coldly, "it does not suit the brother and the rival of Napoleon to play the part of the adventurer Theodore. For our own parts, we never can have any thing to do with a project whose object is to cut off a department from France; and if we were obliged to declare ourselves on one side or the other, it would be against your majesty" The king only smiled at this patriotic frankness, and changed the subject of conversation.

The troops that had been sent against Vescovato were over-awed by the multitude of people, who voluntarily assembled round Murat, and returned to Bastia; but those who had come forward to protect the king thought that prudence required them not to separate, and thus lay themselves open to the vengeance of the government. The king's situation became every day more critical. He wished for nothing but a secure retreat, and was now in reality at the head of an armed multitude. It would appear that in this state of things, the uncertainty of his prospects, the impossibility of remaining much longer in such a situation, and more than all his desire of bettering the fate of those who had bound themselves to his fortunes, drew him in to the adoption of hazardous measures. He sold some diamonds he had kept on his person, and took measures to provide for the maintenance of his followers.

We set out for Ajaccio with about four hundred men, whom we had been unable to persuade to leave him. When he reached that town he went to an inn, to avoid any appearance of hostility to the government; he then purchased five small vessels, and provided them with arms and ammunition. It was now evident that he was going to make a hostile attempt. No one doubted the matter for a moment; when he was heard to say, "that a king who could not keep his crown, had no other alternative than the death of a soldier."

"He is right!" I exclaimed, on hearing it; and I was firmly resolved to go with him.

Whilst the final preparations were making, one of his aid-de-camps came from France, and had many secret interviews with him; and there was a report in circulation that he had at length brought to Joachim the offer of an asylum in Austria, which he had so often asked for in vain; but a month's time had greatly altered circumstances. Murat no longer considered himself master of his own actions.

"The die is cast," he said; "those who lately sought for my alliance have abandoned me to the fury of obscure enemies. They acknowledged me king of Naples: I have not abdicated my crown, and am now going to resume it. The result of my enterprise may be doubtful, but this I care not for. I have often faced death since I became a king; as a soldier—I despise it."

Such language inflamed us with enthusiasm, and we were all ready to shed our last drop of blood in his service.

On the 28th September, at one o'clock in the morning, our little fleet set sail, under the command of Captain Barbara, a man devoted to Murat, and who joined him in Corsica. The military commandant of Ajaccio had withdrawn into the fort, the moment the king of Naples appeared in the town. He thought it his duty to assume a hostile attitude, by firing some cannon balls at us when we set sail. His shot was not returned, and we moved on. It was not without regret that I had the evening before taken farewell of the gallant fellows with whom I had come to Corsica. They were waiting to go to Toulon by the first packet The king embraced them with tears in his eyes, and promised to provide for them if his enterprise succeeded.

The wind was fair, and we soon got into the open sea; but it became contrary on the 2nd October, and we were forced to put into a small island. Advantage was taken of our stay here to form the companies on the shore. The king did not include me in any of them, but kept me employed near his person. We got under weigh again on the 3rd, and Captain Barbara, who commanded the expedition, called the masters of the different vessels together to give them the necessary orders.

In the course of the next day the weather became boisterous. We were opposite the island of Stromboli, off Policastro, on the Calabrian coast, and endeavoured to approach it as near as possible, but the wind blew more violent than ever, and the sea became rough, so that the vessels were dispersed during the night. At daybreak we could scarcely perceive two or three of the vessels on the verge of the horizon. One little *felucca* was the only vessel that kept constantly by the one that conveyed the king, on board of which I was.

In the morning the king ordered the two vessels to move up along the coast, to give the scattered vessels time to join; but he was only joined by one small sloop that had forty men of his old guard on board. Two of their officers came on board on the 7th, to remain nearer the king's person. We were now off the bay of Santa Euphemia.

In the evening the king ordered the felucca to take the sloop that had joined us in tow, and to sail towards Pizzo, a village we already perceived on the coast. About the middle of the night it was found that the sloop had cut off its moorings, and had driven out to sea, which was a clear proof that the crew had deserted the king. This news afflicted him deeply. We did not sail so close to the shore as before, and waited impatiently for the next day.

On the 8th the felucca had entirely disappeared. Out of the whole expedition there now remained only Captain Barbara's vessel, having on board about thirty soldiers and sailors, and the one that had first joined the king, with no more than twenty sailors on board. In the morning the king had a very animated conference with Captain Barbara. As no-one was present, the only reason we had for thinking that it had mightily displeased Joachim, was the thoughtfulness and anxiety he displayed immediately afterwards. It was thought that he would give orders to go along the coast as far as Salerno, the place of meeting appointed for the expedition, and where his purpose would be aided by the presence of some Neapolitan troops; but his impatience carried everything before it, and he resolved to land in the neighbourhood of Pizzo.

But as it was probable the custom-house officers would become alarmed, and fire on the vessels that were hovering on the coast, an officer was sent to sound their intentions, but he was detained. The boat came back without him, and brought a notice that if we did not leave the coast, the custom-house officers would fire upon our vessel.

The king then called Captain Barbara into the cabin, and a moment afterwards I was also sent for: I went below. The king gave the captain orders to cruise off the bay till he could send him information of the result of the enterprise he was about to attempt; and then said to me:

"Captain, I wish I could take you with me; but your intelligence, and the confidence you have inspired me with, incite me to send you on a mission which I consider of the very highest importance. As soon as inform Captain Barbara that I am going to march to Naples, you will set out as speedily as possible, and convey to the queen the despatches I now put into your hands. Captain Barbara has funds for the purpose at your disposal. If I fall, I require your word of honour that you will destroy them."

He then put a sealed packet into my hands, and I promised, though with regret, to execute an order which prevented me from following him in his hazardous enterprise. I was retiring, when he called me back, and gave me another parcel:

"These are papers," said he, "which in case of misfortune you will transmit to my family."

He then went upon deck, and accompanied by all the military men on board, landed on the shore. He was dressed in a splendid uniform, as in the days of his prosperity. At the moment he set foot on the shore, a shout of joy saluted the Neapolitan soil, and the monarch who came to take possession of it. It was returned by the crew of the *felucca*. It was now twelve o'clock. Murat immediately marched towards Pizzo, and was soon out of sight.

The longboat came back in about an hour with the sailors who had gone with it, and who had followed the king as far as Pizzo. It was on a Sunday, and all the inhabitants were in the public square. When they saw the arrival of the little detachment, in the midst of whom the king was, and heard shouts of *Viva Gioachino,* they came out to meet him, and repeated the shout. Even the surgeon of the port came to receive the king. A detachment of artillerymen, who were in the square, put themselves in military array, and presented arms to him. The king ordered them to follow him, which they did; and, without stopping at Pizzo, he continued his march to Monte-Leone.

Our sailors had not ventured to go farther, but their account inspired us with the highest confidence in the result of the king's enterprise. They had scarcely been an hour on board when we heard some shots fired in the direction of Monte-Leone, and we had no doubt that they were fired in honour of the king. However, Captain Barbara thought proper to send the mate in the longboat, with orders to land a considerable distance below Pizzo, and to learn what was going on towards Monte-Leone. The long-boat doubled a small point to the south of us, and entered into a bay, when we lost sight of it, and never heard more about boat or crew.

Whilst our minds were thus wavering between hopes and fears of the success of the expedition, we saw several persons rushing from Pizzo towards the shore. Amongst them we distinguished a uniform, which seemed to me very like the king's. I then told Captain Barbara to send a boat on shore; but he had none but the one he had sent away some hours before. He made signals to the other vessel, which was farther off, to send theirs. They neither sent their boat nor answered the signal.

Meanwhile the king, if it really was he, had got into a boat, and people were struggling round him. This confusion continued for some time, while Captain Barbara looked on the scene with his telescope, but neither said anything nor gave any orders. I then told him that the king might be exposed to the greatest danger amidst the confusion, and that it was his duty to run his vessel as close to the land as possible, at the risk even of running on shore, that he might give assistance to the king in case of need.

Barbara said to me that what we saw on the shore was nothing; that he had orders to keep off the land, and that he could not endanger his vessel by any movement of the kind. I still pressed him, but he told me sternly that he was master on board his own vessel, and then turned upon his heel.

During this discussion the crowd I had seen on the shore had withdrawn towards Pizzo, and the greatest quiet had taken place. We remained in the bay the rest of the day and the following night. No boat came near us, and our longboat did not return from the coast, where it had in all probability been seized; and we could learn nothing concerning what was going on on shore.

Next day things remained in precisely the same situation. I burned with impatience to learn what had become of the king of Naples; and with regret that I had been unable to reach the shore at the moment I thought I saw him return to it. We were obliged to go farther off from the coast to avoid becoming suspected.

We beat about in this painful and monotonous manner for five long days, when we heard a number of shots fired on the coast, and conjectured that Murat was attacking his enemies, after collecting some troops; but if he fought, we felt no doubt of his success; or rather we thought that the shots we heard were fired to celebrate his victory.

A mixture of joy and restless expectation succeeded our anxiety. We approached the shore to wait for the official account of the events we had been expecting. At the approach of night no news had yet arrived; but at ten o'clock we hailed a small boat that was passing near us, and the only man who was in it came on board, and we eagerly inquired of him if he had heard any news.

"Nothing," replied he, with the careless tone so common among the Neapolitans, "but by the bye, do you know that Murat was shot this afternoon?"

We looked at each other in silence, and were completely overwhelmed with the shock. We were so confounded at his words, that he was getting into his boat again before we thought of detaining him, or of inquiring into the particulars of the alleged catastrophe.

He told us that the king, after being repulsed from Monte-Leone, and fruitlessly endeavouring to embark again, had fallen into the hands of a body of custom-house officers, against whom he had fought with extraordinary courage; that the telegraph had transmitted to Naples the news of his arrest, and had brought back an order to try him by a court-martial, which condemned him without a moment's delay, with all the twenty-nine men who were along with him. They had then, he said, been shot immediately, according to the alphabetical order of their names, and without attention paid to rank or command. The king was the seventh who was shot. He gave, himself, the word of command to fire.

The fisherman's boat had long left us before we recovered from the stupefaction we were thrown into; and we remained crowded together on the poop, overwhelmed with the weight of his story.

Yet, we thought that the shots we had heard were not sufficiently numerous to persuade us that the twenty-nine men, who went with the king, were shot at the same time. This appearance of inconsistency between facts and the fisherman's story, led us to doubt the truth of what we had heard; and then we would not believe at all in the king's misfortune; we thought the best thing we could do was to wait near the shore during the night, that we might ascertain the truth or falsehood of the melancholy intelligence. We had no boat, and had no means of sending anyone on shore. The remainder of the night passed away very tediously, for we were burning with impatience and anxiety.

At daylight a boat came from the custom-house to order us to leave the coast. The officer who was sent to give us this notice, said to us with a melancholy tone:

"You belong to Joachim's expedition; I cannot help telling you that you will be exposed to the most imminent danger if you remain near the coast. Besides, you can do nothing now, for the king is dead. Go away as quick as you can."

When we heard these words we saw at length the melancholy truth of what we had heard. The manner in which this officer spoke to us intimated that he was a partisan of Joachim's, and we enquired of him concerning the events of the last few days.

He informed us that the king was unexpectedly attacked near Monte-Leone, by Trentacapelli, a captain of *gens d'armes*, and attempted to storm the position the latter had taken; but that seven of his men were wounded and one killed, and he had been forced to retreat towards the shore. Crowds of the inhabitants took arms against him the moment they saw him retreating.

When he reached the shore at Pizzo he could not find his longboat as he expected, but got into a boat and was endeavouring to push off, when a crowd of people rushed upon him, and in spite of his powerful resistance, took him prisoner. The greater part of those who went with him were similarly overpowered. As soon as the king was taken to the fort, Captain Trentacapelli had the impertinence to reproach him with his enterprise, and ordered him to be searched. But these insults were, fortunately, not of long duration; for General Nunziante arrived on the 8th at night, und took the direction of affairs.

He treated the king with the respect due to an unfortunate prince, and allowed him to accept the offer of a Spaniard, the agent of the estates of the Duke de l'Infantado, who engaged to procure him everything in his power.

No news came from Naples for several days; at length on the evening of the 18th, a telegraphic despatch was received, but owing to the state of the weather, only the words, *Murat to be* could be deciphered. During the night a courier came with orders to try him by a court-martial; and this was instantly done.

Under the pretext of examining them separately, Generals Franceschetti and Natali, and then his valet, Armand, were removed from his presence. When the secretary of the court came, according to custom, to ask him his name and rank, the prisoner proudly replied:

"I am Joachim Napoleon, king of the Two Sicilies—go about your business!"

This was pronouncing sentence on himself.

Whilst the court-martial was sitting, the canon Masdea, a parish priest, came to the gates of the fort. When admitted he said to the king:

"Sire, this is the second time that I appear before you; when your Majesty came to Pizzo, I asked you for a sum of money to finish the cathedral, and you gave me more than I asked for. With a heart full of gratitude, I now offer you my assistance in time of need."

The king then asked for paper, and wrote to the queen and his children. He put a lock of his hair in the letter, and prepared himself for the execution of his sentence, which he underwent by himself at the door of his room, in the calmest and most dignified manner. He had on his breast a portrait of the queen, and said to the soldiers with a smile: "Avoid the face—aim at the heart."

His body was buried without ceremony in that very church of Pizzo, which he had restored by his munificence.

Chapter 20
Court-Martialed in Corsica

As soon as the custom-house officer left us, Captain Barbara without asking the consent of anyone, set sail for Corsica. I saw this done with the most profound indifference. Nothing merely personal could affect me at such a moment, for I was completely overwhelmed with the melancholy fate of Joachim. When he had spoken to me about the dangers of the enterprise, I had conceived that he might fall in battle; but it never for a moment came into my mind, that he would be sacrificed in cold blood, by the orders of a sovereign, who had never suffered the slightest personal injury from him.

Meanwhile I thought of executing his orders. In presence of the captain and his mate, I burned the packet, which I once hoped to deliver into the hands of a lovely and beautiful woman, to whom I should have brought intelligence that she was to re-ascend the throne. I carefully preserved the other parcel given me by the king, with the intention of conveying it to his family.

When I had fulfilled the duties imposed on me by the king of Naples, and paid a just tribute of grief to his memory, I began to reflect upon my own situation. All my hopes had been once more dashed away, and I saw myself thrown back for the rest of my life among the lower ranks of society; to complete my misfortune, in endeavouring to perform a duty called upon by humanity, and with my honour unstained, I had reason to fear that I could not set foot on the soil of France with impunity.

Amidst the depression these painful reflections threw me into, one all-powerful idea occupied my mind—I bitterly regretted that I had not been one of the twenty-nine gallant fellows who followed the king—perhaps I should have been killed, in fighting gloriously beside him, or by a fortunate effort have prevented his defeat, and changed the scene of Monte-Leone. What difference there would then have been in my lot? And if like them I had been taken prisoner, and condemned to death, I should have died the death of a soldier, and worn the insignia of my rank. But now I had no home, and no means of subsistence abroad! I knew not even what my military rank was, nor what my prospects would be after this period of alarm was over.

These sad reflections occupied me during the passage from Pizzo to Corsica, which we made in three days, and landed at Porto-Vecchio, on the eastern side of the island. I immediately purchased plain clothes, and knowing that I should want for nothing, as the king had given me six months pay before leaving Ajaccio, I advanced into the interior. On the same day I arrived at San Paolo, where I put up at a wretched inn, the only one the country could boast of.

At first I complained of an inflammation of the chest, which rendered it necessary for me to breathe the air of the country; but enquiries were soon instituted concerning those who bad gone with Murat, and I was forced to tell my real situation to my hosts. They felt for me, and declared that I might remain perfectly at my ease for I should be beyond all danger as long as I remained with them. I passed -the remainder of the winter at San Paolo, dull enough; for I had no news from my family, who must have been afflicted at my sudden disappearance, and dared not write them, for fear of discovering the place of my retreat, and besides this the news I heard from France was very rare and correct. At the return of spring, Scalotti, the worthy Corsican in whose house I lodged, invited me to go with him, to spend some time with his brother, who was the proprietor of a farm among the mountains. I joyfully accepted-the invitation.

I passed more than a year in this place, and had every day more reason to be satisfied with the hospitably of the Corsican. If these memoirs had not at the period they have now reached, assumed a historical hue, I might attempt to describe their courageous hospitality: one of the distinguishing features of the manners of the island: I should do justice to the energetic character of the men, and the kind humanity and amiable feelings of the women, and should tell how often I forgot the sorrows of my nation in the charms of their conversation.

Whilst I remained in the mountains, I had opportunities of seeing several persons who had been engaged in Murats, expedition. They had returned separately, to Corsica, and several of them thought it necessary to live in a very secluded manner in the country, to avoid the consequences of having taken up arms. They came from all parts of Europe as to a place of rendezvous. Sone came from the kingdom of Naples, where they were not allowed to stay; others came from Sardinia, where the vessels that conveyed Murat's last expedition had put in when they were dispersed by a gale and never again got sight of their consorts. The greater part belonged to families in the island, who sent them regularly everything they could need, that is, all but news. The brave fellows adopted the mode of life of the Corsican mountaineers, and like them went out always armed.

Hunting was our chief amusement, and then we met together, and talked of our past adventures and our future prospects. It was in this way that I became intimate with an officer of rank attached to the king's staff. He soon saw what my real situation was, and showed me a great deal of friendship, partly, he said, because I had sacrificed more in his cause than the rest, as I was not in his service previously.

I related to him all the particulars of our escape from Toulon, and in return (for he had been attached to Joachim's person for many years) he gave me an account of the events that bad brought about that prince's downfall, and that last campaign which has given rise to such a diversity of opinion.

I lived like a mountaineer for more than a twelve. month, but I began to be tired of this monotonous kind of life, and felt great anxiety on account of the awkward situation in which I was placed by circumstances. In fact, no situation could be more painful, for I saw no end to it, and in spite of the kindness of my hosts, and my own parsimony, my means decreased in an alarming manner. I saw that I must decide at last, and that it would finally become dishonourable for a man of principle to conceal himself like a malefactor. This idea instantly settled the matter in my own mind. At the moment they had not the slightest idea of my intention, I bade farewell to the Scalotti family, who fruitlessly endeavoured to detain me, and set out for Ajaccio, with the consolatory reflection, that nothing worse could happen to me than to be shot.

Whilst I was travelling to my destination, I felt a load of anxiety removed from my mind by the resolution I had adopted, and it was almost with pleasure that I went, on my arrival, immediately to the commandant's, where, thanks to my unmilitary dress, I was at first received very politely. I instantly went to the point, told him who I was, and all that had happened to me since I left Toulon.

After reflecting for a moment, this officer, whose conduct towards me has always been exemplary, said to me:

"I shall he obliged to send you to the fort, till I receive orders from the minister of war, whom I shall instantly inform of your situation; but you may be assured that I shall not forget to speak favourably of you, as you have come forward of your own accord."

During the twenty days that elapsed before the minister of war's answer arrived, I was busy in preparing my defence, as I had no doubt that I should be tried by a court-martial, which actually met to try me for desertion and bearing arms in foreign countries. I knew but one individual among all the members who composed the court. He was a captain, and had formerly been a harbinger in the 67th regiment, which was present with us at the siege of Stralsund. He knew me again, and I saw in his countenance an air of goodwill that seemed to me of good omen.

When I had answered the questions put to me by the president, about my name, age, and place of birth, I felt some embarrassment in mentioning my rank; a short discussion took place, and the secretary was ordered to put me down as a Sergeant. After my examination, I asked the favour of pleading my own cause, and showed to them that having met in the evening near Toulon, a general officer, who ordered me to follow him, I thought it my duty to obey. I had embarked with him, and had been taken to Corsica, scarcely knowing whither I was going; it was there only that I learned that this officer was the ex-king of Naples; and amidst the important political struggles in which we were engaged, I could not think otherwise than that he acted for the interests of legitimacy, in whose cause he was engaged the year before; and, finally, that it had never entered into my mind to engage in foreign service, and that I had never belonged to any corps.

This defence, it will be seen, was not strictly conformable to truth; but, in fact, I had no right to accuse myself; and if I had yielded to a feeling of humanity, or to the brilliant prospects that were offered to me, the reader has already seen how very different my intentions were from being hostile to the new government that had established in France.

No witnesses were called, and yet the court deliberated a long time; but I was called in at last, and confess that I was not without dread of the result. I was declared not guilty by three votes out of seven, so that I had but a bare chance of acquittal. The president admonished me in a way that was by no means severe, but which I felt more than if I had been condemned, and concluded by ordering me to be sent to my regiment.

But what was my regiment, and where was it quartered?

I asked the president, but he knew nothing about it; I was referred to the general, and he knew not what to say; and in truth it was not an easy matter, amidst the general breaking up of the army, to tell what my regiment was. I knew very well they would find one out for me, but what rank was I to hold in it? It was evident that the captain appointed by a fugitive king would not retain his rank in the French army; but would not the ensign promoted by Napoleon in person, at the battle of Borodino, at last obtain the rank he had so long gained?

Whilst I sent forward my claims to this rank, the military governor ordered me to enter as a Sergeant into the departmental legion which was then in Corsica. In a short time it was sent to France, and employed to garrison various places. When the new organisation of the army was accomplished, I still received no answer to my numerous petitions.

The legion landed at Toulon, on their arrival from Corsica. After the sufferings I had lately been exposed to, I thought my feelings completely blunted, but I had a painful proof of the reverse, when I learned that my worthy father had died a fortnight before, in consequence of a cold he had caught in shooting quails at Les Sablettes. I had cherished the hope of forgetting for a short period, in his society, the misfortunes to which I had been exposed for the last two years. This painful loss took from me the only friend who could understand my feelings, and renewed the sorrow I had felt at the loss of my mother. My brother Peter had disposed of his business, and lived in the country; and I did not receive from him the consolatory attentions I expected. In fact, I could open my mind to no-one except my kind sister Henrietta.

I have not mentioned the regiment which I entered in 1805, though it has often been honourably mentioned in our military annals. Neither shall I give the name of the regiment which I entered after the disbanding of the departmental legions; the Memoirs I am giving are personal, and I have no right to extend to others the responsibility of the facts I relate.

I led for several years an insipid garrison life, and marched over part of the south of France. I had at first made every effort to obtain the rank of ensign, formerly bestowed on me, but my petitions had led to nothing but dispute. As if my rank had not been acquired on the field of battle, and I was petitioning for a favour, I was asked what claims I had to be made an officer, and was told of my conduct at Toulon, and my voyage to Corsica, as though a good action performed in 1815 could prevent me from gaining a commission three years before. After harassing myself with writing letters, memorials, and petitions, I at length gave up the idea of soliciting any farther, and consoled myself with the thought of obtaining my discharge at the end of my five years' service.

There was a profound peace with foreign nations, but there was always great alarm in the interior; troops were continually sent on to the frontiers, and the moment they were sent away from any central point alarm broke forth again. From time to time reports of war were spread through the army, and I, as credulous and full of my favourite idea as ever, thought that I might again conquer, before the termination of my military career, that commission I had so long and so ardently desired.

But, alas, how different was this hope from what we should have formed in former days! That commission, which I had so long considered as merely the first step towards the obtainment of honours and glory, I now consider as the final object of my ambition, as a haven of rest, the period at which it was my duty to leave my colours with honour. I no longer called upon fortune for its favours, but merely a situation suitable to my time of life, my services, and my experience.

In 1821, the yellow fever at Barcelona, led to the formation of a *sanitary cordon* in the Pyrenees; but this I shall have occasion to notice in the sequel. In the beginning of 1822, the troops were set in motion more than ever, and it was observed that a great many regiments were sent from their garrisons to the frontiers. We were in Dauphiny in March; in May we marched down to Toulon, and I had the happiness of again seeing my native place.

But I do not wish to tire the reader by relating all that I saw at this period. It may be easily imagined that after the events I had witnessed for some years past, I was no longer the same soldier as I was at Stralsund and Wagram. At this time what I saw left a more durable impression on my mind, and had a necessary effect upon my conduct. I studied mankind at my expense; but what benefit did I ever derive from all this study, these comparisons of the present with the past? Nothing! My whole life has been spent in expectation, in hope deferred; and after many a turn I have at last reached pretty nearly the point from which I set out.

In a word, if posterity could interest themselves about the fortunes of a sergeant, they would say of me what can be said of very few of my brothers in arms, and what can be said of but one solitary general.

This personage I had often seen at different places, and I met him at Toulon in 1822, on his return from Languedoc. As his story is not very long, I may be allowed to mention it here.

The Revolution found him a major-general, and he was still a major-general at the restoration of the Bourbons. During these twenty years of prodigies, in which Sergeants became kings, he had not advanced a step, not mounted a single notch in the ladder of ambition; his motionless stupidity amidst the whirlwind which gave rise to so many exploits and such distinguished rewards, would not allow him to be noticed sufficiently to merit even a removal. He was allowed to enjoy his pay at his ease far from the theatre of war, and to show himself off at some reviews in the provinces. It was in one of those places that the only exploit he was ever known to have performed is said to have occurred. At the head of a company of grenadiers and a troop of *gens d'armes*, he sprung sword in hand into the pit of the theatre to fight some students who were hissing an actress, and by this brilliant act of valour was so fortunate as to restore the silence and quiet which had been troubled for more than the space of a quarter of an hour.

The historians who will one day examine into the memoirs of our time, will imagine they have discovered an error or an omission, when, among so many names renowned for their exploits, they will find a name of rank unaccompanied by a single deed of glory. They will then say: "this was perhaps the individual whom a contemporary author, the trustworthy Guillemard, meant to point out, but unfortunately he has not thought proper to name him, for some reason we are unacquainted with."

To illustrate the matter farther, I shall tell them that this gallant fellow must have had many heavy sins weighing on his conscience; for I have seen him in all the splendour of his uniform, with an enormous prayer book under his arm, groaning and striking his breast, and roaring out most devoutly,, *mea culpa*, while listening to the sermons of the Abbé Guyon *on repentance*.

CHAPTER 21

The Trial of Valle

Were I writing anything but mere memoirs of my life, I should gladly take advantage of the want of important incidents to describe circumstantially the aspect which France presented at this period. It truly offered a most curious and interesting sight.

In the time of the empire I had merely marched through it during a space of ten years, and yet I saw that my countrymen looked forward to the close of the war as a happy period that would allow them to display their industry and commerce. After terrible disasters the war had ceased at last, and the future prospects of France were changed by the overthrow of its supremacy; but peace soon restored its energies, and it was soon urged forward on all sides by a most extraordinary activity.

As its career was not yet firmly laid down, it rushed with ardour towards every unbeaten path; and its future prosperity would have appeared to me to be infallible, had the nation been as powerful abroad as it was rich and productive at home; but its political position seemed to me totally inadequate to its proper rank. In foreign countries, the nations who had lately adopted the constitutional regime, instead of being considered as its natural allies, were almost regarded as its enemies: at home, the echo of the cries for liberty that came from the south and west of Europe, gave an ill-timed alarm to some, and roused in others recollections of past times and hopes that had long been slumbering in oblivion.

Amidst these feelings, people's minds became alarmed in various parts of the interior. The terror of some cowardly friends of the new government, and the inconsiderate zeal of others, had found criminality in the recollection of the past, and rebellion in the language of remonstrance. They accused men of forming revolutionary plans, while they were merely discontented. General uneasiness and alarm prevailed; and it may he that some men may have been rendered desperate by the persecution they suffered for their opinions, and have dreamed of a system by which they would not be neglected. In fact, the last expiring shocks of society, in passing from an old to a new state of things, still agitated the community.

On such an occasion it was natural that some individuals, exasperated by the disappointment of their hopes, or by having suffered actual oppression, and governed by a feeling of duty which sometimes leads men strangely astray in political conflicts, should give themselves up conscientiously to the performance of acts which in the then state of affairs were really criminal.

Whilst I was at Toulon, at the beginning of the year 1822, I had the misfortune to witness an event which these passions had given rise to, and which bore the stamp of them in its most minute particulars.

A report was spread that an officer had been arrested at Toulon, for having conspired to destroy the king' government; and that other persons were put in prison immediately afterwards, and would be speedily brought to trial.

I felt no surprise when I heard the news; for if on one hand I saw the political violence that governed men's minds and made them believe in any report, however absurd, I saw on the other a great probability that at such a moment similar plans might have been formed.

The government had committed various blunders, not perhaps of much importance in themselves, but quite sufficient to urge its enemies to a furious opposition. Such a contest would necessarily lead to violence and confusion;

and in a crisis like this I thought it not unlikely that the real importance of events would be greatly-exaggerated by misapplied zeal.

At any rate we have often seen in our civil commotions the different branches of government giving events a fictitious importance, and acting as if the very existence of the government depended on some trifling struggle, just as the soldier considers the capture of the battery before him as the decision of a battle. How can men in those circumstances refrain from that violence and exaggeration, which holds moderation to be high treason, or spreads a feeling of ill-will among the people that betrays them into violence, instead of following the peaceful path pointed out by the laws?

General attention was anxiously fixed upon the trial I allude to; which reminded the inhabitants of one that bad taken place at Toulon in 1815, of some persons accused of a similar offence. The pleadings that take place at a criminal trial, which so powerfully affect the multitude, and always attract their presence, have always bad a painful effect upon my mind. I know nothing more afflicting than to see an unfortunate being placed before his judges, who may be prejudiced against him by the nature of the offence, and the ruling opinion of the day, and before an audience fond of strong emotions, and who often desire to see the prisoner's situation more desperate, that they may be more strongly affected.

I had myself but lately escaped from one of those terrible trials in which the honour and liberty of a man depend upon a quarter of an hour's deliberation; and though the result of my examination had been favourable, I had not been less powerfully affected by the consequences it might have brought upon me, if those who were to decide my fate had not thought of the force of controlling circumstances, und the pardonable zeal of an old soldier in favour of his old commander. This circumstance had at first determined me not to go to the trial of Valle; but when it came near its close, and I was informed that the prisoner was a young officer, whose language, tone, and appearance, presented a most extraordinary aspect, I felt a great desire to see him, and went to the court on the day before, and the same day that his sentence was pronounced.

I shall not enter upon the circumstances of the trial nor the causes that led to it, though the provincial journals gave them in a very imperfect and unsatisfactory manner. Yet the particulars that took place at the trial, such even as they were given in the public journals, are sufficient to prove one important fact: but this period of history would not be accurately described, were we not to show the real character of the men who brought about certain events, or who shone among the front ranks of combatants. Private memoirs can alone make for the omissions of history, for they alone can describe a host of minute particulars despised by the former, but which after all show the real features of men and measures.

I was not acquainted with the particulars of this affair, so that I could neither judge of its importance, the merit of the defence offered, nor the degree of truth there might be in the charges of his accusers. The prisoner, Fidele-Armand Vallé, seemed to be about thirty-two years of age; his countenance was handsome and manly; his language indicated a mind of strong conception, but the style was not altogether appropriate to the dignity of his demeanour.

His defence reminded the court that in the retreat from Moscow, he was the only man in his regiment who succeeded in saving his horse and arms; and this extraordinary act of courage, when everyone else was rendered perfectly powerless and improvident through cold and hunger, had caused him to be raised to the rank of captain. It stated farther, that he had been decorated with the star of the brave for an act of heroism, and that he had received seventeen wounds in the service of his country.

Vallé paid little attention to the suspicious circumstances that were urged against his innocence. He seemed not to dread their influence. Though accused of a regular conspiracy to overthrow the government, and though the agents of the crown made every effort to prove that such a plot existed, he seemed never to think for a moment that such an idea could enter the mind of the jury. In fact, the evidence seemed to me to be far from conclusive, and the second charge of engaging people to enter into a secret association for revolutionary purposes, was not supported by the evidence of any individual who had ever been a member of such body. I asked those who had been present during the whole of the proceedings, what they thought of the result; but they generally believed that Vallé would be acquitted, though I heard some fanatical scoundrels assert, that in a case like this *suspicions were as good as proofs!*

Vallé seemed sure of gaining his cause, and examined all the charges with the utmost boldness, and seemed to feel happy in finding an opportunity of boasting of independent principles. He did not pretend to conceal his attachment to an order of things that was no more.

However, as the time approached when the sentence of the court was to be delivered, the trial assumed greater solemnity; while Vallé, full of blind confidence, seemed pleased with the idea of acting a part in history; but the scene became appalling when the clerk read with a trembling voice the sentence that condemned Vallé to death. Amidst the cries of surprise which a much more lenient sentence drew from one of his fellow prisoners, Vallé continued calm and serene; a smile played on his lips; like Lavalette, he said:

"It's a thunderbolt!" Then said to one of his companions who was bewailing his lot, "Be silent! I am condemned to die, and say nothing. I would give the order to fire, if necessary."

I had no idea that the trial would have ended thus; and the opinion of the jury must have been formed in a very different manner from mine—perhaps because they had cognizance of facts I knew nothing of. From that moment Vallé seemed powerfully affected by the important scene of which he was the chief actor, and rose at once to a height of bold and impetuous eloquence, such as he had been described to possess in the indictment; and he was now wrought up to a pitch of zeal and enthusiasm that remained with him to the last.

He declared his innocence, and said that he was the victim of men who wished to accomplish the slavery of their country. He bitterly reproached the judge and jury for their conduct.

"I certainly did not expect to he the consecrated victim," he then observed, "but I shall die worthy of the cause for which I am sacrificed. It is not a criminal that you wish to punish in my person, but an apostle of the ideas of liberty and equality. You know your real objects. But what avails it to kill one man, since liberty is immortal? In spite of judges and executioners, it will flourish afresh on the soil sprinkled with my blood, as religion sprung up anew from the tombs of the martyrs." He then chanted some lines of a patriotic hymn.

My attention was intensely directed upon the prisoner, whose situation now became more and more interesting. The court wished to keep him silent, and he was interrupted by the united efforts of the judge, the counsel, and the *gens d'armes*. This restraint excited his indignation; and when they talked to him of the obedience due to the laws, he burst forth into a torrent of invective.

According to the usual practice on such occasions, the order he wore was to be snatched off his breast; but when the judge gave orders for this purpose, Vallé rose, and said:

"This part of the sentence is more painful to me than death. Who dare raise his sacrilegious hand against the ribbon that I have honourably won in fighting the battles of my country—that ribbon which your soldiers saluted for the last time as I entered these walls? I alone have a right to touch it." He then tore the decoration from his breast, crumbled it together in his hands, and swallowed it with this exclamation: "That order, which the enemy even respected, is now safe from insult. No! My honour is unstained, my name is inscribed on the pillar erected in honour of the brave. I die innocent!"

This heart-rending scene closed at last; it filled me with the most painful emotions. I wished to drive it from my mind; but how can one erase from the memory things that have made so powerful an impression? It was impossible not to learn one important lesson from this scene, to see the fatal consequences that are produced by the violence of party spirit. Those who from prejudice feel no pity for the victims of criminal law, can scarcely, if they reflect at all upon the matter, refrain from sympathising with those who are condemned for political subjects; for whether guilty or not, they always interest the public mind, because they almost invariably die without dishonour.

In the course of a few weeks the legal steps adopted after Value's condemnation were terminated; and we learned one evening that our company, along with nearly the whole of the garrison, was to be present at the execution, which was to take place next day, the 10th of June. We were sent to the prison to escort Vallé early in the morning, and he left it at twelve o'clock.

When he came out his countenance glistened with enthusiasm; his dress displayed a sort of martial foppery; his cloak was thrown gracefully over his shoulders, the collar of his shirt was thrown back, and left his bosom bare, and his hair was carefully cut. He marched forward with a firm step, and looked steadfastly upon the crowd. Two of our officers, who saw with sorrow one of their companions about to die on the scaffold, went up to him and said:

"Valle, die like a hero!"

"Be not afraid," he replied, with a smile on his countenance; "I shall not dishonour my brothers in arms—the innocent fear not death!"

The drums beat; he walked forward with a commanding look, and universal silence prevailed around him. Some women began crying when they saw him, so young and handsome, marching on to death.

"Weep not for me," he said to them; "I die for my country." A little farther on, a woman was taking away her son from the sight, when he said to her, "Let him come near—let him see how the brave die. It may be a useful lesson to him in future life."

He several times addressed the crowd, and invited them to come and see him die, in the same tone he would have asked them to come and dine with him.

About half way to the scaffold the troops halted on some occasion, and Vallé marked the military step just as if he had been at the head of his company. He was opposite to a coffee-house, and asked for something to drink. The man who brought the glass trembled on presenting it.

"Be calm," said, he to him, "do as I do." He took three separate draughts, exclaiming at the first, "To France!" At the second, "To the Brave!" And at the third, "To God!"

He would not submit to any religious ceremony, but conversed politely with the priests who came to visit him, and who likewise went with him to the scaffold; but they had no occasion to support his courage.

The scaffold was erected in a small square in front the gate of Italy. When Vallé turned the corner of the street he perceived it, smiled, and hurried forward. He wished to address the multitude, but was prevented by the beating of drums and the executioners. What he said is not known, except that he requested the executioner not to show his head after it fell.

Very few people could reach the square where the execution took place, or get into the neighbouring houses. The square, and all the streets and passages that led to it, were nearly filled by the troops. The rest of the spectators were chiefly country people; for the inhabitants of Toulon were too afflicted at Vallé's fate to go to see him executed.

This dreadful scene shocked us all. Military men smile at the fire of musketry, but feel degraded by the scaffold. The law that altered the former military punishment, has doubled the severity inflicted upon the soldier.

The last moments of Vallé were all distinguished by that

energy and enthusiasm he could only have derived from a profound conviction of his innocence, or from the influence of political fanaticism. Neither Sand, nor the young man who attempted to assassinate Napoleon in Germany, in 1809, were to be compared to him; for though animated by similar zeal, the former avowed criminal plans, while the latter indignantly denied every charge made against him, and held himself out as the victim of party spirit. Like them, he displayed the same self-devotion, the same desire of obtaining what he called martyrdom.

If he were innocent, he was the victim of great injustice, and his heroism deserving of our pity and admiration. If he were guilty, he knew at least how to die honourably for the cause he had espoused; and in this age of words, where interest and selfish feelings are the guides of political faith, he forms an anomaly sufficiently remarkable to be recorded, without considering to what party he belonged.

CHAPTER 22

The Spanish War & My Discharge

We left Toulon in the beginning of July, 1822, and marched to take up positions at the foot of the Pyrenees, as part of the army of observation that had been lately formed.

Our object was no longer to preserve France from the contagion that afflicted Barcelona, but to prevent the civil war that was going on in Catalonia and Navarre from spreading disorder to our side of the frontiers. Precautions increased the more that the Constitutionalists defeated the Absolutists; and, in fact, the latter would in all probability have been completely annihilated had they not been able to find an inviolable shelter in the French territory. They came to us in bands, all covered, with filth and rags, and then soon took flight again for Spain, whence they were driven back by new defeats behind our lines.

We remained quiet spectators of the contest, which never would have been doubtful for a single moment had both sides been left to their own resources, particularly since French and foreign refugees, quartered in the frontier towns, had been formed into regiments, and had marched against the *factious*. The malcontents of Biscay and Navarre had been exterminated in a short time; but in Catalonia, on the other hand. Mina, in spite of his renown, had obtained but very doubtful successes, partly because he had not yet armed the French *emigrants,* and partly because it was against that province that most of the factious Spaniards concealed in our territory made their attacks.

Whilst our battalion was at the mouth of one of the passes that leads into the valley of Andorra, and our company in advance of Hospitalet, where our troops suffered greatly from the wind and the cold, several members of the Regency of Urgel, and the famous Trappist, passed the frontiers on their return to Spain. Every one of these men engaged our warmest curiosity, and the young soldiers laughed heartily at the Trappists singular dress. One of our companions, the only soldier but myself who had been engaged in the former war, restrained their gaiety by informing them that these very monks, so ridiculous in appearance, were the best hands in Spain in using the poignard, and had done more injury to the French army than all the rest of the nation put together.

"But," he added, with a smile, "they were then our enemies, and now we are their protectors."

"Yes," said a young soldier, "but have not the Constitutionalists got monks among them also?"

"No."

"Well," said I, "they are very wrong; they should have brought fanaticism to oppose fanaticism; this is one of their bad arrangements, and it is far from being the only one."

One of the men of the Army of the *Faith,* who then attracted the curiosity of our troops more than any other, was Bessieres; this was because he was a Frenchman, because he was said to be General Bessieres, or his son, or at any rate an officer, the most extraordinary things had happened; in fact, it was *very* difficult to tell precisely what he was. I afterwards learned that he bad been a servant to General M—M—, whom he attempted to rob and murder, but through mistake he killed his secretary instead, and then ran off to Spain, where, after the lapse of years, he became a freemason, but was seized, tried, and condemned to death for conspiring to restore the Constitution.

His life was saved in consequence of some popular insurrection that took place, and he was sent to the castle of Figuèras; in moving about from one prison to another he became a convert to the cause of royalism; and had since, particularly at Madrid, supported the king's cause with as great violence as he had formerly defended the cause of the Constitution. He now shone forth as a martyr of fidelity, supported more by his audacity than by the confidence of his own party, and indebted for his popularity solely to the well-known hatred of the Constitutionalists against him, the only title among the Spanish royalists that could obtain from them any respect to a foreigner.

Meanwhile, amidst the daily contests of the factious and the Constitutionalists, the Army of Observation assumed a threatening attitude, and it became evident that war would soon break out. The appearance of the army then underwent a change, and we really became soldiers.

We calculated among ourselves the enemy who were to be opposed to us, our auxiliaries, and the obstacles we had to surmount. Those amongst us who had been engaged in the grand war told their companions all that had been done in it. These particulars formed the subject of all our conversations. They were not very satisfactory, it is true; and it was, perhaps, for that reason that almost all the old soldiers were removed from their regiments at this time. I was so fortunate as not to be included in this arrangement.

After talking about all the circumstances that occurred during the grand war, we inquired with a half concealed feeling of interest about those countrymen of ours whom misfortune or discontent had transplanted into the service of the Constitutionalists. They were pitied for their ill fortune rather than blamed for their folly. In party quarrels it is difficult to say where duty lies. These refugees were the objects of our curiosity, as the bands of the *Faith* were of our contempt. But we could obtain very little information concerning their situation.

Several divisions of the army were already formed in the beginning of 1823. Our regiment formed part of the 4th corps, commanded by Marshal Moncey, and destined to act against Catalonia.

We daily expected orders to cross the frontiers, but the Spaniards did not believe that war was approaching them. Their troops that were in the neighbourhood of our advanced posts constantly told us that it would not take place; and when we marched into their territory about the middle of April, they retreated in the greatest confusion, with the usual exclamation, *"No importo"*, a consolatory saying, which Spanish pride applies to everything, indiscriminately. It appears that General Milans had no idea of our movement, for he immediately abandoned the positions he held on the frontiers, and retired in the utmost disorder.

Our young men became the bed of the stream, which was dry, and the cavalry galloped to the foot of the hills to cut off their retreat. At daylight we perceived the regiment of Cordova before us, but it was not without a strong feeling of regret and sorrow that we perceived the Italian Liberal regiment near, and some men retreating with the uniform of the old imperial guard.

Whilst we charged the rear companies of the regiment of Cordova, the Italians made so well timed a movement on our right, that they cut down the front ranks of our company. Whilst I was bringing the company into close file, I was separated from the main body along with a few men. We made as obstinate a resistance as if we had been supported by the whole strength of the battalion. Two of my companions were killed beside me, my arm was wounded by the thrust of a bayonet, and my gun fell from my hands; in spite of all my resistance I was carried off, along with the three soldiers, by a body of the enemy who were retreating.

I was once more a prisoner! I had formerly been so nearly on the same spot, and might, without cowardice, feel some alarm for my fate when in the hands of men governed by such violent passions, had I not more honourable reasons for being afflicted. An old soldier like me falls into the enemy's hands almost at the first shot! Three different times in my life a similar event had thrown me back into the crowd from which I was on the point of elevating myself. A fourth time, after eighteen years' service, when favours are no longer exclusively reserved for the old and experienced, I am going to be thrown back for ever, beyond the line of promotion. All my efforts and intelligence, and even, perhaps, talents superior to the common run of non-commissioned officers, were of no avail against the strokes of chance; since 1805 my life had been nothing but a aeries of well-founded hopes, all scattered by a breath of wind.

It was not enough that I was condemned to the drudgery of the service since the peace, but must at the first ray of hope and promotion again become a prisoner of war, I knew not even how long I might be a captive, for many of my unfortunate companions had been ten years on board the English guard-ships. Such melancholy reflections rendered me desperate, and had I not been deprived of my sabre, I should have speedily put an end to my sorrows by running myself through the body.

The Italians who took me, carried me off along with them. When the rapid march we made, and more mature reflection, had somewhat dissipated my sorrow, I began to pay some attention to the movements of the two armies. The enemy retreated from one position to another, and were strongly pursued by the French I should have been happy had one of their balls struck me to the earth.

A man who has been in the army ten years during the imperial sway, knows a little of all languages. I entered into conversation with an Italian non-commissioned officer. He eagerly informed me that I was in perfect safety, and ran no risk of suffering the treatment we were exposed to during the grand war, when we were so unfortunate as to be taken prisoners. I had not fallen into the hands of a guerrilla; and the fury of the Spaniards was no longer directed against foreigners, but solely against their countrymen of the opposite side, whom they put to the sword without mercy.

I was taken from village to village till we reached the neighbourhood of Manresa, and put into a sort of fort along with some Frenchmen. The day after our arrival we were visited by some French refugees, who came to enquire into our wants, and to offer us their services. We told them our names.

The same evening I saw, with equal surprise and pleasure, Sergeant-Major Ricaud, with whom I had escaped from Cabrera. He had on the uniform of the old imperial guard, and had left France in consequence of a quarrel with his captain. We threw ourselves into each others arms; and I know not how it was, but we were more affected than if we had met in any other situation.

"My dear fellow," said Ricaud to me, after the first burst of joy was over, "you will no longer be a prisoner, but will be incorporated in the battalion of refugees."

"What! You force prisoners to enter your service."

"No, Robert, we have no right to do so; but they may recover their liberty by entering into the battalion."

"But I do not wish to enter into the service of Spain."

"And do you think that we are serving Spain? Look at this uniform. Come, you know that though I am no more than a sergeant, I have formed a just opinion of events; and if my wont of prudence has prevented me from being promoted, it was not because I knew less than those who commanded us. Come, listen to me, and judge for yourself."

His narrative was long, I learned things that greatly surprised me, and which would probably surprise the reader much more, though related long after they occurred; but I cannot and ought not to tell them here.

Some facts should not be published till ten years after their occurrence. At some future period, if these memoirs are favourably received by the public, I shall give a supplement, exclusively devoted to the state of Spain in 1823. I shall endeavour to show in it all that I learned then and afterwards, concerning the foreign refugees, whose story is so eventful and interesting; also concerning the secret societies of the country: but as the greater part of these facts necessarily require very full political illustrations, and I am indebted to Ricaud for them, it will not be thought wrong for me not to be thought wrong for me to take upon myself the responsibility of their publication.

When my friend had concluded his narrative, I said to him, "My friend, I cannot yield to your request. I have long ago learned, in the words of the old song, that *a good soldier must suffer injustice without complaint.* I cannot enter into the battalion, I will never consent to imitate those emigrants who have borne arms against their country."

"But I know that you have suffered great injustice."

"At every period of my life."

"That you love your native country."

"Above all things."

"That at the remembrance of French glory, and. the sight of my uniform ——."

"Tears would come into my eyes; but my judgment restrains the impulse of my heart."

"Come, be one of us?"

"I would join you tomorrow, were it necessary only to die; but I will not fight except under the colours of France."

"Is that your last word?"

"It must be the invariable rule of my conduct."

Ricaud left me with tears in his eyes.

I saw him every day during the time he remained here; but he never mentioned the subject again. I even thought sometimes that he was glad that I had firmness enough to resist his offers, I was afterwards enabled to appreciate the high generosity he had shown by urging me no farther.

The refugees, whom misfortune or the persecution of the laws had forced to cross the frontiers, were the first victims of the yellow fever of Barcelona, and were unable when the war broke out to remove to another country. They were forced to gain a living to enter the Spanish service along with some other foreigners, and experienced in all its bitterness the misfortune of being subject to Spanish pride, and the caprices of the guerrilla leader, Mina. By how many sufferings and humiliations did they purchase the fatal honour of forming a peculiar corps, which was subsequently annihilated in the fields of Llado and Llers! At the latter battle, the flying column of Fernandes, which marched out from Barcelona for the purpose of entering Figueras, was surrounded by the French army, and forced to lay down their arms. But the legion of foreign liberals refused to capitulate, and defended themselves with heroic perseverance; when almost entirely destroyed, the survivors fought as gallantly as ever. It is said that one of their officers blew out his brains when he was on the point of being taken. My unfortunate friend, Ricaud, who once wished to enrol me in it, received three bayonet wounds, and was left for dead on the field of battle. Two of his intimate friends were killed by his side. At this sight, cries of pity burst forth from the French ranks; the officers threw themselves into the midst of the vanquished, and lowered their swords, while the brave General Damas, who commanded the division, advanced in person, and promised them, if they surrendered, his powerful intercession with the prince, whose subjects these gallant adventurers were. Upon the word of that warrior, whose noble character is worthy of the times of chivalry, they laid down their arms, and surrendered to those in whose ranks they had gloriously fought during a period of twenty years.

At the same period a second column, composed of the remains of the refugees of different nations in Catalonia, marched from Tarragona towards Lerida, under the orders of Evariste San Miguel, and was cut to pieces, along with their commander, in an action with the French.

Such was the deplorable end of these unfortunate beings, who had assembled from the extremities of Europe upon a foreign soil.

Some days after I was taken prisoner, the refugees left the district, and the Spaniards themselves went out to meet the French, who seemed desirous of taking possession of the banks of the Llobregat. The small fort we were kept in was only guarded by some volunteers, who went away at night, after locking up my three fellow prisoners and myself in a large hall. At one of the large windows which lighted it, we discovered some loose bars, and by our united efforts we succeeded in pulling one of them out, and lowered ourselves out of the fort by means of a rope. The most profound silence reigned all round us, We entered the narrow streets of the village, and found our way to the fields.

At daybreak we had crossed the Llobregat, and approached the mountains beyond which the river Ter flows. We were then forced to conceal ourselves among some bushes, and to wait for the approach of night; we again continued our journey, and soon came to the Ter, along the banks of which we marched till we came to the neighbourhood of Geronna, still alarmed with the thought of meeting a party of Spaniards, though we did not see a single uniform for two whole days.

When we came in sight of Geronna, we fell into the very midst of the outposts of the army of the Faith. We were immediately known to be French; but some took us for emigrants acting as spies, and wanted to shoot us; and others thought we were deserting to the enemy, and were ready to subject us to the same fate. Though we were worn out with want and fatigue, we cried as loud as them, and at last succeeded in obtaining a hearing. We were taken to headquarters, and much praised for our conduct.

I had latterly suffered a great deal, particularly during our two days of flight; the wound in my arm was greatly inflamed. By the advice of the head surgeon, I was sent to the ambulance, and had scarcely reached it before I was attacked with a violent fever. When it was nearly removed, I was sent from one fort to another along the frontiers, and arrived in a very bad state at Tech, near Ceret, in the beginning of July.

As there was no hospital in the village, I was quartered in a private house. My arm was swelled to a great size, and I was afraid of gangrene breaking forth.

A surgeon came every other day to visit me, and some

other wounded men at Tech; but his attendance seemed of very little avail, and I was overwhelmed with a depressing melancholy. Many weeks elapsed before my wound made any sensible progress, but it began, to heal at last, and I recovered in some degree my fortitude and strength of mind.

More than two months had elapsed since the battle of Mataro, the army was engaged in besieging Barcelona; but the war went on slowly in that province, and fighting was scarcely heard of. For the first time in my life I felt no desire of returning to my regiment. It was this period that I received notice from my colonel that the minister of war had sent my discharge.

The unusual manner in which the thing was done surprised me at first; but I recollected that I had often talked to my fellow soldiers about the war of 1808; that I had been a prisoner for some days, and during that time had been excellently treated by the French refugees, and I thought there might be some suspicion at the bottom of all this business. Assuredly the only claims I had to be discharged were ten years service in the time of the empire, and the eternal grief of not receiving the commission which I legally held by Napoleon's order.

I conceived that the soldiers of the emperor were now merely tolerated in the ranks of an army that was to be bent to other recollections than ours, and in which we involuntarily spread regret that our brilliant career of conquest was no more. They and we were neither of the same period, nor of the same turn of mind. It was doing a great deal to retain the officers, whose experience rendered them necessary; but it would, perhaps, have been impolitic to keep the private soldiers, who could not so easily bend their ideas to the system of the new government; but I had always done my duty without reproach, and had no right to expect to be turned away so unceremoniously.

Three months sooner I should have been in despair had I been included among the old soldiers, who were then nearly all discharged; but now that it was certain that all the fortified places surrendered almost without firing a shot, and that the war would be ended before I could make up for lost time, I thought it of little consequence that I was to be sent home a few days sooner than I would have asked for. I was, therefore, resigned to my fate; and without complaint or unavailing regret for the past, I quitted the service nearly on the same spot where, eighteen years before, I had entered it, full of youth, and burning with hope.

About the middle of September I had nearly recovered from my wound, and I burned with the desire of seeing my home at last. I travelled by the *diligence* to Toulon, and arrived at my native village on the 2nd of October, 1833.

Chapter 24

Conclusion

I am now at Sixfour, and shall never again leave my native place; here my lot, so long precarious and uncertain, is fixed at last. I shall perhaps enjoy in the course of time the peace I have so much need of; but nothing can ever fill up the void which so many emotions have left in my heart.

Many prospects of fortune and glory have opened upon me during my military career; and the moment I thought they were on the point of being realized, the whole edifice disappeared before my eyes. I had also left pleasing illusions at Sixfour, and on my return find they also have disappeared, and that everything has undergone a change.

I left my family happy and flourishing, and it is nearly extinct at the present day. My worthy father, followed my mother to the grave, and left but little property to his children.

My uncle, Eyguier, left the service at the restoration of the Bourbons, and went to the West Indies, where be, amassed a fortune. He made his last voyage in 1821, in a brig of his own, intending to retire from business on his return. The outward-bound voyage and his commercial speculations were all favourable, but a hurricane caught him on his return, and the brig and all on board went to the bottom. About half a dozen little mulattoes and quadroons now came forward, pretending to be his children, and they obtained all the property he had in the West Indies.

My brother is solely devoted to the mean labours of agriculture, and speaks a language foreign to my heart; he is quite absorbed by his daily habits, and despises a soldier who cannot sow a field of grain. Yet my father had educated him for labours somewhat more important. He contemptuously calls me, *his learned brother* or *the officer;* and is, perhaps, the only man in existence who never found anything amusing in the stories of an old soldier.

None could be more affectionate towards me in my infancy than my sister, Henrietta; but now, thanks to the difference of tastes, we no longer feel that soft and easy intimacy that springs from mutual sympathy with each other's joys and sorrows; she still loves me, however, and it is along with her that I live on the feeble remains of our patrimony.

Of the group which old friendships had gathered round our family, I find that very few remember me at all; and even these are divided by interests or political opinions, and live in a state of constant quarrelling among themselves.

M. Rymbaud died long ago. I saw his son killed at Trafalgar.

Miette is the mother of five children, and cares about as little as I do for the remembrance of our former love; she is, in my eyes, nothing more than the good housewife of a retired citizen. I am sometimes surprised at finding myself preferring her husband's conversation to hers. He was formerly employed in the Davy victualling office, and like me, had his prospects ruined by being forced to quit the service. Frank and straight-forward, he coincides with me in deploring the distrust and discord which reign in a country, whose principal charm was wont to be an openness of manners and general harmony we once thought peculiar to our neighbourhood.

Social parties between the inhabitants of the surrounding villages are now unknown.

The fetes have lost their freedom and their gaiety.

After such a shock as that we have witnessed, these habits, will not return before the lapse of many years. It will require twenty years to calm the waves of this mighty tempest; and in twenty years everything will have undergone a change, for the very scenes themselves are no longer what they once were.

Thus wherever my heart turns for consolation, it finds a dreary void; and I can find no other subject for my thoughts than the melancholy recollections of the past.

I have been the perpetual sport of events, and have been placed too low to command any of them. I have been borne involuntarily along by the movements of the multitude, and have never been able to raise myself above the sphere into which I was thrown by chance, in spite of the constant efforts of twenty years, and the concurrence of a host of circumstances that were all favourable to my elevation.

At Trafalgar, I gave the hero of England his mortal wound; and that circumstance, which would have made the fortune of any other man, was completely neglected. I then became the secretary of Admiral Villeneuve, who, trusting to his innocence, returned home to solicit a new command; and when I had every reason to depend on his influence, he fell by the hand of an assassin. His tragical end, which I witnessed, procured me one of those interviews with the emperor which were never unproductive to any other; but it was equally so to the victim and to me.

I marched over Germany and Sweden. After many fruitless fatigues, I attached myself to a man who pursued fortune with all the vigour of youth and genius, and who was likely to insure my own; yet Oudet was killed beside me at Wagram. I fell from one disaster to another, till I was thrown upon the barren rocks of Cabrera. There the love of liberty and the desire of promotion never left me for a moment. With the versatility of Figaro, I bent my mind to the pursuit of a singular but gainful business; and my unwearied activity was devoted to the pursuit of every chance of escape. I succeeded at last in getting away from the island with three of my friends.

I had scarcely escaped before I gained that cross, which I then thought the forerunner of future eminence—the cross which now forms my sole consolation, and which I can at any rate proudly show wherever I go.

How great and glorious did France appear to me on my first return to my home! How far did I then think misfortune from my country and from me, when with six hundred thousand fellow soldiers, we entered the Russian territories, gained the famous battle of Borodino; and I was appointed an officer by the emperor in person!

Yet a few hours afterwards I fell never to rise again. I became a prisoner of the Russians; and two disastrous campaigns took place without its being in my power to share in their perils or their glory.

At my return I was present at two revolutions. My obscurity—which I had made every effort to shun, that obscurity which is considered a safeguard in civil commotions—delivered me up to the murderers of Nismes. After escaping from them, as if by a miracle, I march to Toulon to save the life of a king. At the moment I had received the rank I thought myself qualified honour, I saw that prince perish miserably; and I again became the sergeant of 1810.

Henceforth, as the obscure soldier of a garrison, and an unknown spectator, I looked forth upon the politics of the world. I tried to study mankind, but it was of no avail. Yet a ray of hope broke upon my mind when I heard the cannon of the Bidassoa; I thought I should at length be enabled to conquer, for the third time, that commission so ardently desired, and which I might have had fifteen years sooner.

I fell again into the hands of the enemy, and saw Spain once more, only to pity the lot of those unfortunate Frenchmen to whom she had offered a fatal asylum; I succeeded in escaping from my prison; but as I was henceforth hopeless of the future, it was with indifference that I received that discharge I had formerly flattered myself with obtaining only to enter into the upper ranks of society.

But if fortune has always been hostile to me, this I can safely assert, that I never did anything dishonourable to obtain her favours; and this will, perhaps, at some future day console me for having been neglected.

The trade of a soldier is the only one I ever knew; and now I can carry it on no longer.

I learned to judge mankind; and this knowledge is totally useless to me.

I had latterly even paid attention to politics, and I am now confined to an obscure village.

In a word, during the whole of the last twenty years, I have been an alien to the affections of my own family, and a stranger to the feelings of the farmer, the citizen, in fact, of every one of the industrious classes; and, wherever I go, I am out of place.

Yet I cannot make up my mind to be totally useless—my recollections may not be wholly uninteresting at this moment, when everyone is looking back with avidity to that brilliant period which will long claim the attention of the present generation. The profound impression it left on my mind forms the leading object of my thoughts; I feel a strong necessity of communicating them to others; and it is this impulse which has led me to compose the unimportant, but authentic, Memoirs, I now submit to the candour of the public.

ALSO FROM LEONAUR
AVAILABLE IN SOFTCOVER OR HARDCOVER WITH DUST JACKET

THE COMPLEAT RIFLEMAN HARRIS *by Benjamin Harris as told to & transcribed by Captain Henry Curling*—The adventures of a soldier of the 95th (Rifles) during the Peninsular Campaign of the Napoleonic Wars

WITH WELLINGTON'S LIGHT CAVALRY *by William Tomkinson*—The Experiences of an officer of the 16th Light Dragoons in the Peninsular and Waterloo campaigns of the Napoleonic Wars.

SERGEANT BOURGOGNE *by Adrien Bourgogne*—With Napoleon's Imperial Guard in the Russian Campaign and on the Retreat from Moscow 1812 - 13.

SWORDS OF HONOUR *by Henry Newbolt & Stanley L. Wood*—The Careers of Six Outstanding Officers from the Napoleonic Wars, the Wars for India and the American Civil War, with dozens of illustrations by Stanley L. Wood.

SURTEES OF THE RIFLES *by William Surtees*—A Soldier of the 95th (Rifles) in the Peninsular campaign of the Napoleonic Wars.

ENSIGN BELL IN THE PENINSULAR WAR *by George Bell*—The Experiences of a young British Soldier of the 34th Regiment 'The Cumberland Gentlemen' in the Napoleonic wars.

HUSSAR IN WINTER *by Alexander Gordon*—A British Cavalry Officer during the retreat to Corunna in the Peninsular campaign of the Napoleonic Wars.

NAPOLEONIC WAR STORIES *by Sir Arthur Quiller-Couch*—Tales of soldiers, spies, battles & sieges from the Peninsular & Waterloo campaingns.

JOURNALS OF ROBERT ROGERS OF THE RANGERS *by Robert Rogers*—The exploits of Rogers & the Rangers in his own words during 1755-1761 in the French & Indian War.

KERSHAW'S BRIGADE VOLUME 1 *by D. Augustus Dickert*—Manassas, Seven Pines, Sharpsburg (Antietam), Fredricksburg, Chancellorsville, Gettysburg, Chickamauga, Chattanooga, Fort Sanders & Bean Station..

KERSHAW'S BRIGADE VOLUME 2 *by D. Augustus Dickert*—At the wilderness, Cold Harbour, Petersburg, The Shenandoah Valley and Cedar Creek.

A TIGER ON HORSEBACK *by L. March Phillips*—The Experiences of a Trooper & Officer of Rimington's Guides - The Tigers - during the Anglo-Boer war 1899 - 1902.

AVAILABLE ONLINE AT
www.leonaur.com
AND OTHER GOOD BOOK STORES

www.ingramcontent.com/pod-product-compliance
Lightning Source LLC
Chambersburg PA
CBHW031624160426
43196CB00006B/269